MAJOR TRENDS AND DEVELOPMENT IN DALIT POLITICS

MAJOR TRENDS AND DEVELOPMENT IN DALIT POLITICS

Ram Sharan Masania

2008

CYBER TECH PUBLICATIONS
4264/3, Ansari Road, Daryaganj, New Delhi-110002 (India)
Ph.: 011-23244078. Fax: 011-23280028
E-Mail: cyberpublicationsdelhi@yahoo.com

MAJOR TRENDS AND DEVELOPMENT IN DALIT POLITICS

First Edition 2008

Published by G.S. Rawat

For Cyber Tech Publications

4264/3, Ansari Road, Daryaganj, New Delhi - 110 002

E-mail : cyberpublicationsdelhi@yahoo.com

Phone : 011-23244078,

Fax : 011-23280028

Printed at

Amit Enterprises, Moujpur, Delhi. Ph. - 9810878184

Preface

It is in this context that studies establishing a connection between the Dalit movement and the above concepts bring out the latent contradictions of a socio-economic and political nature. Moreover, such studies also reveal that relative deprivation leading to socio-economic mobility has after all a democratising impact on the socio-economic, political and bureaucratic structure of India.

Even to-day discrimination against the Scheduled Castes and the practice of untouchability persist tho'only in certain parts of the country. Even today, serfdom and bonded labour implicating dalit families continues. All the laws and constitutional prescriptions notwithstanding, enforcement is a flop, a fraud. Investigation into offences against the Scheduled Castes and Tribes is often done by hostile policemen. Gang rapes of these backward women rarely reach the court and if they do they hardly survive to end in conviction. The truth is that neither the Police nor the Court has any emotional involvement or sufficient social commitment where, on the one side, is the feudal order and, on the other side, is the dalit brother or sister. What is of moment and accounts for the law's betrayal is the implicit hostility of the dominant classes to legislative measures which are merely the skin-deep homage paid to social justice.

The publisher and their staffmembers have assisted in every possible way and have worked hard for its timely completion of the book.

—Editor

Contents

1

Caste System in India

The *Bhagavad Gita*, probably the best known Hindu religious work, teaches that it is better to do one's own caste duty badly rather than the duty of another caste well. Vangala J. Ram, in a recent analysis of he themes in North Indian village culture, emphasizes the importance of dharma or duty, He says: "This theme of dharma runs so deep into Indian culture that many regard it as synonymous with it. Almost every form of social action is attributable to this overriding concept...A fieldworker in an Indian village, very early in his field work, is confronted with dharma as the explanation of actions for which the informant can offer no other explanation. But when he stops to ask what this dharma is, he comes across only vague and nebulous responses. Dharma is a strong motivating force which even those who one's dharma is unthinkable. The charge of "*adharma*" (contravention of *dharma*) is one of he most serious charges that can be leveled against anyone.

Hindu philosophies and religious beliefs and practices are directed toward winning salvation, or freedom from rebirth; but only some support directly the caste system. The various approaches to salvation are called *marg*. There is, for example, the *dharma marg*, the path of duty which mot clearly supports the caste system; the karma marg, the pat of ritual activity, which supports the caste system because of the great ritual importance of the Brahman; the *jnana marg*, the path of mysticism; and the bakti margs do not support the caste system directly. However, in their preoccupation with divine powers, they do not advocate concern with or attack upon the caste social order.

All behaviour is viewed in the context of duty or dharma. The Brahman avoids contact with Camars, devotes himself to learning, and accepts gifts, because it is his dharma to do so; a Camar serves his Thakur, often at his own expense, because that his Thakur, often at his on expense, because that is his dharma; A Camar defers to his Thakur, stands up when the latter passes, lets him initiate a conversation, and addresses his respectfully, because that is what he has been told is his dharma. However much it might displease him.. he will continue to do it, because dharma cannot be violated. One's opinions, attitudes and feelings cannot stand up against the overwhelming power of dharma.

The prominent Indologist, Heinrich Zimmer, recounts this story as an illustration of the ancient Hindu belief that the perfect performance of dharma not only leads to salvation but to immense personal power. The story is this: The great emperor Ashok was standing by the river Ganges with his ministers and people, near his capital city of Pataliputra (Patna, Bihar) He asked if any of his very gifted colleagues could make the river run backwards, in the opposite direction. None could but there was standing within earshot a courtesan, Bindumati, who performed the feat—the river reversed its flow. The emperor in amazement asked the courtesan how it was she had performed this "act of truth." She explained that she had always fulfilled her dharma consistently, unquestioningly. She served whomever gave her money, she said, whether he be a Kshatriya, a Brahman, a Vaishya, or a Shudra. She treated all her customers exactly alike, did her duty, and thus through her perfect dharma had great magical power.

Brahmanism. Orthodox Brahmanism states that only Brahmans can gain salvation; those of other castes must wait until they are reborn as Brahmans and then perhaps they will be able to transcend the rebirth process by becoming part of the Absolute. The path of works, the karma marg, which includes the performance by brahmans of the prescribed religious sacrifices, is the most orthodox path. Higher caste families are regular clients of household preceptors who perform the various annual Hindu rites for them. The very important Hindu Pollution Concept which is so basic to the ranking of castes in local caste systems is connected with the predominance of the Brahman priest. He must be kept pure, so there must be others in other castes to absorb impurity for him.

Buddhism, Jainism, and the Upanishads. As early as 500 B.C. there were teaches who rejected the Brahmans priests claims of superiority and the exclusive truth of the Brahmans' ritual tradition, they Vedas. One of these teaches was Buddha; another was Mahavira, the founder of Jainism. The teachings of both were considered by Brahmans to be heresies, and thus, outside of Brahmanism, within the Vedic tradition. However, were the Upanishads, the insights of mystics.

All Upanishads, developed during the same period, and all discounted the Brahman sacrifices as the most important path to salvation. All three held as the ideal a totally religious individual, a mystic Holy Man. Within Hinduism the path to salvation through such mysticism is the Jnana marg.

The individual who renounces village, caste, and family to become a holy man has been released as an individual from the caste system. Louis Dumont has spoken of the ideal of the Renouncer as the individualistic alternative to the collectivistic caste system within Hindu culture. Dumont pints out that it is the renouncers as religious philosophers who have been the creative force within Hinduism; not the orthodox priestly Brahmans. Renouncers as "holy-men" are not totally divorced from society. They both teach ordinary men and depend upon ordinary men for food and shelter as they tour the countryside.

The various bhakti or devotional approaches taught by gurus or "holy-men" held that through love and devotion to a savior one could reach salvation. These holy men rejected the necessity of the Brahman intermediary, as well as the caste ladder of ascent to rebirth. The humans and poems of the bakti cults were written by saints of a variety of caste origins. One of the most popular was a weaver named Kabir; another was a Shoemaker named Ravidas. There were women poets, also, such as Mira Bai.

Thus, much of the inspirational leadership was held by non-brahmans, who were often of humble caste ran. In this sense, the bhakti sects were anti-Brahman—rejecting the priest as intermediary, and holding out hope for direct salvation.

Bhakti marg and caste, bhajan groups which gather for hymn singing in a bhakti mode are often multi-caste in membership. There were such groups in Khalapur. Milton inger also describes these multi-caste groups in the city of Madras. However, the bakti spirit of inter-caste communal devotion does not seem to have affected the local functioning ritual-occupational caste systems; the remain intact. The content of the bhakti beliefs concerns the perfection of the savior and his or her powers of salvation. There is little direct criticism of the social order. In fact, people converting to bhakti sects in past centuries have formed new castes, so that sectarian castes constituted a minor number of castes in the local caste systems. In Khalapur, for example, there were both Weavers and Kabir Panthi Weavers, the latter following the bhakti guru, Kabir. In the state of Karnataka (formerly Mysore) one o the major dominant castes is such a bhakti sect, the Virasaivas, popularly known by the phallic pendant (Lingani, symbol of the god Siva0 which they wear as Lingayats.

Dumont suggests that the religious support for the caste system lies in the purity-impurity syndrome which, in turn, implies the necessity of the Brahman for Vedic study an ritual communication with the gods. Thus, caste is closely related to karma marg (the path of ritual action). To the extent that bhakti and jnana paths reject thee assumptions, such disciplines do not support the caste system as a religious system. However, they allow to continue as a secular order of society. Dumont points out that this religion-social phenomenon, the relationship of these individualistic paths to the caste system, is poorly understood by scholars.

Other religions have also seemingly offered an alternative

to Hindusim and, one might suppose, to the caste system. Thus, during the Muslim rule of large parts of India from the eleventh to the twentieth century, many Hindus converted to Islam, a religion which holds that all are equal in the eyes of Allah. Today, about 10 percent of the population of India is Muslim. Before the partition of the subcontinent into Indian and the Muslim nation of Pakistan, about one-quarter of the population was Muslim. The inspiration of Islam is seen in some of the medieval Bakti cults and in the reform religion, Sikhism, which developed in the fifteenth century in Northwest India, Sikhism was anti-Brahman, anti-caste, and anti-idolatry. In Some parts of India, Christian missionaries were quite successful. In areas such as Kerala and Southern Tamil Nadu, where there were many Untouchables and low castes, and where the rules of pollution wee strong, large numbers converted to Christianity.

Present day Kerala has a relatively high proportion of Christians, about 20 percent. Such religious counter-movements to caste were unsuccessful in that Christians, Muslims and Sikhs were integrated as castes into the caste system. Among Christians, Sikhs, and Muslims, there are also castes—there ranking and separation based upon the Hindu origin of he converts. Thus, Mazahbis were Untouchables converted to Sikhism. Thee are in Tamil Nadu, Nadar Christians and Pariah (untouchable) Christians, and they do not worship together.

Reform Movement

Growing out of the contact wit Christian beliefs, various reform movements within Hinduism developed during the nineteenth century. Among the most important are the Brahmo Samaj, Arya Samaj, and Ramakrishna Mission. All were some what critical of the caste system, but their influences in this respect touched mostly urban western-educated men. There were religious approaches both within Hinduism and in other popular religions that failed to support the religious importance of the Brahman and the ladder to salvation through rebirth into higher an higher castes. However, this lack of support had little effect upon the caste system as a lived in social order because none of the other religions offered or instituted a new alternative social order. All were, in this sense, "other-worldly."

Modern Class System in India

In order to speculate with any degree of fidelity about what the future may hold for nay society some attention must obviously be paid historically speaking to where it has been and where it stands at the present time. The task is compounded in the case of India by the fact that strictly speaking it is more than a nation in the Western sense. In structural terms India is not analogous to Europe as a whole—a very large world composed of myriad, culturally—linguistically differentiated nationalities around whom a single national boundary had been drawn as a consequence of prolonged and complex historical processes.

Therefore, to try and project a scenario for India's future for the rest of this century is equivalent to trying to do it for Europe. Ideally it requires one to apperceive not merely a single history but several histories. It requires that one apperceive not merely a single overall outcome but a number of subsidiary outcomes as well which in an inter related way tend to build towards that overall outcome. This is the task that should be performed, and in some measure we will attempt it. But within the space-limit available full justice cannot be done to this dimension of the complicated subject at hand. Instead, we will proceed on the assumption that despite this underlying complexity, and the need to be constantly aware of it, is nonetheless true that some important general truths about Indian political society are knowable and projectable, as is true for Europe as a whole as well.

In fact, such may be even more true for India than for Europe because unlike the latter Indian can at least be said to have had contralised political and administrative institutions for more tan a century and that within this framework economic, sociological and cultural processes have had opportunities to shape the characteristics of its people in fairly comprehensive terms. Even before the modern era there were what may be called culturally centralizing processes at work in India which generated social structures and value systems (political and economic as well as religious values) that were shared by the people of every region and ethnic community in the subcontinent.

The Hindu religion and its social expressions, such as the caste system and the devotionalistic sects, wee especially instrumental in orienting Indians towards certain basic functional and status relationships, towards certain common structural approaches to the distribution and utilization of power, and towards certain common solutions to the relationship between how life must be lived and how it may be transcended.

India entered her period of full nationhood in 1947 bearing the sociological imprint of her ancient past and the political imprint of her long struggle against imperialism. It was here consciousness of both of these aspects of her history which served as bases for the kind of national society India's emergent leadership proposed to create once the power to do so was in their hands. Through the synthesizing talents of Gandhi, Nehru and many other nationalists, political consciousness was blended with cultural consciousness to produce visions of modernity which had an Indian content. In a very real sense, they mobilized and reshaped Indian Traditions to meet the challenges of a rapidly changing post-colonial world.

By the time of Independence, however, this image of the national whole, of a blend of past and present, was beset by divergent conceptions of how it must be given a contemporary content. Congress had achieved its organizational ascendancy and mandate to rule India by essentially assembling a at coalition of supporters which cut across the entire spectrum of Indian life Beneath the overarching and all-embracing political doctrine of freedom from Great Britain were gathered a mélange of sub-ideologies (from Marxism to Hindu revivalism) which expressed the sociopolitical agendas of the party's numerous factions.

From a programmatic standpoint there was not one Congress Party, there were in fact several. And in the transition from being a nationalist movement to becoming a governing party-machine the structures and policies which congress was compelled to pursue, if it were to hold itself and the country together, had to simultaneously reflect a commitment to large national goals and a cautious regard for the special interest, with diverse and often conflicting agendas, whose allegiance the party had cultivated and whose continued support its survival was sorely dependent upon.

Jawaharlal Nehru incarnated this fundamental dilemma inherent in the Indian National congress born from the approach to successful party-building which history and the realities of trying to crave a modern nation out of a subcontinent had thrust upon it. By ideological predilection he was a Marxist and a democratic socialistic; by sentiment he was the penultimate modern Indian for whom India and all she represented was a kind of metaphysical reality to be cultivated and cherished like a precious family heirloom.

In his Marxist aspect he yearned for the kind of political centralization and freedom of action, leavened, of course, by Gandhian compassion, which he saw the Bolshevik leaders acquire use in the Soviet Union to sweep away the old reactionary regime and propel Russia towards becoming a modern industrial state. In his Indian nationalist aspect he resisted a ruthless shattering of the past as the price of progress and struggled to find a pathway through the thicket of Indian diversity that would enable India to somehow become economically, socially and culturally modern without doing violence to the rights and sensibilities of those who did not share the lineaments of his dream.

The struggles between Nehru and Sardar Patel within he party during the years immediately following Independence vividly show how clearly Nehru perceived the situation and how consistently he, and indeed most of the other principal figures in the party, acted in terms of it. The ideological reluctance and structural incapacity to pursue outright victory over each other resulted in a political standoff through which the social interests and philosophies which each represented were both able to retain viable institutional wellsprings within Indian society.

As the first Five year Plan got underway in the fifties, with Patel personally removed from the scene by his death in late 1950, but with his political legacy still alive, and with Nehru in a politically unassailable position as Prime Minister and idol of the masses, India was being governed by a party which was simultaneously committed to Socialism and to Capitalism (by a pledge to honour the concept of the 'mixed economy'), to centralized economic planning on the Soviet model, on the one hand, and to an open polity on the wet-minister model, on the other.

The consequences of these contradictory tendencies were many and varied and will occupy the attention of the remainder of this chapter. For they have a direct bearing on not only where India is today but where she may find herself tomorrow. From the point where Nehru consolidated his political power following the first General Election in 1952, he found himself in a position to obtain parliamentary assent to this adoption of the Soviet Model of centralized economic planning coupled with a Fabian (i.e., non-tatalitarian) approach to the social mobilization of the resources needed to implement such planning. These undertakings, as is well known, progressively expanded the scope of central and provincial bureaucracies (i.e., the state apparatus) and made the state the dominant player in India's economic life. The sociological ramifications were enormous, of course.

Development became more than a policy and a programme. It became embedded in the contemporary national culture s a symbolic holy grail whose details one debated but whose bona fides one never questioned. In the 1950's and 1960's most Indians poke of the "Socialist Pattern of Society" in hushed and reverential tones.

Evidence of significant shifts in basic social and economic relationships within the decade following the Avadi resolution abounds. But the forms they took reflected not merely the impact of the changes which Nehru, the Socialist, had been able to set in motion. They also reflected the limits of Nehru's power to influences outcomes.

The incapacity of the congress Left to subdue the Congress right during the last phases of the Freedom Movement and (especially) the initial years of Independence was responsible for this. Conservative, traditionalist, anti-Socialist interest, all anathema to Nehru's conception of the future, found sanctuary and political support among substantial sections of the Congress which had been brought under the control of the Patel faction. Moreover, there power was ideally situated to thwart the implementation of policies emanating from the levels of government which Nehru most effectively controlled.

The reification of political stalemate between Socialists (inspired by Soviet and Fabian models of social change) and conservatives (inspired by capitalist and revivalist models of social continuity) determined the course which social change had taken in India since independence and will continue to determine its course for the foreseeable future.

In the broadest terms it has meant that a fundamental cleavage has been implanted in the very fabric of the country's social, governmental and constitutional structure. India is simultaneously a Socialist state and a capitalist society. This has come about under the prevailing structural circumstances because every measure for change and reform initiated to increase the capacity of the Socialist government to mold India society to accord with its Marxist presuppositions about the just and equitable society has had the concomitant effect of increasing the resources available to opposing conservative interests to expand an strengthen their domains of power and influence as well.

Let us take the issue of land reform which was a cause celebrate during the Freedom Movement days and became an item of first priority on the agenda of Socialists within and outside the Congress Party following Independence. Nehru and other leftists envisioned land reforms that would eventuate in a revolutionary new agrarian system for India whose basis would be some form of collective management and resources-sharing benefiting especially the most impoverished and vulnerable classes in rural society. The capacity of the opponents of such policies to modify them and blunt their implementation through the power they exerted within the Congress itself led in fact to the progressive rise of a capitalist agrarian structure throughout rural India. A large ephemeral class of feudal-style landlords (the so-called *zamindars* and taluqdars) who were essentially revenue farmers not centrally relevant to agricultural production were summarily swept away in a blizzard of idealistically phrased legislation while the means of production, never really in their hands anyway, were legally ceded to the middle and elite caste farmers who were their actual users, and who had been the backbone of Congress's political support in rural India since the days of Champaran and Bardoli.

Politically indebted to these nascent peasant farmers and powerless to prevent them from effectively representing their interests through the local and provincial branches of the Congress, which they largely controlled, the Socialist government of India found itself compelled to act essentially as their subsidizers. Subsequent rural reforms such as cooperative banking panchayati raj, community development, joint farming, ultimately 9and especially) the Green Revolution, all promulgated under a Socialist ideological rubric, progressively facilitated in fact the consolidation of the political and economic power of a basically conservative, capitalistic peasantry which found itself able to seriously challenge Socialist political dominance in the provincial capitals and eventually in the national capital itself. Charan Singh and Devraj Urs are after all striking manifestations of this social structural irony.

The creation of this capitalist peasantry came about, in other words, because a Socialist regime which had enough power to raise capital (through taxation and foreign borrowing) to finance public economic undertakings lacked enough corresponding political power to fully determine the class destination of these capital resources. The rise of the caste lobbies in India, which has been so widely discussed and analysed by the scholarly and journalist communities, was a direct sociological consequence of this profound social structural dilemma. Nehru's and other progressive Congressmen's steady stream of denunciations of 'casteism' over the years affords eloquent testimony to the threat which they believed this institution represented to their socialist goals, and a testimony as well to how strongly entrenched the particulars in interests articulated through caste mobilization had become. The caste lobbies of the fifties and sixties competed for access to a growing reservoir of social and economic resources and promoted and supported in the process parochial political and economic goals such as the linguistic reorganization of the provinces (which Nehru bitterly opposed) and the patterning of industrial development in response to political agitation instead of economic rationality alone (which he also resisted). And finally, of course, as noted earlier, the middle-range cultivator castes evolved toward becoming a capitalistically-oriented agrarian class as increasing proportions of the national wealth flowed in their direction and gave them the resources with which to increase not only their material well-being but their political clout as well.

Industrialisation followed a comparable course. State-owned heavy industry of every kind was created under the guidance of Nehru's Planning Commission. The public sector assumed enormous proportions in terms of capital expenditure, goods and service produced, and size of the workforce and bureaucratic-managerial cadres employed. Socialist planning and economic mobilization behind Nehru's dedication and charisma clearly enabled India to become a formidable industrial power by he time of his death, and to progress at an even more rapid rate since. But the private sector of the industrial economy, despite being constricted labyrinthian regulations and heavy taxation, grew tat rates comparable to those of the public sector. While the gross product of the former more than doubled between 1960 and 1970, the latter came within a hair's breadth of doing the same.

Structurally speaking, the mercantile castes were to he commercial and industrial sector of the national economy what the cultivating castes were to its agricultural sector. As the latter had been the de-facto possessors of the means of agricultural production, so the former had been throughout Indian history the de-facto possessors of the means for the production of non-agricultural goods and services. As the *kisans* had found the political means within the Congress to protect their economic resources from confiscation through collectivization, so the '*Baniyas*' had found support from the same category of internal political benefactors for preventing the economic resources which they commanded from being totally nationalized in the name of Karl Marx and Sydney and Beatrice Webb. Having preserved their economic domain by helping to produce political stalemate between the Congress right and Congress Left in the early years of Independence, the old mercantile communities commenced evolving into modern capitalist entrepreneurial lobbies increasingly capable of challenging Socialist policies emanating from the Centre as their wealth and economic complexity (and consequently their political influence) ramified. Wealth and social consolidation grew in direct proportion to the overall successful development of the Indian industrial economy—once again, ironically, made possible to a high degree by the massive public investment in economic promulgated in the name of Socialist ideals by the Nehru government and its successors.

The culmination of this process of growing capitalist entrepreneurial interest-representation within the corpus of the socialist state began, in my opinion, with the rise of Sanjay Gandhi in the seventies. He realized, instinctively perhaps more than intellectually, that a capitalist-entrepreneurial stratum of rapidly increasing wealth, sophistication and power was coming into being within the fabric of India's fructifying industrial economy.

The boundaries between the private and public sectors were becoming increasingly blurred as monetarist philosophies gained the upper-hand in the advanced industrial nations and the world's lending institutions, as economic self-reliance, Performance and fiscal responsibility became consequent essential ingredients of national economic survival. Sanjay Gandhi conferred political legitimacy on this dynamically expanding sector of economic society.

Political Success and Representation of Labour Class

The provincial autonomy under the Government of India

Act.1935 was carried out in 1937, hence the coming election was important and interesting for all the political parties. Dr. Ambedkar founded a new political party named, "Independent Labour Party" in August, 1936. The party was focussing the needs and grievances of the landless, poor tenants and workers. (*Ibid.*285). Dr. Ambedkar launched an election campaign. He concentrated on 'Bombay Province'. He toured all the districts of Maharashtra. He made speech at 'Nasik', 'Ahmednagar', 'Solapur', 'Satara', 'Belgaum' etc. The elections took place on February, 17, 1937. Dr. Ambedkar and his Party got a big success in this election. Out of 17 candidates, put by the Party, 15 candidates got a success. Dr. Ambedkar was elected with a huge majority. (*Ibid.*290-292). During his period at assembly, he introduced number of Bills like, "A Bill to Abolish Khoti System", "A Bill to Abolish the Mahar Vatan" etc. He also gave number of speeches on different issues. Dr. Ambedkar was the first legislator in India to introduce a bill for the abolition of the serfdom of agricultural tenants. (*Ibid.*296).

On 13th May, 1938, Dr. Ambedkar went on a tour of Konkan Maharashtra and addressed number of meets and rallies organised by the tenants and agricultural labourers. The Bill about the Abolition of Khoti System introduced by Dr. Ambedkar was being postponed for ten years by the Congress.(*Ibid.*310-312). But Dr. Ambedkar fought for this issue. He took this issue towards the masses. In September, 1938, 'Industrial Disputes Bill' was brought by the Assembly. Dr. Ambedkar opposed this Bill saying that, this Bill declares the strike as illegal, where as this must be a right of worker. (*Ibid.*313). On another occasion, Dr. Ambedkar had called a strike of workers of Bombay and it was the first successful strike launched against a popular government. (*Ibid.*313). On 6th January, 1939, Dr. Ambedkar addressed a big meeting of agriculturist at 'Mahad'. He explained the ill attitude of Congress Government towards the agriculturists. Thus Dr. Ambedkar could able to establish his leadership among the agricultarists and industrial workers. He represented, in a real sense, the labour class in the Assembly with sincerity.

Dr. Ambedkar founded the "All India Scheduled Castes Federation", a political organisation, in 1942. The organisation was representing the Scheduled Castes. In the year 1945, elections were held and the organisation failed to win a seat. This was very repayment for Ambedkar's services to India. It was something, he was to later experience again, for the record of Dr. Ambedkar's last few years was that of a fruitless campaign for proper political representation for Dalits. (Ramesh Chandra & Sangha Mitra :2003:105)

Harijans' Perception of Caste Hindu Values

In the wide span of human life, a time, a stage comes when perhaps every individual, for reasons known or unknown begins to identify himself with either some other individual or group of individuals. Identity formation of an individual begins right from his childhood. The child learns and develops his beliefs and strong opinions about himself and others as well as his own and other groups in his own family. The members of the family play the most significant part in shaping, moulding and evaluating a child's thoughts and beliefs about himself and the others. With the advancement in age the child's gradual contacts with neighbourhood and outside world makes him add certain other norms and values to his idea of 'who he is' or 'what he considers himself to be.' Nevertheless, the "interpretation and evaluation" by family guides the way. As observed by Lee Rain Water, "As the child tries on identities, announces them, the family sits as judge of his pretensions.

Family members are both the most important judges and the most critical ones, since who he is allowed to become affects them in their own identity striving more crucially that it affects anyone else." While explaining about identity Erickson lays emphasis on two factors, *i.e.*, the 'sense of continuity' and social Sameness' whichin the process links what the individual" was a child and what he is about to become and also reconciles his conception of himself and his comunity's recognition of him." In other words, identity is "self realisation coupled with mutual recognition." With change in circumstances individuals are capable and are in the habit of altering their identifications. But a young person must follow progressive lines of development to "experience wholeness" and evolve into an integrated personality.

There has to be therefore, a "progressive continuity" between the initial stages of his life, what he has come to be after a process of development in childhood and that which he aspires to become in future. He should feel integrity between what be imagines about himself and that which he thinks others visualise about him and 'expect of him.' Similarly interaction with community plays a vital part in shaping an individual's identity. Many a time a person having manifold interests tries to identify himself either with another individual or with a group of individuals who have similar interests or are engaged in work or activities of his liking. He may have certain characteristics, traits or ideas which are still in a formative stage and have not been developed to the fullest possible extent. If these have been developed, to whatever extent, in some other individual or group, the former considers the latter to be an ideal. He tries to identify himself with that individual or group who or which has already achieved some recognition by society. This process of identification varies from individual to individual or group to group depending on their socio-cultural and political background which moulds and shapes their thoughts and ideas.

In the Indian context one can say that the pattern of identification varies from individual to individual or group to group. Some people try to identify themselves with their own caste group, occupational group, etc., whereas some other try to identify themselves with the other caste group, occupational group, etc. It may not sound strange, as we have found in our study, if the illiterate, uneducated and aged Harijans try to identify themselves with their own castemen as well as occupational group. But a small section of the young. Harijans who are highly educated, politically conscious and well placed in jobs prefer—to become identified with the people belonging to higher castes in the same occupational rank.

An individual does not feel at ease when he believes that there is a dichotomy between his own perception about himself and that of others about him. When an individual feels that his self-identity is in danger, he tries to identify himself with a group which may provide social, physical and psychological security. The sense or feeling of insecurity is the basic motivating factor behind such types of identification. But, in order to raise their own social status, the younger, educated and politically conscious persons among Scheduled Castes may try to revolt against the traditional norms and values of society. In our own study, the educated Scheduled Caste reppondent regarded Dr. Ambedkar as their ideal hero, perhaps because, he openly revolted against the norms and values set up by the higher castes people. But a great majority of the uneducated Scheduled Caste respondents (whether young or old) regarded Gandhiji and Mrs. Indira Gandhi as their ideal heros. Perhaps because although Gandhiji preached and practised against some of the traditional norms and values, his constructive work programme for Harijan uplift did not seem to them as rebellious (though equally revolutionary if not more so) in content and technique as the former one. The measures undertaken by the Government for the benefit of Scheduled Castes during the last ten years seem to have strengthened Mrs. Gandhi's image in the minds of illiterate rural Harijans.

The outlook of an individual widens with education, experience and frequent interpersonal contacts, etc. The younger, educated and politically conscious group though do not hesitate in adopting the life style of the people belonging to higher castes they are now openly challenging the traditional relationship which existed between the Scheduled Castes and the higher castes.

The pattern of identify formation was assessed by administering a 'self-identity inventory' to the respondents. It was developed on the pattern of "Personality Trait Inventory" developed by Dr. N.N. Sen of NCERT. It consisted of 24 items. Through the items listed in the instrument we tried to analyse the individual's perception and his reaction to the different kinds of stimuli which reflected the general pattern of identity formation. The main purpose of using this instrument was to measure or estimate them pattern and direction of identity formation in the context of the respondents' perception of: (a) His own caste, (b) Other castes, (c) Hindu community as a whole, (d) Indianness, and (e) Humanity.

One of the great advantages of this inventory was that by one administration as many as five sets of responses could be obtained which elucidated different pattern of identity formation. The respondents indicated their agreement, disagreement or uncertainty about each of the 24 statements of the inventory. From this pattern of endorsement their identities with certain social values were estimated. Their endorsements were then converted into frequencies and the identity measures obtained.

The above mentioned inventory was primarily meant for the educated Scheduled Caste respondents only. However, out of the 24 statement, the nine which have been marked with asterisk (*i.e.*) were administered to the uneducated Scheduled Caste respondents as well. The respondents indicated their 'agreement' and 'disagreements' or 'uncertainty' about each of the statements of the inventory. Their responses in the form of 'yes' or 'no' were obtained. Uncertainty was indicated by '(?).' These responses were converted into positive and negative frequencies. Each of these responses were given + 1 mark for positive response and – I for the negative response. Zero marks were given for responses indicating uncertainty. In other words, the undecided markings were not scored. Here it should be borne in mind that — for two statements under the heading 'towards his own caste' stating: "I dislike the people of my own caste for their servile attitude" and "The fat that I am born in a Scheduled Caste community makes me feel bitter. I wish to detach myself from my ancestry," — 1 making was given if the response was 'yes' and + 1 if the response was 'no'. Similarly, the statement under the head 'towards other castes' stating" "I hate and sometimes feel like paying off the caste Hindus in their own coins for their unkind and inhuman treatment of Scheduled Caste people "was given—I marking, if the response was 'yes' and + 1 if the response was 'no.' The plus and minus frequencies marked for each category were added separately—for example, respondent 'A' might have got an aggregate frequency of +4–2 in regard to category II. After the frequencies were added separately for each of the five categories they were converted into response percentages which have been shown as the 'mean score percentage' in the tables. The three tables given an idea about the individual's appreciation for each of the above mentioned five categories of social values. In psychological term these appreciations are respondents' perception of 'their own castes,' 'other caste,' "Hindu community as a whole,' 'Indianess' and 'Humanity.' The respondents who were uncertain about their views have not been shown in the tables. This is why in some of the columns of the tables to the total sums of pluses and minuses (+ and –) are less than 100. As already mentioned that out of the total number of respondents (282) as many as 181 belonged to Scheduled Castes. Out of these Scheduled Caste respondents, 45 in the urban area and 57 in the rural area were uneducated. And 53 in the urban area and 21 in the rural area were educated. Thus among the Scheduled Castes, the number of educated respondents was greater in the urban area and the number of uneducated respondents was greater in the rural area.

The bulk of the educated Scheduled Caste respondents in the rural as well as in the urban area had a positive appreciation for their own castemen on matters relating to status, intelligence, sense of responsibility, etc. The mean score percentage being 68.47 was fairly high in the urban area and higher still (75.17) in the rural area. Thus we find that the extent of identification of the educated Scheduled Caste respondents with their own castes was fairly high. The wean score percentages showing negative attitude were 22.44 in the rural area and 25.98 in the urban area.

The mean score percentages in the rural and the urban areas being 78.55 and 66.37 respectively shown that the regulated way of life, education, etc., of the caste Hindus were held in great esteem by the majority of the educated Scheduled Caste respondents. Under this category the mean score percentage was also found to be higher in the rural area. Thus their identification with the 'other castes' was fairly high in the urban area and very high in the rural area. The difference in the mean score percentages of the rural and urban respondents not having such high or positive views regarding the caste Hindus was 8.11. The mean score percentage in this regard was found to be higher in the urban area.

The extent of identification of the educated Scheduled Caste respondents with the 'Hindu community as a whole' was very high in the rural area. The mean score percentage showing positive appreciation in the rural area was 83.33 whereas in the urban area it was 55.17. Thus the difference in such percentages between the rural and the urban responses is quite obvious. The mean score percentage of the urban sample showing negative attitude being 37.07 denotes that, as compared to other categories, the minimum level of identification was indicated by the educated Scheduled Caste respondent for the "Hindu community as a whole."

The extent of identification of the educated respondents in relation to 'Indianness' as well as 'humanity' was found to be extremely high. The mean score percentage was 100 each in relation to 'Indianness' and 'Humanity' in the rural area. In the urban area as well it was as much as 91.39 in the caste of "Indianess' and 98.28 in relation to 'Humanity.'

Thus, so far as the educated respondents belonging to Scheduled Castes are concerned, the mean score percentage for positive appreciation in each of the five categories was found to be higher in the rural area than that of the urban area. In other words, the extent of identification of the educated respondents in relation to each of the five categories was found to be higher in the rural area than in the urban area. In the rural area, the extent of identification of the educated respondents was found to be maximum with 'Indianness' as well as with 'Humanity,' followed by that for 'Hindu community as a whole,' 'other castes' and 'his own caste' in descending order. The order of preference was found to be somewhat different in the caste of the educated respondents of the urban area. In this case, the extent of identification in relation to various categories was found to be maximum with 'Humanity' closely followed by 'Indianness' and then followed by that for 'his own caste,' 'other castes' and the 'Hindu community as a whole' showing obvious decline.

So far as the uneducated respondents belonging to Scheduled Castes are concerned, it is evident from Table 5.2 that a great bulk of them in the rural as well as in the urban area had positive appreciation for their own castes. The mean score percentage being 79.44 was very high for the urban responses and higher still for the rural responses (88.15). Thus we find that the extent of identification of the uneducated Schedulé Caste respondents with their own castes was very high.

The extent of identification of the uneducated respondents was found to be minimum with 'other castes.' The mean score percentage calculated for such responses was 52.63 for rural sample and lower still, ire., mere 43.33 for the urban sample. The mean score percentage calculated for showing negative attitude towards 'other castes' was also found to be higher (41.22) in the rural area than that of the urban sample which was 32.22.

The extent of identification of the uneducated respondents with the 'Hindu' community as a whole was extremely high both in the rural as well as in the urban area. The mean score percentages calculated for such rural and urban responses were 94.74 and 95.55 respectively. Thus the difference in the percentage was insignificant.

The extent of identification in view of the uneducated respondents' appreciation of 'Indianness' as well as 'Humanity' was found to be extremely high. The mean score percentage was 100 each in relation to both 'Indianness' and 'Humanity' in the rural as well as in the urban area.

Thus, keeping the overall picture in view we find that both in the rural as well as in the urban area, the extent of identification in view of the uneducated Scheduled Caste respondents' appreciation was maximum in relation to 'Indianness' and 'humanity' followed by that for 'Hindu community as a whole,' 'his own caste' and 'other castes' showing obvious decline.

It has been mentioned earlier that only 9 out of 24 statements, which have been marked with asterisk, were administered to the uneducated respondents belonging to Scheduled Castes. The data regarding these nine statements were tabulated again separately in order to know the views of the educated Scheduled Caste respondents as well on these specific issues. This was done in order to make a comparative analysis of the uneducated and educated Scheduled Caste respondents regarding these nine specific statements. That a majority of the educated respondents, both in the rural as well as in the urban area, had a positive appreciation for their own castes. The mean score percentage being 68.53 was fairly high in the urban area and very high (82.14) in the rural area. Thus, as compared to the urban area the extent of identification of the educated respondents with their own castes was found to be greater in the rural area.

In the case of the educated respondents the extent of identification was found to be minimum with 'other castes.' The means score percentage calculated for showing positive appreciation for 'other castes' was 69.04 in the rural area which may be classified as fairly high but it was only 51.72 for the responses received in the urban area. The mean score percentages calculated for showing negative attitude towards 'other castes' being 30.95 (for the rural responses) and 37.06 (for the urban responses) were higher as compared with other such percentages shown in Table 5.3.

The extent of identification of the educated respondents with the 'Hindu community as a whole' was extremely high in the rural area and was found to be fairly high in the urban area. The mean score percentage in the former case was 100.0 latter it was 67.22. Thus the difference in the rural and the urban responses in fairly obvious.

The extent of identification of the educated respondents in relation to both 'Indianness' and 'Humanity' was found to be extremely high. The mean score percentage was 100 each in relation to 'Indianness' and 'Humanity' in the rural area. In the urban area as well it was as much as 91.37 in the case of 'Indians' and 96.55 in relation to 'Humanity.'

Thus, in the rural area the extent of identification of the educated respondents was found to be maximum with 'Hindu community as a whole.' 'Indianness' and 'Humanity,' followed by the for 'his own caste' and 'other castes.' The order of 'preference was found to be somewhat different in the case of educated respondents of the urban area. In this case, the extent of identification in relation to various categories was found to be maximum with 'Humanity,' followed by that for 'Indian-ness,' 'his own caste,' 'Hindu community as a whole' and 'other castes.'

Thus, keeping only the nine statements marked with asterisk in view, it is apparent that in the case of the educated Scheduled Castes respondents the mean score percentage for showing positive appreciation in each of the five categories was found to be higher in the rural area than in the urban area. This shows that the extent of identification of the educated respondents in relation to each of the five categories of social values was found to be higher in the rural area than in the urban area. But so far as the uneducated respondents are concerned the mean core percentage for positive appreciation (for their extent of identification) was found to be equal in the rural and the urban area in two categories, *i.e.*, in the case of 'Indianness' and 'Humanity'; it was higher in rural area in the case of 'his own caste' and 'other castes' and slightly lower in the rural than in the urban area in the case of 'Hindu community as a whole.'

In the rural as well as in the urban area the extent of identification of the uneducated Scheduled Castes respondents with their own caste was found to be greater than that of the educated respondents. A close observation of the data revealed that all the 45 uneducated respondents in the urban area and 55 out of 57 in the rural area and similarly all the 21 educated respondents in the rural area and 55 out of 58 in the urban area indicated their immense faith in the capabilities of their own castemen. Out of the four statements which were put to them under the head 'his own caste,' the number of respondents mentioned above indicated their agreement for the statement, "Given the equal and proper facilities for higher education. I believe that I could also acquire a cultural status equal to that of upper caste Hindus." Under this category the minimum appreciation, both in the rural as well as in the urban area was indicated for the statement: "I dislike the people of my own caste for their servile attitude.

Though in the case of both the uneducated as well as the educated respondents the extent of identification was found to be minimum with 'other castes' the mean score percentage in the rural as well as in the urban area was found to be higher in the case of the educated respondents. Thus as compared to the uneducated respondents the educated respondents' identification with 'other castes' was found to be, greater. Under this category two statements were put to the respondents. A close look at the data revealed that the percentage of uneducated respondents condemning the unkind and in human treatment by caste Hindus and Scheduled Caste people was greater in the rural area. Among the educated respondents this percentage was found to be greater in the urban area. The percentage of uneducated respondents admiring the clean and regulated way of life of Brahmins and other upper castes was found to be higher in the rural area. In the case of the educated respondents as well, the percentage calculated for this statement was found to be higher in the rural area.

Though the extent of identification with the "Hindu community as a whole" was higher in the case of the educated rural respondents the difference between the mean score percentages of the educated and uneducated responses from the rural area was very little. But the difference between the mean score percentage of uneducated and educated urban responses was found to be 28.33. In other words, the extent of identification of the uneducated urban respondents with the 'Hindu community as a whole' was much grater than that of the educated urban respondents. Among the uneducated sample the difference between the means score percentages of urban and rural responses was only 0.81 whereas in the case of the educated responses the difference between the rural and urban mean score percentages was 32.78.

The extent of identification with 'Indianness' was found to be equal in the case of the uneducated and educated respondents coming from the rural area. But in the case of the urban respondents the uneducated respondents' extent of identification was found to be greater than that of the educated respondents.

That extent of identification with 'Humanity' was also found to be equal in the case of the uneducated and educated respondents coming from the rural area. But in the case of the urban respondents the extent of identification of the uneducated respondent was found to be greater than that of the educated respondents.

From the analysis obvious that the mean score percentage of the educated urban respondents regarding the 'Hindu community as a whole' was lowest as compared to their views about the other four categories. Because of availability of newspapers, radio, etc., are the educated Scheduled Castes people living in the urban area are aware of the social and political developments and happenings in the country. They know that even if the Scheduled Castes people given up their traditional occupations, the stigma of Harijan would still be attached to them and they would not be able to establish proper relationship with the caste Hindus of the same occupational rank. They are also aware of the fact that the people belonging to Scheduled Castes have not been given social recognition by the society in which the people belonging to upper and middle castes wield socio-economic and political power. They have read about Dr. Ambedkar's views on the issues relating to the Scheduled Castes. They also known the way he fought for their betterment. In a later chapter we will see that a very large majority of the educated urban respondents considered him as their 'ideal hero.' They were very much influenced by his views. According to Merton "The person who identifies himself with a reference individual will seek to approximate the behaviour and values of that individual in his several roles."

The views expressed by Dr. Ambedkar from time to time make it clear that he felt that the upper castes 'did not recognise Untouchables as a part of the Hindu community. During the course of data collection these view were expressed to some extent by the educated and politically conscious urban Scheduled Caste respondents. This, perhaps, explains why they did not appreciate the 'Hindu community as a whole' wiın the same intensity as the uneducated respondents belonging to their own castes.

For decade Untouchability was prevalent in the Hindu society and so some castes were excluded from its main stream. Despite the Governmental efforts as well as social reform movements, Untouchability has not yet been completely eradicated from our society. Because of their ignorance and poor socio-economic condition, even now some people belonging to the Scheduled Castes are unable to locate themselves in the "social space." Generally, in the backward rural areas the Scheduled Caste people (from their childhood) are not trained to develop their potentialities and face the social stigma and evils boldly. Circumstances force them to learn to be submissive and accept the verbal and physical assaults of the higher and middle caste people as almost a part of life and thus they have to live with their inadequacies. The family and the neighbourhood inculcate in them a feeling that they are weak, helpless and powerless and for the sake of survival they have to compromise with this unpleasant situation. Under such circumstances, they get very little scope to develop their potentialities.

The life of a vast majority of the rural people revolves around agriculture in which a fairly good number or Scheduled Caste people are engaged as agriculture labourers. Their range of contacts are very limited. By birth they belong to Scheduled Castes and by profession they are mostly engaged in low paying jobs. Thus they are on the lowest rung of the social as well as the economic ladder. Very few of these have learnt any skills. The Jack of skill and technical knowledge do not provide much scope to the rural Scheduled Caste people for raising their standard of living. Hence they find it difficult to break away from their traditional occupations and to a very great extent are economically dependent on caste Hindus. They find it difficult to exercise and assert their rights though they have the protection of the law. The identification a shown by the uneducated Scheduled Caste people perhaps indicates the economic security provided to them by the existing caste system. Under these circumstances, they do not want to be regarded as being outside the fold of the Hindu community and hence their extent of identification with the 'Hindu community as a whole' is higher. It denotes that when it is a question of survival the dominated group would prefer to be identified with the dominant group in order to meet its basic needs. But this raises a question—if all the people belonging to the Scheduled Castes become educated and politically aware, will they reflect the same views on the issues as expressed by our educated urban respondents? This requires further research and probing and the data at hand do not provide scope to go into such details.

2

The Dalit Movement in India

The Dalit Movement has attracted some leading sociologists over the past two decades in India and abroad. The centenary year of B.R. Ambedkar has seen a plethora of publications, thus adding to the growing literature on Ambedkar, Dalit politics and the Dalit Movement. Among sociologists it is possible to discern a dominant ideological current that has bearings on the study of the Dalit Movement. There is a 'liberal' trend among a group of scholars, who believe that it is the ancient Hindu reactionary traditions and the deep-rooted prejudice of the upper-castes against Dalits, that has led to the protest of the latter. Thus, this trend views Dalit protest as a necessary outcome of an obscurantist Hindu tradition. This liberal view also has a strong tendency to assume that the Dalit Movement is limited to achieving a partial advance in the socio-economic, civic and political fields within the existing social order, thus hardly any thought is expended on radical transformation in other respects. It is due to this ideological position, that concepts like 'social mobility,' 'reference group' and 'relative deprivation' figure so prominently in their writings on the Dalit movement thus becoming a major frame of reference in studying the Dalit Movement. Among those notable scholars who fall into this liberal category is M.S.A. Rao who has used similar concepts for understanding the emergence of the protest movement among the backward classes and the Dalits in India (1982:4). Rao, taking a cue from Merton and Runciman, has argued that social mobility forms the major basis of the theory of relative deprivation (1982:4). (Social conflict as a basis of relative deprivation finds mention in Rao's study but without much detailed discussion.) Rao further argues that the relative deprivation is connected with the moment of emulation of a positive reference group (1982:194).

Other scholars too have tried to link the emergence of the Dalit Movement with the issue of relative deprivation, reference groups and social mobility (Joshi, 1987; Issac, 1964; Lynch, 1974; Silverberg, 1968; Singer and Cohen, 1968; Sachchidananda, 1978; Bhat, 1971; Ram, 1988; Patwardhan, 1973). It is obvious from the works of these scholars that terms like social mobility and relative deprivation form and major frame of reference in discussions of the emergence of reform, protest and movement among the Dalits. In studying Dalit mobility it has been suggested by some scholars that the process of Sanskritisation could be a model, *i.e.*, certain Dalit groups or individuals try to adopt either ritually or culturally higher groups or individuals in order to achieve similar social position or to adopt the values that promote the aspirations of an atomised individual in a civil society. According to this view if the Dalits fail in their achievement of thus imitation of the Sanskritisation model of upper mobility, they then suffer from relative deprivation because at the social level their attempt to overcome relative deprivation is restricted by the upper-caste group whom they cite as a reference group existing mostly in a pre-civil social situation which is still dominant in some pars of the country. At another level, the articulation of relative deprivation among the educated Dalits might take place when compared to the Westernised high caste. Thus, in the Indian case, as Oommen has pointed out, the deprivation is multi-faceted (1990:225).

However, studies establishing a link between the emergence of the Dalit movement and relative deprivation, social mobility and reference group theory, though inadequate in understanding the Dalit movement, need to be supported on the following theoretical and strategic grounds. Both historically and dialectically, this concept of relative deprivation could capture social reality at a particular historical juncture when Indian society was trying to release itself from the feudal ethos which was facing an ever-increasing threat from the advancing civil society in India. In this transitional process, the Dalits who were aspiring towards mobility of various kinds but were unable to achieve it due to the restrictions imposed by the feudal as well as colonial vested interests felt deprived, a fact which time and again prompted the Dalit movement, for example in the 1930s in Maharashtra, to challenge feudal values through a process of emulation and Sanskritisation (see Omvedt, 1994). This attempt to imitate the upper-caste values particularly in the case of the Maharas of Maharashtra, certainly contributed to the development of a negative consciousness which according to Gramsci may not constitute a mature and fully evolved class consciousness, but certainly is the first glimmer of such consciousness constituting the basic negative, polemical attitude (see Guha, 1983: 20). Gramsci further argues that the lower classes, historically on the defensive, can only achieve self-awareness through the identity and class limits of their enemy (Guha, 1983).

Taking a cue from Gramsci, Ranajit Guha tries to understand this consciousness of the insurgent peasantry in colonial India. He says, it was only by attacking the material symbols of governmental and landlords authority that the insurgents upset the established order. They did so by undermining its dominant semifeudal culture as well. Insofar as religion constituted the most expressive sign of this culture in many if its essential aspects, the peasants' defiance of the rural elite often involved an attempt to appropriate the dominant religion or to destroy it. To those who were high up in society the emulation of their culture by the lower strata seemed always fraught with danger. There have been occasions when, thanks to the stimuli given to casteism by British colonial policy, Sanskritising movements among the lower castes to upgrade themselves by adopting the rituals and religious idioms of their superiors were resisted by the latter and generated much social tension and even some actual violence (1983:20). (This is also borne out by Ambedkar's Chowder Tank movement at Mahad in 1927 and temple entry movement in 1929 at Nasik.)

In the same vein, the Dalit social protest of 1930s, under the leadership of Ambedkar focused its attention on entering the *Savarna* temples and tried to improve the status of Dalits through the imitation of Hindu lifestyle by adopting gods and rituals of the upper-castes, *i.e.,* through the process of Sanskirtisation (see Srinivas, 1962). Although the usual tendency is to view Sanskritisation as a cultural process aimed at bringing about changes in the lifestyle of Dalits, it had important structural ramifications in that the protest orientation and counter-mobilisation were necessary attributes of Sanskritisation movements since the Dalits often did so in a spirit of recalcitrance and the upper-castes invariably opposed such attempts (see Oommen, 1990:255).

Second, studies understanding the Dalit movement in terms of relative deprivation and social mobility helped to reveal the role of castes and inherited status that have for long influenced the monopolising of the available jobs by the upper-castes which viewed caste mobility as dangerous and disruptive of the social fabric. It is in this context that studies establishing a connection between the Dalit movement and the above concepts bring out the latent contradictions of a socio-economic and political nature. Moreover, such studies also reveal that relative deprivation leading to socio-economic mobility has after all a democratising impact on the socio-economic, political and bureaucratic structure of India, (Shah, 1991:603).

Studies linking relative deprivation and social mobility with the Dalit movement assume importance at least for tactical and strategic reasons especially when the studies of these movements are denied their legitimate place in the academic world and are considered to be deviations from the mainstream and irrelevant in the Indian context (Oommen, 1990: 30). Oommen, while criticising this approach as historical and biased, has argued that an adequate framework for the study of social movements should take into account the historicity, the elements of social structure and the future vision of the society in which they originate and operate and it is the dialectics between these which provides the focal point for the analysis of social movements (Oommen, 1990: 30).

However, the present scenario, highlighted by three major developments of the total marginalisation and annihilation of the rural Dalits, Hinduisation of the Dalit masses and the growing crisis of the Indian welfare state seems to be questioning the theoretical validity of relative deprivation both as a conceptualisation and as a form of consciousness. Concepts of relative deprivation and also social mobility are quite inadequate to capture this reality at the theoretical level. Given the happenings in the rural areas where the upper-castes or class forces are committing brutal atrocities on the Dalits, and when the state's response is either callous or repressive, the Dalits do not feel a sense or relative deprivation so much as a total alienation and exclusion and the threat of physical liquidation. What one observes in rural Maharashtra and also in the rest of the country is the complete alienation of the Dalits from resources like land, water and agricultural implements. Thus, the Dalits do not find sufficient access to either the natural and human resources and, therefore, feel totally marginalised in relation to the so-called decentralisation of political power in rural India. Such a situation where the Dalits are collectively and absolutely worse off, questions the validity of the concept of relative deprivation which primarily presupposes the perception of contrasting one's situation, even at the most trivial level, with that of others worse off than oneself (Runciman, 1966:9). Moreover, it is this perception of total exclusion from the developmental processes that forces the Dalits to protests in the most militant way, ranging from radical reaction to physical retaliation in self-defence. This militancy is evident among the Dalits of Andhra Pradesh, Bihar and Maharashtra.

However, in the urban setting in Maharashtra, the concept of relative deprivation and social mobility has some relevance to the new educated employed Dalit class that is emerging from among the Mahars and Mangs. It is true that the Mahars do feel relative deprivation at two levels. First, at the vertical level, the Mahars feel relatively deprived both socially and materially in comparison with the upwardly mobile upper castes. To assuage this feeling of deprivation, these Dalits, particularly officers, float some kinds of welfare associations to gain, among other things, more patronage from the system. This is to overcome their relative deprivation by raising the material and social status of the individual up to the level of those who are immediately above them. Thus, at the vertical level, the reference group for the Mahars is the upwardly mobile upper-castes.

However, at the horizontal level, for the Mahars and for the Mangs the reference group is the emerging Mahar elites. The Mahars and even the Mangs in the urban setting seem to have developed a sense of relative deprivation often reflecting the feeling of hatred, contempt and jealousy towards those Mahars who according to the group under reference are more fortunate in raising their material status. This feeling of relative deprivation among the less fortunate Mahars and Mangs is now being openly articulated—an articulation that can lead to the formation of a sub-group or a social category based on the region-specific identity of these Mahars. The Marathawada Mitra Mandal (the organisation of the Dalit teachers from Marathawada University) is a case in point. It is alleged that the members of this Mitra Mandal feel relatively deprived in comparison with the Dalits of north Maharashtra and Vidarbha (see Jondhale, 1992). It is interesting to note here that this is true of the Dalits of Telangana who feel relatively deprived in comparison with the Dalits of coastal Andhra Pradesh, particularly of the Guntur region, who, according to the former, are far ahead in terms of socio-economic and educational achievements.

This relative deprivation and social mobility performs a very important function for the stability of the system. First, the feeling of relative deprivation, if assuaged successfully, has an inbuilt atomising tendency which isolates the Dalits under reference from the large Dalitness. Second, the concept of relative deprivation tends to prevent the formation of a critical consciousness which involves the critique of the Indian state and the lopsided economic development. Instead, it fetters itself to the narrow contours of envy, contempt and hatred against persons from the same social situation. For example, the Dalits (Mahars, Buddhists) of Marathawada who, in educational and material terms, are relatively backward as compared with the Dalits of Vidarbha consider this relative advance of their counterparts from Vidarbha as the major cause of their own backwardness. They, however, do not consider their backwardness as being a result of the feudal ethos that dominated the socio-economic life of Marathawada for 500 years which eventually led to the late arrival of these Dalits in the main channels of advancement.

Similarly, the feeling of relative deprivation makes the Mangs (Dalit) overlook the connection between their backwardness and their traditional skilled occupation which had bound them to the feudal agrarian structure. Due to the socio-economic and technological changes in Indian agriculture and state intervention in the condition of the Dalits in general, the Mangs are now being displaced from the agrarian economy and are compelled to take to education and to the subsequent quest for jobs. This compulsion and displacement is a result of the replacement of the old agricultural implements which were made by the Mangs, by the more sophisticated implements manufactured by the Garwares. In this situation, the Mangs are lagging behind the Mahars owing to their late response to the state which, as we wills see, seems to have lost the capacity to accommodate these latecomers in its rather obsolete network of patronage. Why do the Mangs no question the capacity of the Indian state and find faults with the markets society which underlines and renews the structures of inequality? Why does their feeling of relative deprivation revolve around the relative advance of the microscopic section of Mahar elites? The answer to this question lies in the politicisation of relative deprivation.

The politics of relative deprivation finds expression among the Mang elites. These elites, though emerging on a very small scale, are now found vocalising the sense of relative deprivation of the common Mangs with the intention of sharing the spoils with the Mahars by forcing a bargain with the power centres. (This was evident at the state-level conference organised by one of the important Mang leaders at Tehalkaranji in November 1991)

This political expression of relative deprivation aimed at creating a constituency among the ignorant but innocent Mangs surfaced in one of the state-level conferences organised by the Mang elites in Maharashtra at Ichalkaranji in November 1991. It is interesting to note that in this particular conference the feeling of relative deprivation with a negative reference to the Mahars was articulated by the Mangs with the encouragement and patronage of the upper-caste political forces which are alleged to be instrumental informing hostilities between the two communities for the electoral politics of the reformer in the state.

Needless to say, this feeling of relative deprivation, suspends, if not eliminates completely, the possibility of the development of a homogeneous Dalit unity cutting across castes as well as regions. Second, since relative deprivation underlines the quest for social mobility, this mobility syndrome of Dalits has the potential of diffusing the formation of social consciousness by promoting individual consciousness which has atomising dimensions leading to the isolation and independence of the Dalits from their community. Thus, this feeling of deprivation and the element of mobility inherent in its pushes the Dalits away from the centre of collective struggles to the periphery (participating in the struggle by paying only lip sympathy to the Dalit cause), thus bypassing the assumption of the historical responsibility that Ambedkar and rested on their shoulders of their emancipation and that of the common Dalits from their dehumanising conditions. Therefore, while studying the Dalit movement in terms of relative deprivation or social mobility one should not lose sight of the fact that social mobility has sustained the belief in functionalism which has a stabilising influence on society and polity.

The real serious damage that the concept of relative deprivation can cause to the Dalit movement today is that it represents a negative Utopia in two major senses. First, this concept at the theoretical level, attempts to describe 'what is' without behind the Mahars owing to their late response to the state which, as we will see, seems to have lost the capacity to accommodate these latecomers in its rather absolete network of patronage. Why do the Mangs not question the capacity of the Indian state and find faults with the market society which underlines and renews the structures of inequality? why does their feeling of relative deprivation revolve around the relative advance of the microscopic section of Mahar elites? The answer to this question lies in the politicisation of relative deprivation.

The politics of relative deprivation finds expression among the Mang elites. These elites, though emerging on a very small scale, are now found vocalising the sense of relative deprivation of the common Mangs with the intention of sharing the spoils with the Mahars by forcing a bargain with the power centres. This political expression of relative deprivation aimed at creating a constituency among the ignorant but innocent Mangs surfaced in one of the state-level conferences organised by the Mang elites in Maharashtra at Ichalkaranji in November 1991. It is interesting to note that in this particular conference the feeling of relative deprivation with a negative reference to the Mahars was articulated by the Mangs with the encouragement and patronage of the upper-caste political forces which are alleged to be instrumental in farming hostilities between the two communities for the electoral politics of the former in the state.

Needless to say, this feeling of relative deprivation, suspends, if not eliminates completely the possibility of the development of a homogeneous Dalit unity cutting across castes as well as regions. Second, since relative deprivation underlines the quest for social mobility, this mobility syndrome of Dalits has the potential of diffusing the formation of social consciousness by promoting individual consciousness which has atomising dimensions leading to the isolation and independence of the Dalits from their community. Thus, this feeling of deprivation and the element of mobility inherent in it pushes the Dalits away from the centre of collective struggles to the periphery (participating in the struggle by paying only lip sympathy to the Dalit cause), thus bypassing the assumption of the historical responsibility that Ambedkar had rested on their shoulders for their emancipation and that of the the common Dalits from their dehumanising conditions. Therefore, while studying the Dalit movement in terms of relative deprivation or social mobility one should not lose sight of the fact that social mobility has sustained he belief in functionalism which has a stabilising influence on society and polity.

The real serious damage that the concept of relative deprivation can cause to the Dalit movement today is tha it represents a negative Utopia in two major senses. First, this concept at the theoretical level, attempts to describe 'what is' without linking it with the question 'what can be' and, thus, results in an adequate description of social phenomena. While it denies to sociology a critically subversive character it also denies an emancipatory consciousness to the groups under reference. It impels the Dalit groups to organise their thought and action not in their own authentic terms but in terms of those privileged sections whose hegemonic world-view underlines the structures of domination.

The state plays an extremely important role in keeping the sense of relative deprivation vital. This is done systematically and shrewdly by transferring resources from the more privilege sections to the underprivileged sections as a part of its welfaristic strategies. In doing so the state not only weerkens the critical consciousness that had begun to articulate itself against the structure of domination but as a corollary also discredits the movement by co-opting the most vocal and assertive elements into the pacification structures built around the welfare state.

For example, in the 1960s in Maharashtra, the state seems to have, time and again, effectively scattered Dalit consciousness which in the process of its development had opened up the possibility of reaching the level of a broad social consciousness. In Maharashtra this was exemplified by Dadasaheb Gaikwad in the early 1960s in the Dalit movement. Later, there was an alliance of the Dalit Panthers with the Left and democratic forces. However, this integrating consciousness got dissolved into separating individual consciousness which brought about the fragmentation of the Dalits into at least a dozen small groups of the Republican Party of India (RPI) in Maharashtra. This diffusion was effected through the introduction of the Integrated Rural Development Programme (IRDP) and National Rural Employment Programme (NREP) package and the discrediting was achieved through the co-option of important Dalit leaders, including Gaikwad, by the state.[1]

But scholars studying the Dalit movement have not focused much attention on such a vital aspect of the movement which involved the subversive role of state. Oommen has tried to locate the state response to the Dalit movement, but he seems to have given a more formal and legalistic explanation of the state response to the Dalit movement or any other movement of the weaker sections of the population (Oommen, 1990: 187). For example, he tenders to argue that the state becomes either repressive or it discredits the movement because the latter defies its authority (Oommen, 1990: 187). But an emasculation of any movement, particularly the Dalit movement in Maharashtra in the late 1960s and early 1970s, was done by the state not solely because the Dalit Movement had undermined its authority but more because this has of the dalit movement which focused only on the question of redistribution of land has seriously threatened the material interests of the rural rich as a result of the Dalit demand for government land and land declared surplus under the ceiling law.

Though the concepts of relative deprivation and social mobility play a diffusionist role as they render the formation of an integral Dalit consciousness difficult in the urban setting, they were relevant inasmuch as they could capture the social reality, although fractionally. However, it seems now that the growing crisis of the Indian welfare state, the systematic attempt by the Hindutva forces to Hinduism the Dalits and the revitalising of Buddhist culture among the Dalits all seem to have rendered the concept of relative deprivation too fragile to lead to new initiatives.

The levels of the feeling relating to relative deprivation and social mobility are conditioned by the capacity of the state to intervene in the conditions of the population sections concerned. This can be corroborated by citing Runciman, who observes that in Europe the welfare provisions of the inter-war period helped to keep the level of relative deprivation lower than the actual hardships imposed by the depression might appear to warrant (1966:70). Moreover, in the Indian context, the experience is quite contrary to that stated by Runciman because, in view of the absolute deprivation of the Dalits it was politically imperative for the Indian state to nurture the feeling of relative deprivation among them by shifting resource (this includes various constitutional provisions and different welfare programmes for the Dalits) from the more privileged sections thus reducting the absolute deprivation into relative deprivation. And this tends towards atomisation, thus denying a collectively critical subversive consciousness to the community as a whole.

In the last few years—particularly in the urban setting—developments in Maharashtra in the sphere of state and religion are likely to conduce towards the initiation of the reverse process: a shift from relative to absolute deprivation. This is so because the current fiscal crisis of the Indian state renders it difficult to shift resources from the privileged to the under-privileged. This impels the state to withdraw largely from the social sphere. This with drawal is evident from two facts. First, according to a rough estimate, the budgetary provision for social welfare is 1 percent. Infact, the percentage outlay on the Scheduled Castes had increased only marginally from 0.35 percent in the First Five Year Plan to 0.84 percent in the Fifth Five Year Plan. Thus, we find that the Scheduled Castes, who constitute 15 percent of India's population and a much greater proportion of the poor, have been provided a disproportionately low share of the plan resources. Second, the state's thrust towards privatisation means practically a total marginalisation of the Indian Dalits because the private sectors would hardly be interested in accommodating them. This growing privatisation and the resultant exclusion of the Dalits from the urban settings also is likely to lead towards an articulation of their critical consciousness as a collectivity. At any rate, this is a likely consequence when deprivation tends towards absolution under present circumstances. However, as of today, such an articulation of corporate Dalit consciousness has not found any organised expression among the urbanite Dalits. Unfortunately, the growing privatisation of the Indian economy and the crisis of the welfare state in India did to figure at all in the state conference recently organised by the Backward, Adivasi and

Muslim Caste Federation (BMCEF) at Nasik.

Moreover, the sense of relative deprivation which emanated as a reaction to the upper-caste restrictions against the Dalits adopting certain high-caste social norms had led the Dalits in the later 1930s to overcome it through collective mobilisation. But today, the Hindutva forces are taking the initiative in accommodating the Dalits in the Savarna culture. The notable example of this deceitful elevation of the Dalits was marked by the laying of bricks during the Ram Shilanyas at Ayodhya by two Dalits who were pressed into god Rama's service by the BJP-VHP combine a couple of years go. In this particular case it was certainly not a genuine desire to overcome the relative deprivation of the Dalits that led to their mobilisation. However, whatever the reasons, this certainly suspends the necessity for the Dalits to initiate movements towards Sanskritisation. Further, since this concept or relative deprivation has meaning only in the hierarchised socio-economic situation, it cannot explain the phenomenon of the Buddhist conversion movement in Maharashtra and of late in the Andhra Pradesh.

Dr. Ambedkar established '*Independent Labour Party*' in 1936, which got tremendous success in the elections. His party served for the development of agriculturists, industrial labourers and the Untouchables. In the later phase, Dr. Ambedkar established 'Scheduled Castes Federation' in 1942. Through this federation, he started to fight for the equality and freedom for the Untouchables. Dr. Ambedkar wanted to create a new political party named "Republican Party", but due his sad demise, he could not do it. However, the followers of Dr. Ambedkar established '*Republican Party of India*' in 1957. But this was not a party as expected by Dr. Ambedkar. It was a mere a political party of the 'Mahars'. 'Dadasaheb Gaikwad', 'B.C. Kamble', 'Khobragade' and others were being holding the Ambedkarite movement. They could establish the popularity to some extent. But, after 1964-65, the party went for number of splits. Some of the leaders joined 'Congress Party'. The Ambedkarite movement lost their strength. The Ambedkarite community was devided into number of groups.

It led to number of problems in the movement. (Nimbalkar Waman: 1990:63-65). The Ambedkarite community was without strong leader. In the meanwhile, a strong political organisation called '*Dalit panther*' was established by '*Raja Dhale*', '*Namdev Dhasal*' and others, which went for highest popularity among the Ambedkarites.

Ambedkarite Movement in Maharashtra had been strong in the seventies. The movement was monitored by '*Dalit Panthers*'. It was a result of increasing serious atrocities in Maharashtra and as result of these, '*Dalit Panther*', an organisation was established in 1972. '*Raja Dhale*' and '*Namdev Dhasal*' , the two leaders establishing popularity among the Scheduled Castes in Maharashtra. The whole movement was captured by the '*Panthers*'. The '*Dalit Panther*' had declared and protested against silver jubilee of India's Independence by calling it '*Black Day*' (in 1972). This organisation was banned during emergency period for demonstration of any revolt. (Naik C.D.:2003:354) This organisation opposed the social injustice and atrocities with an aggressive and violent agitation. The organisation created enthusiastic environment among the SCs. 'J.V.Pawar', 'Arjun Kasabe', 'Vijay Girkar' and others were also associated with the '*Panthers*'. The '*Dalit Panther*' got a mass base in the society. But unfortunately, the first split among the '*Panthers*' took place in 1974, and since then number of splits have been taken place. '*Namdev Dhasal*' and '*Raja Dhale*' had a differences, which led the end of mass based organisation. Ultimately, in the year 1989, the '*Dalit Panther*' was dissolved and absorbed in the 'Republican Party'. (Jadhav Raja :2000:72-73)

Nimbalkar Waman (1990:30-32) has explained the the popularity, achievements and drawbacks of '*Dalit Panther*' in Maharashtra as below:-

"The branches of '*Dalit Panther*' were being established in all the towns and villages of Maharashtra. The large majority of the dalit youths were attracted towards this organisation. Since the leaders of the organisation, were creating the literature, the flame of the movement went up. It was a complete unity of the dalit leaders, which gave a big blow to the established society. The speeches of the '*Panthers*' were aggressive and attractive. The activists were reaching at every atrocity in every village and were conducting strong agitation. The best achievement of the '*Dalit Panthers*' was renaming the 'Marathwada University' as 'Dr. Babasaheb Ambedkar Marathwada University'. This organisation was a real mass based organisation in Maharashtra. But the activists of the '*Panthers*' were in disciplined. They had no perfect social goal. They were lacking maturity. They believed in violence. Hence they were framed by the police department. Number of cases were registered on the names of 'Panthers' , they were sent to the prison. Some of them were killed. Ultimately, the '*Dalit Panther*' went for a first split in 1974 and continued with number of splits".

Even now, the period of '*Dalit Panther*' is remembered by the 'Ambedkarites'. Dr. Ambedkar never supported the violent agitation, but he believed in democratic agitation. Some of the scholars have criticized the way of '*Panthers*'. But it is a fact that, there was a strong social unity among the 'Ambedkarites'. In the present time, the existence of '*Dalit Panther*' organisation is at negligible sense. 'Namdev Dhasal', holds his group of Panthers, but the organisation has no mass base.

In the contemporary period, the Ambedkarite movement has been monitored by number of '*Republican Parties*', but in general, there are four strong major groups or parties of 'Republicans', which holds the movement. They are- "*Republican Party of India* (Athavale)", "*Republican Party of India* (Gavai)", " *People's Republican Party of India* (Kawade)" and "*Republican Party of India-Bahujan Mahasangh* (Prakash Ambedkar)". The first group of 'Ramdas Athavale', has a coaliation with 'Nationalistic Congress Party' of Sharad Pawar., the second group of 'R.S. Gavai' has attachment with the 'Congress Party', the third group of 'Jogendra Kawade' and the fourth group of 'Prakash Ambedkar' operating the movement independently. None of the leader has got strong mass base. Comparatively, 'Prakash Ambedkar' has been monitoring the movement with wide vision of the backward castes. Coincidently, he happens to be a grandson of Dr. Babasaheb Ambedkar, hence this has been important factor in monitoring the Ambedkarite movement. It must be stated that, Prakash Ambedkar is an intellectual and matured leader of the Ambedkarite movement. However, he could not establish a strong political success in Maharashtra. None of the leaders have established a strong political success, independently, in Maharashtra. This has been a major limitation of the Ambedkarite Movement. Apart from these, there have been number of small political groups established at the local level, who believes in their idea. During last few years, the political parties like '*Bahujan Samajwadi Party*' (Kashiram and Mayavati), "*Lokjan Shakti Party*" (Ramvilas Paswan) and others also entered in Maharashtra to capture the Ambedkarite community. Although, so far, they could not establish their place among the Ambedkarites, but they have been able to give an alternative way. In the crowd of these political groups, the Ambedkarite movement has lost its political strength. Therefore, insignificant size of Ambedkarites also have joined 'Congress Party', 'Nationalist Congress Party', 'Bharatiya Janata Party' and 'Shiv Sena'. This all led the movement towards the confused environment. Ambedkarite community has been devided into number of groups, and each group differs from others. There has been absence of unity over the ideology. Interestingly, all the political leaders from Ambedkarite community always addresses the meet, function with the name of Dr. Babasaheb Ambedkar. There has been one important blame over the 'Republicans', i.e., although there have been number of groups in Ambedkarite movement, it is said that, these have been concentrated among the 'Mahars' or 'Neo-Buddhists'. It is a fact to some extent. It is also a fact, that, this dominated Ambedkarites have been fighting for number of social and economic problems of the Scheduled Castes, and the fruits have been given to all the segments of the Scheduled Castes.

Dalit Literature

The 'Dalit Literature' created by the Ambedkarites has been popular in the India, especially in Maharashtra. The reason for the popularity of '*Dalit Panther*' organisation was that, the leaders like 'Namdev Dhasal', 'Raja Dhale' and others were the writers. This branch of literature has been throwing a light on the social life of untouchables in India. The writers demands aggressive change in the social situation. The writing was in 'Marathi', the regional language of Maharashtra. Some of the well-known writers are- 'Namdev Dhasal', 'Raja Dhale', 'Gangadhar Pantavane', 'Shankarrao Kharat', 'Daya Pawar', 'Narayan Surve' and others. The '*Dalit Literature*' has been so powerfull that, it has crossed the region of Maharashtra and India. Number of translations of '*Marathi Dalit Literature*' have been carried out in various Indian languages, like 'Kannada', 'Gujarati' etc. Not only that, the literature also has been translated in 'English'. The English writers like 'Eleanor Zelliot', 'Milton Israel', 'Gunther Sontheimer' etc. have translated the '*Dalit Literature*' into English. (Naik C.D.:2003:365-366). Interestingly, this literature has been popular even in the contemporary period of times.

Avinash Dolas (1995:9-11), an eminent scholar of Ambedkarite Movement in Maharashtra, has reviewed the '*Marathi Dalit Literature*'. He writes that, "The Dalit Literature began from Ambedkarite Movement. The movement could establish enthusiastic environment and a new approach among the Dalits. The beginning was as back as in 1927. The speeches of Dr. Ambedkar was presented by the artists in the form of poems and stories. Number of News papers and journals were started and through which various writes were being putting their views towards the dalits". The author has reviewed the dalit literature created by 'Anna Bhau Sathe' (Fakira), 'Shankarrao Kharat' (Manuskichi Haak), 'Sukharam Hivarale' (Gaavkari), 'Baburao Bagal' (Jevha Mee Jaat Chorali), 'Vaman Hoval' (Benayad) and others. The author says that, some of the writers from the Upper Castes, like 'V.M. Joshi', 'Mama Varekar', 'V.S. Khandekar', 'Kolhatkar' and others, were inspired by the 'Gandhi's Philosophy', whereas some of the writers (from the upper castes) like, 'V.V. Shirvadkar', 'Anant Kanekar', 'Karandikar', 'Bedekar' and other were inspired by the 'Marx's Philosophy'. But the writers from the Panthers and others from Dalit Community have created anti-Hindu social literature. Further the author points out that, "During 1970-1980, the Dalit literature was dominated by the writers from the wing of '*Dalit Panthers*' 'Namdev Dhasal', 'Raja Dhale', 'J.V.Pawar', 'Arjun Dangle', 'Avinash Mahatekar' and others had created an appealing literature in the form of poems and stories, which attracted the dalit youths". (*Ibid.* pp.58-59)

NOTES & REFERENCE

1. *Sugawa*, a special number on the theme 'Ambedkar and Hindurvavadi' was published by Sugawa Publications at Pune, 1991. (in Marathi).

3

Caste Impact in Indian Politics

During the seventh General Elections in 1980, with the Janata coalition which had swept the field two years earlier now defunct, the Lok Dal believed they had a strategy in hand that would exploit class feelings to their advantage. Since becoming Chief Minister I 1977, Karpoori Thakur had promoted a job reservations scheme whose purpose was to provide greater access to government employees for the Backward Castes and to other 'downtrodden' elements in Bihari society. It was anticipated that the more than fifty percent of the province's population which comprised the middle-caste category would respond to this policy and vote their class interests.

Only it did not tour out that way, because Yadav politicians got control of the Bihar branch of the party and transformed it into a patronage machine for their own caste to the exclusion of middle-range cultivators from other castes. Under this parochial leadership, the Lok Dal, in one commentator's view, acted like a small regional party. It fielded only 36 parliamentary candidates (out of a possible 54) and garnered a mere 15.6 percent of the vote in the elections. It came to be perceived by the public as an ethnically-based listed of class-based organisation with the result that most of its hoped-for constituencies turned away from it. They supported Congress (1) "because [the loc Dal] came to be branded by all sections of the electorate, including the non-Yadav backward castes, as a 'Gope Dal', (a party of the Yadav's alone.)" What this suggests is that where a single caste is large enough to convert numerical dominance into political dominance, and for any reason undertakes to do so, this in effect transforms class into an ethnic category which for the length of time this situation persists results in class disintegration. But this is clearly not the major trend under current Indian political conditions.

The Bharatiya Kranti Dal /Lok Dal/Dalit Mazadoor Krishak party is a political organization with firm roots in the Backward Caste Communities of the entire Hindi Belt. The Urs-Hedge phenomenon in Karnataka, the Shared Pawer phenomenon in Maharashtra, and the anti-Solanki phenomenon in Gujarat are structurally comparable manifestations of awakening class. Consciousness among smaller-scale cultivators and economic and status concerns. The potentiality exists in these formations for a peasant party national in scope, expanded to coterminate with the limits of the national economic environment.

The application of the Westminster system to a highly pluralistic society of sub-continental proportions and European cultural dimensions, beset wit scarce resources and limited mobility opportunities, has placed a premium on political office-holding not as a means of public service but as a means of social mobility through access to a system of spoils. With thousands of political offices ranging from more than500 parliamentary seats, over 3,500 provincial assembly seats, and seemingly limitless numbers of local elective offices, a vast national mosaic of access-points to the public larger now exists.

Political careerism has become a way of life in itself for thousands of Indians, and the cherished goal f many thousands more as attested by the astonishing number of persons who run for office as independents in almost every constituency at every level of the polity at election time.

In the recently concluded parliamentary and assembly elections as many as thirty-five to forty constituencies and generally speaking independents outnumbered all party-selected candidates by rations of three or four tone. While most of these candidacies could be dismissed as frivolous from the standpoint of realistic chances of being elected, their number bespeaks of how strongly the profession of politics has come to be viewed in India as a pathway to fame and fortune.

Dalit Vision of A Just Society in India

The word 'Dalit' in Sanskrit means 'broken,' and 'downtrodden.' Dr. Babasaheb Bhimrao Ramji Ambedkar often described the 'Untouchables' as broken people. The Dalits are socially weak, economically needy and politically powerless, despite the protective policies followed by the Government under provisions of the Constitution (guaranteeing them educational concessions and scholarships, employment and political reservations and socio-economic welfare benefits). The term 'Dalit' thus describes a condition of being underprivileged and deprived of basic rights and refers to people who are suppressed on grounds of their lowly birth. The word 'Dalit' is a descriptive word evocative of bondage and agony, the anguish and frustrated aspirations of a vast victimised section of the Indian population right down the ages. The word as such was first used as far back as 1931 in journalistic writings. Following this, the Dalit Panther Movement of Maharashtra in the early 1970s gave currency to the concept and the word 'Dalit' to highlight the sufferings and struggles of the untouchables to begin with, but later extending it to include all the oppressed groups, namely the Scheduled Castes, the tribes, the workers, landless labourers, small farmers and other poor, and also the neo-Buddhist converts. However, more recently, the Scheduled Castes (earlier called Depressed Classes under the British and Harijans by Gandhiji) prefer calling themselves 'Dalits' or 'the oppressed,' while the tribals prefer to call themselves '*shoshits*' or the exploited. Both the words are evocative of the anguish and frustrated aspirations of these victims of social injustice for several thousand years. The word 'Dalit' particularly emphasises the dehumanising "caste oppression' that makes them outcastes and Untouchables (a degradation not shared by the tribals or *shoshits*), within the context of the Hindu caste system with its religion-social organising principle of 'purity and pollution' (see Zelliot, 1992; Prabhakar, 1990: 24–25; Massey, 1990: 40–41; Irudayaraj, 1990).

The ideology of the Dalits for a just society has mainly been developed by eminent personalities like Mahatma Jotirao Phule (1826–90), E.V. Ramaswamy Periyar (1879–1973) and Babasaheb Ambedkar (1991–1956), with many others throughout India (Narayanswami Guru in Kerala, Acchutanand in U.P. and Mangoo Ram in Punjab) (See Omvedt, 1996). They attacked the system of exploitation at all levels—cultural, economical and political. They developed their vision of Indian society as an alternative to the upper-caste understanding of India. Hence it is important to pay some attention to this historical context in which the Dalit ideology has been developed.

Two Visions of Indian Nationhood

During its almost 5,000 years of history, the vast Indian subcontinent has nourished the growth of a great civilisation, characterised by the diversities of many cultural and racial groups, castes, religions and languages, and vitalised through cross-cultural contacts.

In the early stages, unity was achieved by recognising this plurality and the autonomy of various groups. According to Kothari, 'in the absence of centralised political authority 'it was the Indian civilisational enterprise' which "over the centuries achieved a remarkable degree of cohesion and held together different sub-systems in a continental-size society" (Kothari, 1988:2223). Thus, the unifying force of Indian civilisations was the acceptance of multi-culturality and linguistic diversity rather than political ideology.

Modern nationalism which emerged in Western Europe in the second half of the 18th century quickly spread throughout the world in the 19th. In India, it can be traced to the political and administrative unification which was later followed by economic unification. The first expression of national consciousness in India was in the form of social and religious reform movements. The important question then was—what was the cultural foundation of Indian society and how was it to be reconstructed as a modern nation on par with other modern nation states? Two strands of thought emerged: one led to an attempt at reconstructing Indian society on the basis of Western ideas originating in the 'Ages' of Reason, the Enlightenment and Liberalism, and the other wanted the reconstruction to take place on the foundation of ancient upper-caste Brahminic Hindu traditions.

The enlightenment philosophy of the West began to have its impact on the newly Western-educated Indian during the colonial period. It gave rise to the 'Indian renaissance.' The spirit of English education was liberal, rational and utilitarian, a spirit that challenged the very presuppositions on which the orthodox Hindu systems of conduct were based. With ruthless self-criticism reformers sought to lay the ground for a total social transformation, to weld science and rationality to Indian culture, to recreate India.

The beginning of this social revolt can be easily identified with the thought of Rammohun Roy (1772–1833). Roy vividly described the degraded state of society and acknowledged without embarrassment the virtues of Western learning, liberal, legal and social institutions, and the Western social ethic (see Damle and Aikara, 1982: 77). With a view to cleansing Hindu culture and society of its weaknesses and incongruities, he founded the Brahmo Samaj. The purpose of the Brahmo Samaj was to restructure Hindu culture in terms of modernity. His revolt against contemporary Hindu society and his appeal to Indian to purify their religion and reconstitute their social institutions echoed throughout the century after his death.

Indian Nation Built on Aryan Vedic Culture

While Rammohun Roy envisioned an Indian society ultimately renovated by centuries of exposure to Western science and Christian morality, Dayananda Saraswati (1824–83) on the other hand urged a regeneration of Hindus through adherence to a purified 'Vedic faith.' The Arya Samaj was founded by Dayananda Saraswati in 1875. Its aim was to bring about social and religious reform through a renewal of early Hindu doctrines, its favourite dictum ran thus: "Back to the Vedas" and Aryavarta for the Aryans' (William Roy Smith, 1938:57). It is in this context of the upper caste Hindus' identifying the 'nation' and the 'national culture' as basically Hindu, as deriving from Vedic times, and as fundamentally a creation of the Aryan people that we should view the alternative vision provided by Jotirao Phule who was bom in a Shudra caste.

The Vision of Jotirao Phule (1826–90) for a Just Society

Jotirao Phule was the first Indian to proclaim in modern India the dawn of a new age for the common man, the down-trodden, the underdog and for the Indian women. It was his aim to reconstruct the social order on the basis of social equality, justice and reason. As we have just seen, the 'Aryan theory of race' constituted the most influential common discourse for discussing caste and society in Phule's time. European 'Orientalists' like William Jones, Charles Wilkins, James Prinsep and others (see Marshall, 1970: 1–44) conveniently used it to assert an ethnic kinship between Europeans and the ancient Vedic peoples (see O'Hanlon, 1985:57–59). The constant interest of European scholars like H.H. Wilson, C.Lassen, H.T. Colebrooke, Monier Williams, Max Mueller and others (see Kejariwal, 1988) in ancient Aryan society and their appreciation and praise of this society provided an important moral boost to high-caste Indians. Thus, Indian civilisation was seen as primarily derivative from Aryan civilisation, and the caste system was lauded as a means by which people of diverse racial and cultural backgrounds were brought together and subjected to the civilising influence of the Aryans (Omvedt, 1976: 103).

At one level, Phule simply reversed this notion, arguing that the low castes, whom he sometimes called 'Shudras and Atishudras' and were simply listed as 'Kunbis, Malis, Dhangars . . . Bhils, Kolis, Mahars and Mangs,' were the original inhabitants of the country, enslaved and exploited by conquering Aryans who had formulated a caste-based Hinduism as a means of deceiving the teeming masses and legitimising their own power. It was the confirmed and sincere view of Jotirao that the ancient history of India was nothing but the struggle between

Brahmins and non-Brahmins (Keer, 1964:120). Hence, Phule consciously sought to bring together the major peasant castes (these were, besides the Kunbis or cultivators, the Malis or 'garden' cultivators and Dhangars or shepherds) along with the large Untouchable castes of Mahars and Mangs in a common 'front' against Brahmin domination (see O'Hanlon, 1985:131).

Jotirao's attack on Brahminism was uncompromising. He realised that the seeds of the Brahmins' power, supremacy and privileges lay in their scriptures and Puranas; and these works and the caste system were created to exploit the lower classes (see O'Hanlon, 1985: 122–132). Phule also reinterpreted sacred religious literature. To give an example: by reading the nine avatars of Vishnu as stages of the Aryan conquest and using King Bali as a counter-symbol to the elite's use of Ram, Ganapati or Kali (see O'Hanlon,1985: 137; Keer, 1964 : 90–125). Thus, Jotirao attacked the Brahminical scriptures and Puranas, revolted against priestcraft and the caste system and set on foot a social movement for the liberation of the Shudras, Atishudras (Untouchables) and women.

Phule realised that the strongest hold of religious tradition on the people derived from the extensive integration of Hindu religious literature into the popular culture and oral traditions. Phule's answer to this was to provide alternative accounts of the texts, myths, and stories most common in popular Hinduism. He linked these with important symbols and structures from contemporary Maharashtrian society in order to convey the real community of culture and interest that united all lower castes against their historical and cultural adversaries: the Brahmins.

To fulfill his life's ambition to establish a casteless society, Phule founded the *Satya Shodhak Samaj* (truth-seeking society) on 24 September, 1873. The Samaj set up the first school for girls and untouchables. Phule also organised marriages without Brahmin priests, widow remarriages, etc. According to Phule, the performance of any religious ceremony by a Brahmin priests for a member of another caste expresses in a concrete form the relations of purity between them which make up the basis for

Hindu religious hierarchy. It is the Brahmin priest alone who, in his ritual purity, has the power to mediate between the human world and that of the high gods, and so it is he who controls the entry of divine power into the world (see Babb, 1975:31–67). For this season, Phule felt that the employment of Brahmin priests negated the very principle upon which he hoped a community of the lower castes would be based. Thus, the Satya Shodhak Samaj actively encouraged marriages without Brahmin priests. Thus, the Salya Shodhak Samaj assumed a vital role as the ideological conscience for all those who identified themselves with the lower castes, whether they belonged to the Samaj or to one of the numerous other groups working for lower caste uplift.

A fundamental difference between the 'historical' religions, Christianity and Islam, and Hinduism, consists in their attitudes to history. While the latter conceives of human history as the eternal recurrence of illusion, the historical religion works out its destiny within those very processes, organised around the Church, the visible body of the faithful, the book and the incarnated Saviour. All human history takes its meaning from the struggle (Weber, 1958:167). As we have seen, one of Phule's main concerns was to locate the struggle of the lower castes within history, to transform myth into history and establish a diachronic relation between present and past oppression. King Bali had stood as they symbol and mainstay of the pre-Aryan realm. Here, it is possible to see how Phule's perception of human history strengthened his scheme more generally. On the mass level, history became purposive (see O'Hanlon, 1985: 203–205).

Thus, the 19th century saw the beginning of a violent and controversial movement of protest amongst western India's low and untouchable castes, aimed at the effects of their lowly position within the Hindu caste hierarchy (see O'Hanlon, 1985).

Cultural Controversies in the National Congress

A second stage is the modern development of Indian nationalism emerged in 1885 with the foundation of the Indian National

Congress by an Englishman, Allan Octavian Hume. The Indian National Congress tried to define a new India in terms of ideas borrowed from European political experience and Western social ethics (see Donald Eugene Smith, 1963:880). All the same, by the end of the 19th century there was a mighty struggle for the control of the Congress. The two factions, namely the moderates and the extremists, held radically different views about the proper ends and means of the nationalist movement. While the moderates the National Congress like Dadabhai Naoraji, Mahadeva Govinda Ranade and Gopal Krishna Gokhale stood up for reforms in Hindu culture, the extremists like B.G. Tilak glorified Hindu culture and opposed any kind of reform. While the moderates or liberals envisioned a modernisation of India through the adoption of the Western parameters of justice, order, rationality and the secular state, Tilak on the other hand glorified the deeds of the Vedic civilisation (Parvate, 1959:463). Tilak's overall consideration was the promotion of solidarity and unity among the Hindus, and hence he emphasised the superiority of their religion, encouraged revivalism, politicised the Ganapati festival and converted Shivaji into a cult Figure, thus serving both religious and political objectives (Michael, 1986:91–116). The style of the revivalists was aggressive and tended to reflect a Kshatriya (Warrior) world-view.

When Mohandas Gandhi publicly emerged on the Indian political scene after World War I as the Mahatma, he received widespread revivalist support, Indeed, many believed him to be one of themselves. While Gandhi had much in common with the revivalists, many came to oppose him as they gradually became better acquainted with his ideas. Gandhi declared that his Hinduism included all that he knew to be best in Islam, Christianity, Buddhism and Zoroastrianism. Gandhi strove unceasingly for Hindu-Muslim unity, convinced that ultimately both religions were true and valid (see Gandhi, 1949). His deepest conviction was that God, Truth and *ahimsa* (non-violence) were all one and the same. *Satyagraha* (truth-force, non-violent resistance) was thus based on Gandhi's personal religious faith and outlook.

The revivalists were disturbed by Gandhi's ascetic non-

Kshatriya style of leadership, his definition of dharma as the non-violent pursuit of 'truth,' and his assimilationist conception of the Indian nation, which he saw as a brotherhood or a confederation of communities. Dr. Kurtakoti, Sankaracharya (a Hindu spiritual guide) of Karvir Perth implored Hindus to return to the militancy advocated by Tilak, Vivekananda Gose (Anderson and Damle, 1987: 20).

The Equality Question Among the Revivalist

As a result of the intensification of Hindu-Muslim tension between 1921 and 1923, the dormant Hindus Mahasabha, formed in 1915 as a forum for a variety of Hindus interests (*e.g.*, cow protection, Hindu in the Devangiri script, caste reforms, etc.), was revitalised. It is in this setting of "Hinduism in danger' that a new, more influential Hindu militant organisation known as the Rashtriya Swayamsevak Sangh (RSS) was established in 1925 by Dr. Keshab Baliram Hedgewar, who was deeply influenced by Tilak.

The RSS claims to defend Hinduism against its so-called antagonists. Its avowed objective is the unification of the Hindu community and the inculation of a militant awareness of its common heritage and destiny—One of the most influential books in the development of Hindu nationalist ideology was the treatise on Hindutva by V.D. Savarkar, a close associate of Tilak. Hindutva refers to a people united by a common country, blood, history, religion, culture and language. This idea become the foundation and basis of the RSS's activities. Members of all castes are welcomed into the RSS if they conform to behavioural standards considered proper by the RSS leaders. Those standards continue to reflect, to a larger extent, the Maharashtrian Brahmin cultural values of the founders of the RSS.

According to M.R. Golwalkar who succeeded Dr. Hedgewar as the chief of the RSS, at the heart of Hindu culture is Hindu religion, and at the heart of Hindu religion are the noble ideas of the Vedas. He also asserted that the diverse languages of India are the offshoots of Sanskrit, the dialect of the gods and the enlightened Aryans (Golwalkar, 1947). Golwalkar regretted the fall of the Brahmin in Hindu society which, according to him, was deliberately brought about by the British. Thus he presents what may be called the Golwalkar notion of social structure in these terms: The unique feature of our society is its diverse functional groups (castes). The present-day mind accustomed to viewing through foreign 'isms' and their high-sounding slogans of equality, has failed to grasp this unique feature and talks of classless society. The glorious main feature which once distinguished our society was the *varna vyavastha*. 'But it is being dubbed as casteism and scoffed at.' There are some who never tired of propagating the idea that the caste system was responsible for our downfall. This is not ture, the so-called caste-ridden society has remained intact and firm and alive and unconquerable whereas the so-called 'casteless' societies crumbled at the very outset before foreign conquests (Golwalkar, 1968 : 89–120).

Gandhian Approach to Caste and Varna

Hindu reformers, including Gandhi, were of the opinion that the Untouchables could maintain a Hindu as well as a Vankar or Malliga identity without the stigma of being untouchables. The Hindu reformers delinked the problem of untouchability from the caste system. Untouchability, according to them, was not an essential part of Hinduism or, for that matter, of the caste system. It resulted from a violation of the basic spirit of Hinduism. 'Vamashram,' Gandhi asserted, 'was for the preservation of harmony and growth of soul' (Shah, 1995:28). Gandhi repeatedly harped on the evils of untouchability. He himself adopted a Dalit girl as his daughter. He voluntarily decided to live with the Untouchables to become one with them. He symbolically called Untouchables Harijans, that is, people of God. He started the Harijan Sevak Sangh to launch programmes to remove untouchability and improve the economic conditions of the Untouchables (Shah, 1995: 28–29).

It is in this context of Hindu revivalism and the Gandhian approach to caste and varna that one has to view the ideas and visions of non-Brahmin leaders like Periyar and Ambedkar.

Periyar's (1879–1973) Vision for Justice

E.V. Ramaswamy Naicker, known as Periyar (Great Sage), was born in 1879 in Erode into a respectable middle-class family of artisans. He married at the age of 13, but after six years he became a *Sanyasi*, travelling as a religious mendicant over the whole of India. In his visits to pilgrim centres, he gained an intimate knowledge of the evils of popular Hinduism and also of the exploitation of the masses by Brahmin priests.

Periyar became convinced that casteism and Hinduism were one and the same. He wanted Hinduism, as he saw it, to be removed altogether. His movement took a turn towards racial consciousness and became a 'Dravidian' movement, seeking to defend the rights of the Dravidians against Aryans domination. It blamed the Aryans for introducing an unjust and oppressive social system in the country (see Hardgrave, 1965: 17). Periyar realised that the important feature of all new ideologies of the elite was the 'Aryan view of race.' The 'Aryan view' was adopted enthusiastically by the Indian elite as a new model for understanding caste. That is, Brahmins, Kshatriyas and Vaishyas were held almost as a matter of definition to be the descendants of invading Aryans, while Shudras and Untouchables were those of the native conquered inhabitants. In this new language of caste and race, to claim, 'Aryan' descent was equivalent to claiming 'twice-born' status to say 'Dravidian' or 'non-Aryan' almost equivalent to saying 'Shudra.'

The high-caste elite of Indian began to take Aryan and Sanskritic culture as the basis of 'Indian nationality,' but in so doing they were in fact taking a part—the culture of the upper castes and roughly more northern groups—for the whole. Periyar's movement sought to defend the rights of the Dravidians against Aryan domination. He saw in the Brahmins the representatives of Hindu arrogance and the stronghold of social injustice (see Devanandan, 1960).

Naicker quit the Congress and attacked it as a tool of Brahmin domination. In 1925, he organised the 'Self-respect Movement.' designed as Dravidian Uplift, seeking to expose Brahmin tyranny and the deceptive methods by which they controlled all spheres of Hindu life. Naicker publicly ridiculed the Puranas as fairy tales, not only imaginary and irrational, but grossly immoral as well. Naicker attacked the Hindu religion as the tool of Brahmin domination.

Under the Congress ministry of C. Rajagopalachari in 1937, Hindi was introduced to the South as a compulsory subject in schools. Taking this as an affront to Tamil Culture and its rich literary tradition, Tamil patriots like Annadurai, Karunanithi and others under the leadership of Naicker reacted with violent protest. Naicker saw the imposition of Hindi as a step towards subjugation of the Tamil peoples by the North Indian Aryans.

The Hindu religion was denounced as an opiate by which the Brahmins had dulled and controlled the masses. "A Hindu in the present concept may be a Dravidian, but a Dravidian in the real sense of the term cannot and shall not to be a Hindu" (A.S. Venu, cited in Harrison, 1960:127). Pains were taken to destroy images of Hindu deities such as Rama and Ganesha. According to Periya, 'Rama and Sita are despicable characters, not worthy of imitation or admiration even by the lowest of fourth-rate humans. "Ravana, on the other hand, is depicted as a Dravidian of 'excellent character." In his preface to The Ramayana: A True Reading he states that "the veneration of the story any longer in Tamil Nadu is injurious and ignominious to the self-respect of the community and other country" (Naicker, 1959 : iii–iv).

On the eve of Independence, Naicker called upon the Dravidians people of South India 'to guard against the transfer of power from the British to the Aryans' (The Hindu: 11 February 1946). Fearing Brahmin dominance under Aryan 'imperialism,' Naicker called for the formation of a separate South Indian state, Dravidasthan. Today, the several Dravidian political parties in Tamil Nadu trace back their inspiration to Periyar in their programme to build a Dravidian civilisation the Indian subcontinent.

Ambedkar (1891–1956): A Revolutionary

It is indeed impossible to understand the contemporary Dalit revolt without understanding the ideas of Dr. Bhimrao Ramji Ambedkar. For a growing number of Young Dalits across Indian, many born after his death in 1956, he has become a symbol of a vision that can be achieved, a vision of freedom from social and economic injustice. Ambedkar attacked two central features of the Indian order: culturally enforced inequality and economic inequality. Throughout his writings and actions there is one common thread, *i.e.,* socio-economic transformation in India requires a cultural revolution, one that will not only destroy the culture of the past but also built something of value in its place.

Ambedkar was inspired and guided by the noble example set by Mahatma Jotirao Phule. Phule was no longer there to guide Ambedkar. Nevertheless, his example had an indelible imprint on Ambedkar's mind. He was determined to complete the work started by Jotirao and it is not surprising that it became his life's mission (Rajasekhariah, 1971: 18–19; also seen Keer, 1974: vii).

Ambedkar was a revolutionary. He led the fight against untouchability, Hinduism, and the Brahmin caste. He was convinced that the caste system was not only unjust but also immoral. He established a new dispensation, a new religion (neo-Buddhism) whose foundation is its unequivocal rejection of Hinduism. Ambedkar criticised the caste system vehemently. For him, the fight against casteism and untouchability was central, at the heart of his agenda. Hence, he was very critical of the two contemporary approaches to reform the caste system, namely Dayananda Sarasvati's and Gandhi's. According him neither could bring about a real solution to casteism. He held that society should be based on the three fundamental principles of liberty, equality and fraternity.

If caste was to be destroyed, he said, then its religious foundation in the Vedas and Shastras must also be destroyed. Faith in these scriptures was nothing more than a legalised class ethic favouring the Brahmins. If you wish to bring about a breach in the system, then you have got to apply the dynamite to the Vedas and the Shastras, which deny any part to reason, to the Vedas and Shastras, which deny any part to morality. You most destroy the Religion of the Smritis' (Ambedkar, 1945a; 70).

Ambedkar also rejected the position of Gandhi with regard to caste and its reform. Gandhi felt that the ancient Hindus had already achieved an ideal social system with *varna vyavastha*. According to Gandhi, 'The law of varna means that everyone will follow as a matter of *dharma-duty* the hereditary calling of this forefathers... he will earn his livelihood by following that calling (Zelliot, 1992:154). In contrast, Ambedkar believed that an ideal society had yet to be achieved India. For him, the priority was not making 'Hinduism' or Hindu society 'shine forth' but building a new, equal, free, open non-hierarchical, modern India.

According to Ambedkar: 'It is wrong to say that the problem of the Untouchables is a social problem...the problem of the Untouchables is fundamentally a political problem (of minority versus majority groups)' (Ambedkar, 1945b: 190). Hence, Ambedkar launched his revolutionary movement for the liberation and advancement of the Dalits. On 20 July, 1942, he declared at Nagpur. With justice on our side, I do not see how can lose our battle. The battle to me is a matter of full joy. The battle is in the fullest sense spiritual. There is nothing material or sordid in it. For our struggle is our freedom. It is a battle for the reclamation of human respectability which has been suppressed and mutilated by the Hindu social system and will continue to be suppressed and mutilated if in the political struggle the Hindus win and we lose. My final word of advice to you is, 'educate, organise and agitate;' have faith in yourselves and never lose hope (see das and Massey, 1995: viii).

Thus Ambedkar was able to put the untouchability issue on the centre stage of Indian politics (see Shashi, 1992).

Ambedkar painfully realised that within Hinduism the Untouchables would never be able to get equal status and receive just treatment. He was also convinced that individual and group mobility was difficult for the Untouchables within the Hindu social system. In this context, he saw two possibilities for social emancipation: the political unity of Untouchables and an en masse conversion. Hence, in 1936 he talked of conversion to another religion: though I have been born a Hindu, I shall not the as a Hindu' (31 May 1936, Bombay). He had already made a first mention of conversion in the Yeola Conference of 1935.

The conversion call of Ambedkar disturbed the Hindu leadership very much. Several leaders tried to persuade him not to go ahead. Ambedkar expressed surprise that the caste-Hindus, who had never shown any fellow-feeling for the Untouchables were suddenly beseeching them to stay within Hinduism. Since Untouchables had been for centuries ill-treated and humiliated by caste-Hindus, why did they now suddenly take such an interest in keeping them within the Hindu fold?

On 14 October 1956, after long deliberation and a conscious choice in favour of Buddhism, Ambedkar took his *diksha* at Nagpur at 9.30 a.m. Assembled were about five lakh Mahars, who all converted to Buddhism on that day. Ambedkar's embracing of Buddhism was a strong protest against all that the Hindus had failed to do. For him *swaraj* did not mean anything if it did not also put an end to the slavery of the Untouchables (Gore, 1993: 144).

Ambedkar's legacy at the time of his death were a large body of writings; a political party for all oppressed Indians, the Republican Party; a nascent Buddhist conversion movement; a system of higher education begun with Siddharth College in Bombay and which was spreading to other cities; a host of reserved places for Scheduled castes in education, administration and legislative bodies; and a critical mass of awakened ex-Untouchables (Zelliot, 1996: 12).

The above Phule-Ambedkar-Periyar tradition represents the effort to construct an alternative identity of the people, based on non-Aryan and low-caste perspectives, that was critical not only of the oppressiveness of the dominant Hindu caste society but also of its claims to antiquity and to being the dominant Indian tradition (see Omvedt, 1994; 1996).

Politics of Numbers in Independent India

With the growth of democratic institutions and the 'politics of numbers' in contemporary India, the Dalits began to assume some importance in national politics. The Dalit leaders in different political parties, in order to take advantage of the situation and bring about their liberation, began to mobilise forces.

To fight untouchability, which was spread throughout the country and was deeply rooted in the minds of the people, was not a simple task. First, the Dalit leaders had to lift their brothers and sisters from their ignorance; to teach them to agitate against injustice and to organise them into a pulsating force. The response was at first weak, clumsy and slow, but later it became positive and healthy. Second, the leaders had to face and stand up against the reactionary caste-Hindus. Every step towards the liberation of the Dalits was followed by a sharpe reaction from the caste-Hindus in the form of boycotts, atrocities, arson and other crimes. In all such critical situations, the Dalit leaders had to stand by their poor brethren, raise their morale and help them wage a peaceful and legal battle against the forces of reactionaries. Third, the Dalit leadership had to convince the government to accept their demands of human rights.

An Unfinished Revolution

All these things, certainly, have an impact on the socio-economic and cultural life of the Dalits. Economic development in general as well as the reservation policy and the special component plan have led to some improvement in the educational and economic status of the Dalits. Their literacy rate increased from 10.2 percent in 1961 to 37.41 percent in 1991 and their enrollment in schools doubled between 1981 and 1991. The reservation policy has also had a positive impact. The number of Dalit employees in government service has risen from 212,000 in 1956 to 604,000 in 1992, while those employed in public sector undertakings have increased in number from 40,000 in 1970 to 369,000 in 1992 (see S.K. Rhorat, 1996:1). These and other positive trends led to some decline in the percentage of poor Dalits, In rural areas the percentage of the poor among the Dalits declined from 58.07 percent in 1983–84 to 50 percent in 1987–88, while in urban areas this percentage went down from 56.52 percent to 46.95 percent during the same period (see S.K. Thorat, 1996:1).

Despite these improvements, Dalits still lag far behind other groups in Indian society. While their literacy rate is now 37 percent, that of non-Dalits is 57 percent. In rural areas, where most Dalits live, their economic base continues to be weak. In the late 1980s, 63 percent of the Dalit households were landless or near-landless wage labourers, but only 31 percent of non-Dalit households were. Only a fraction of Dalits owned land and 73 percent of those who did were marginal farmers with too little to live on. The cumulative result has been a high incidence of poverty among Dalits, 50 percent as compared with 37 percent among non-Dalits in 1987–88. Meanwhile, civil rights violations and atrocities against Dalits continued to increase. In1966–76 there were 40,000 such atrocity cases or 4,000 per year; in 1976–87 there were 17,000 or 8,500 per year; in 1981–86 there were 91,097 or 18,000 per year (S.K. Throat, 1996:4)! The Government admitted in Parliament on 22 April 1994 that there were 62,113 cases of atrocities against Dalits and tribals between 1991 and 1993. The annual report of the Ministry of Welfare for 1995–96 shows that the number of cases of crimes against SCs and STs committed by members of non-Scheduled Castes and non-Scheduled Tribes has shown a continuous increase with the number of cases going up from 25,352 in 1992 to 38,926 in 1994. The increase in crimes against SCs and STs in 1994, as compared with crimes into the preceding year, was as high as 36 and 27.4 percent respectively (Godbole, 1997:14). Studies indicate that atrocities were committed over land disputes and minimum wages as well as to prevent Dalits from securing justice under civil rights laws.

With regard to Dalit women, in all respects, they are at the lowest level of the socio-economic and educational hierarchy. Dalit women tend to be concentrated in areas of work in which wages are lowest and regular employment least certain. In 1991, about 74 percent of them were agricultural labourers, whereas only 43 percent of the non-Dalit women were agricultural labourers. Even in urban areas, 28 percent of the Dalit women were employed as agricultural labour, as compared to only 5 percent of the non-Dalit women (Vimal Thorat, 1997:1).

The New Economic Policy also affects the Dalits adversely. After the new reforms were implemented in 1990, both unemployment and the poverty level increased. The poverty ratio increased from 38 percent to 48 percent in 1992. Since the Dalits constitute the bulk of the poor and unemployed, they have suffered most. The number of Dalit employes in government service declined from 628,000 in 1991 to 604,000 in 1992, while those in the pubic sector dropped from 432,000 in 1990 to 369,000 in 1992 (see S.K. Throat, 1996:4). What is most disturbing is that most of this decline has occurred in the lower-level posts. Thus the burden of the New Economic Policy has fallen most heavily upon the poor.

Thus, the persistence of poverty and caste injustice remain a shameful blot on Indian society. Over the past 10 years, an emerging Dalit identity and social consciousness has created a new political consciousness among poor rural Dalits. The consciousness is by no means limited to the Scheduled Castes. It has begun to symbolise a much broader spectre of the oppressed and hitherto excluded social strata. It is based on an attempted, though by no means still realised, solidarity of the poor and the discriminated classes of the people.

Today's political cent in India cannot be understood without taking into consideration the phenomenon of the upsurge of Dalit-OBC self-consciousness that has spread from the South and the West to the North. Among the northern states, the meteoroic rise of the Bahujan Samaj Party in Uttar Pradesh since the 1980s is almost unprecedented. Of late, the Bahujan Samaj Party has also made significant inroads in Punjab and Madhya Pradesh. The desecration of an Ambedkar statue in Mumbai on 11 July, 1997, resulted not only in several deaths in police firings but caused widespread protests and bandhs (strikes and lockouts) throughout Maharashtra and Gujarat. This suggests that Dalit consciousness has become assertive. This new spirit of independence among Dalits is not confined only to economically developed western states of India, but is a country-wide phenomenon. This together with the logic of fresh realignments of political parties has made the Dalits the new pivotal players in Indian politics. The Dalits and the backward castes hold immense political potential. If they could be united into a powerful force, they would bring about a true social revolution or equality and justice.

There are some signs of this today. The Dalits are asserting themselves much more than before (Vanaik, 1997:323–26). They have decided that they will not call themselves 'Harijans'—simply because it is a paternalistic expression. There are numerous small and large organisations of Dalits all over the country such as the Dalit Sangharsh Samiti in Karnataka; Indian Dalit Federation in Kerala; Dalit Maha Sabha in Andhra Pradesh; Bahujan Samaj in Uttar Pradesh, Bihar and other northern states; Dalits Sena consisting of Dalits of several states, etc. The Dalits are trying to get organised into a well-coordinated political movement with an all-India organisation and all-India leadership that can challenge the established socio-political order. This aim is inspired by their resentment against the existing social system which expresses itself through various forms of agitation and struggle and is bound to acquire the momentum of a national movement in the years to come (Ayrookuzhel, 1990: 14–23).

However, the movement is always opposed by external and sometimes by internal forces. Every more of Dalit mobilisation is virtually followed by a counter upper-caste assemblage. The on-going controversy centred around Aambedkar and his detractors is one of this kind (see Shourie, 1997). While there is a concerted attempt by the Brahminical forces to co-opt Jotirao Phule and Ambedkar as 'Hindu reformers,' a sustained attack has been launched by Hindutva/Brahminical ideologies like Arun Shourie's to denigrate and maling these great Dalit bahujan personalities. In reality this controversy centred around Ambedkar and his detractors should be analysed in the broader perspective of the emerging sociopolitical trends in the country. As discussed earlier, the social justice movement has been one of the most remarkable and relevant sociopolitical movements of modern India. In fact it is evolving into a democratic, em-powering and assertive mass movement against the Brahminical social order. Ambedkar is of central relevance to the growing human rights movement and is fast emerging as the pan-Indian leader, symbol of the Dalits and other oppressed masses. Precisely because of this, Ambedkar has been chosen as their prime target since he best symbolises the aspirations of the Dalitbahujan masses. The Phule-Ambedkar ideology has challenged the very legitimacy of Hindutva/Brahminism as a social order or religion.

Unfortunately, Dalits are also divided among themselves and their leadership too is riven with both confusion and schism. The Dalit movement is beset by the virus of endemic co-option—from the old days of the Scheduled Caste Federation and the Republican Party to the Dalit Panthers to the various anti-reservation movement to the recent controversy on Arun Shourie's book on Ambedkar (Shourie, 1997). In spite of this experience of continuing let downs and reactions, there are also signs of new hope emerging, namely the Dalit-Bahujan alliance of Scheduled Castes (SCs) and Other Backward Castes (OBCs), offshoots of the Mandal slogan couched not only in terms of achieving social justice but also capturing political power (see Kothari, 1997:439–58). There is also no shortage of sensitive and committed people in the Dalit movement to take forward the vision of Phule, Periyar and Ambedkar. Hence, what is required is a strong unity among the poor, the marginalised and the outcastes. This will not be an easy task because they are internally divided into several castes and sub-castes, externally scattered almost throughout the vast country and prone to be a prey of divisive forces. Therefore, the Dalit leadership has to strive constantly for bringing about unity among the Dalits and other oppressed groups to fight against their common foes and enemies (see Kshirsagar, 1994).

Conclusion

The pioneers who worked for the liberation of the Dalits and other backward castes, like phule, periyar and Ambedkar, propagated the idea of the need for a cultural revolution or a total transformation of Indian society. They rejected the vision of the upper castes which identified the Indian nation as basically Hindu, deriving from Vedic times, and fundamentally a creation of the Aryan people. While rejecting the ideals of the upper-caste notion of Indian society based on the ideas and values of Manu and *varna vyavastha*, they propagated the principles of equality, justice, liberty and rationality. This broad-based standpoint is widely accepted among the Dalits.

There is, however, much discussion and dispute on the means of attaining these ideals of social justice. This problem worsened by the multiple divisions existing in the Dalit ranks; for example, the Dalits are divided among themselves along sub-caste lines and like the proverbial crabs keep clawing at each other, pulling down those who move up, so that all of them remain in their lowly position. They are also hindered by the present political climate where the upper castes are trying to establish a unified Hindu cultural nationalism.

All the same, it is true that if the goals of a movement are clearly outlined and well-defined, and if it finds active support, first in its own ranks, and second, in those of others likely to be sympathetic to their cause, the movement will become an organically living one. What is needed is good and able leadership. If the cause is right and the leadership is good, then the movement will certainly grow even if faced with antagonism and hostility. Every step ahead will encourage the Dalits to move forward towards final victory.

Caste Sentiments are Fashioned by Class Interests[1]

Mayawati was Chief Minister twice and is on the roll for a possible third stint if the elections work out her way. Her success is not because she is across opportunity or an increable megalomaniac a she is made out to be in the popular press, but because she is a careful strategist. Unlike many other Dalit leaders, she knows that one way of getting around the obstinate arithmetic of caste numbers is to fox the opposition with the chemistry of alliances. It must be recognized that Mayawati thinks along class lines even though she gives the impression for being a caste-obsessed politician. She has gone off the beaten tracks and actively wooed the upper castes, including the Brahmins, because she knows that the Dalits have no immediate class contradictions among them. In fact, there are large areas of concordance between the upper castes and the Dalits for whom, in both instances, the common enemy is the aggressive OBC. True, the Dalits are mostly in villages and the upper castes in cities, but because contemporary politics has given an overbearing presence to OBCs in both these locales, a most unusual class alliance has emerged.

Brahmins, Baniyas and Kyasthas do not see the Dalits as antagonists as they do the rising factor capitalists' led by Mulayam Singh. The Yadvas, JATS and Gujjars are competing against Brahmins and Baniyas for urban jobs. These traditionally privileged urban upper castes do not mind the Dalits for they are reconciled to reservations for them, and have been so for years. Their immediate combatants are the mandal-energised OBCs. This may come as a surprise to many urban observers who have been bred on traditional textual renditions of Brahmin caste oppression. It is here that Mayawati's genius kicks in She Knows from intimate experience that it is the same cluster of OBCs that threaten and terrorise he scheduled Castes in India's villages in act, the Yadavs. Kurmis, Jats and The vars are probably more cruel and rapacious in their relationship with the Scheduled Castes than the traditional upper castes were. I have been told by Dalits in western Uttar Pradesh that they would be happer in erstwhile zamindari areas of east Uttar Pradesh because the Jats and Gujjars (the leading OBCs) are not the dominant communities there. This is the rationale behind Mayawati's attempt to get traditional upper castes on her side for she knows that a deal of this sort would not hurt the scheduled Castes as a naïve understanding might propose.

So what we have is a grand alliance that brings together urban and all of India like never before and yet all of this lies the beauty and elegance of her scheme, It I like a classic one two punch in boxing that totally disortents the opposition. Mayawati can think innovatively because she lives at ground level reality whereas her deractors only read about it second hand. She knows grandstanding on purist themes would sound good to the literate classes but would be of little use in advancing Dalit interests. In this she is mohallas ahead of her competitors including the communists and her fellow travelers in Ministers and her fellow travelers in Maharashtra and elsewhere. She has no time for preening before the UN commissariats in Durban, nor does she treame before the ghosts of Gandhi and Ambedkar.

Mayawati's moves have a Maoist touch to them though their stated ideologies were far apart. Like the Chiologies were far apart. Like the Chinese leader. Mayawati too is a great strategist. She is constantly on the lookout for alliance partners and finds them in places where purists would not even deign to look For those with long term memories it may be recalled that Mao, too, was attacked by Russian and European marzist for he allied with the rich peasants when it resulted him and occasionally with landlords too –the somewhat improverished ones.

Through all this, Mao never took his eyes of the ball. The poor peasants were always his most durable friends, just as the Scheduled Castes are for Mayawati. Many communists in the West berated Mao for his unorthodox peasant Marxism, but he made the revolution whereas his detractors did not. Likewise, there are many today who see only an opportunist in Mayawati, but she became Chief Minister twice and is readying herself for many more stints in that chair.

It is true that Mayawati learnt her basic lessons from her mentor Kanshi Ram. But she soon outstripped him as a strategist and tactician. She knew that the terms as Chief Minister were going to be tenuous leaving her little room to make a long-term dent on the uplift of the Dalits. Big things can hardly be done at such sort notice.

Once again she though out of the box. Time was short but she wanted to leave behind a legacy of her chief ministership that would be hard to over look no mater which political high street one took. In a few months she set up Ambedkar's statues all over UP. She may no longer be the boss anymore, but every time you see Ambedkar's stylized icon you cannot help but think Mayawati. Through hundreds of these concrete Ambedkar memorials. Mayawati has solid life her reputation with Dalits in the cities and villages of UP. I know from my own field experience in rural UP that OBCs resent this consistant in your face Ambedkar/ Mayawati presence much more than the Brahmins or other members of the upper castes, do. If I could sense It, I am sure Mayawati knows all about it and revels in her ability to haunt the OBCs as a perennial spectre and alloming eminence grise Brahmins and other upper castes are of little consequence in the villages but can tip the scales in terms of numbers and can also be unuseful if one could leaverage on their social networks. Unlike many other Dalit hotheads, Mayawati does not demonise these so-called upper castes for she seems them essentially as toothless and effete tigers. Even so if their reputation, such as it is, can be mobilized to advance the Dalit cause where is the harm?

Nowhere in this very careful reasoning, does Mayawati ever betray her mass base which continues to be the Scheduled castes, whether in urban Lucknow or in rural Mirzapore. There will always be the very poor village bund OBCs who would find Mayawati a possible alternative, and then there are the strays that the SP can pickup from factional wars in the ranks of the Samajwadi Party and the BJP. She has, therefore nothing.to lose in her strategic pursuit to win over the upper caste bloc.

We must hand it to Mayawati that she is not blinded by caste passions. Her political strategy is premised on the belief that caste sentiments are fashioned by class interests. This is what allowed her to forge an alliance between traditionally antagonistic castes for she recognized that they had a common enemy in the OBCs. This truth along with the political opportunities it presented, was much dear to her than any elevated copy book morality. After al, her commitment is to the Dalits and not to the read relate brokers of ivory towers.

NOTES

1. Dipankar Gupta, *Hindustan Times*, 10-4-2007, Page 10).

4

Rural Dalit and Social Development

The ancient varnas function as a pan-Indian scheme. They can be Considered to form an all-India caste system. In khalapur, for example, one can identify the Brahman as Bahmans, the Rajputs as Kshatriyas, the Banias as Vaishya, and the Gold smiths, Carpenters, Blacksmiths and Gosains as Shudras, and the Shoemakers, the Chamar Leather workers, and the sweepers as Panchalas or Untouchables. In South India, it is said that there are no Kshatriyas or Vaishya, although some rulers have legitimized themselves as Kshatriyas through Brahmanical rites of mobility.

Dalits represents a larger social category and includes Scheduled Castes, Scheduled Tribes including nomadic tribes (*vicharati jati*), Other Backward Castes (OBCs) and minorities. They also include Dalit women who suffer from dual disadvantages, *i.e.*, being Dalits and being women. The burden of the argument is that rural development has generated processes and patterns which have tended to subordinate and marginalise the masses including the Dalits, their men, women and children (Brara, 1983; Breman, 1994). We address ourselves to two questions. (i) What are these subordinating processes and patterns?; and (ii) What are the perceptions and experiences of the masses, and how do they cope with emerging crises and challenges? In answering the first question, we try to note down and discuss the conditions of the rural poor at the ground level. These processes, we believe, have their roots in the macro developments in the spheres of policy and delivery package (Adelman, 1975; Frankel, 1978; Haque *et al.*, 1977). These decisions are taken at a distance farthest from the village, taluka or the district. Thus, when the Dalits and other poverty-stricken groups come face to face with this 'development'; the question before them is whether to take it or leave it. There is hardly and third option before them. But how do they perceive and interpret these changes occurring around them? Do they mutely accept the message of the 'development-doers,' without searching for rejoinders? This constitutes our second question, and we try to explore this on the basis of our field experience in the region. In this section, we will discuss briefly the developments in two states in western India, namely Maharashtra and Gujarat, and argue the nature of contradictions and paradoxes underlying development. For this I will utilise my own field work experiences in both states in 1985–86, and also other documentary evidence available including literary sources such as autobiographical narratives of the Dalits and the downtrodden men and women (Punalekar, 1985b; 1986; 1988). In an empirical survey, I had covered eight villages; four from Maharashtra and four from Gujarat. The Maharashtra villages (MVs) are: Kasbe Digraj and Tung from Miraj taluka of Sangli district, and Bargaon Nandur and Digras from Rahuri taluka of Ahmednagar district. The Gujarat Villages *(GVs)* are: Vankaner and Mota from Bardoli taluka of Surat district, and Narsanda and Pij from Anand taluka of Kheda district.

All the four districts were involved in varying degrees in contributing to and shaping the social fabric of this region. Ideas of independence from foreign rule, social reform and moral uprightness of the individuals were quite popular and pronounced in this region. Protest against dominance and misrule was not an alien experience to the people of these districts (Omvedt, 1976; Hardiman, 1981). Political contacts and experiences of the nationalist workers and the freedom fighters helped many of them later, *i.e.*, on the eve of Independence to consolidate their position in the Congress Party, the only party which had a broad mass base. The rich and vocal sections of the peasantry dominated the rural institutions like gram panchayat, co-operative societies, development banks, etc., albeit with the support of the lower ranks of peasantry (Jugale, 1987).

The more influential and powerful the leader in the ruling party hierarchy, the more his village and the surrounding area benefited in terms of development schemes. Villages such as Kasbe Digraj of Sangli district and Bargaon Nandur of Ahmadnagar district provide a vivid testimony of this process. Facilities such as roads, electricity, banks, post offices, telephone, state transport etc., are more developed in these politically advanced and influential areas. All eight villages covered in this study share certain common developmental attributes. All these villages have extensive irrigation facilities. They receive water through canals, tube-wells rivers, rivulets, etc. Out of a total land of over 20,233 acres in eight villages, 9,641 acres (48%) are under canal irrigation. This has helped to increase agricultural production. Cash crops such as sugarcane, tobacco, etc., are now grown on an extensive scale. In recent years, lemon and grape orchards have also come up. A network of local and regional markets have enabled the farmers to sell their produce at favourable prices.

In addition to these regulated marketing outlets, there are co-operatives of sugar and milk producers in these villages. the farmers are members of these co-operatives which are vertically linked to taluka and district-level organisations. These institutions have provided opportunities for village elites to gain political positions and influence. There are well-developed multipurpose co-operative societies in all four Maharashtra villages we surveyed. They are locally known as VIKAS agencies, an abbreviation for the *Vividh Karyakari Sahakari Mandal* (multipurpose co-operative society). Annual transactions of these VIKAS agencies or multi-purpose co-operative societies run into several lakhs of rupees. They distributes annual 'gifts' to their members in the form of cash certificates, utensils or other household utility, items, out of a surplus generated in the co-operative venture.

Land distributions is quite skewed. The advantage of co-operatives and the allied network has largely been secured by the Upper and Middle Strata (UMS) of the peasantry. The UMS are known as the progressive farmers. In local parlance, they are referred to as 'Dhanik' (rich), 'Pragatishil' (progressive) and 'Mota Khedut' (big farmer). Most of the developments relating to crop-pattern, water management, agricultural technology, credit distribution, marketing, etc. have taken place in the last 15–20 years. Since the mid-1970s, this development has intensified, providing sharp contrasts between the rich and the poor in MVs and GVs. Rising productivity in agriculture, and its commercialisation has increased the net cash inflow in these villages. There is perceptible rise in the demand for consumer goods and services, especially from among the upper and middle strata. The latter group seem to be keenly imitating the lifestyle of their urban counterparts residing in the nearby towns like Bardoli, Surat, Anand, Vallabh Vidyanagar (in Gujarat); and Sangli, Miraj, Kolhapur, Ahmadnagar, Rahuri, etc. (In Maharashtra) (Breman, 1974; Punalekar, 1980; Shah, 1985).

In Kasbe Digraj and Tung together, between 2,000 to 3,000 migrant labourers live in the tents on village fields. These labourers have migrated from the drought-prone region, namely from the districts of Beed, Osmanabad and Latur from Marathawada region. There are some from the neighbouring districts of Karnataka state also. This number swells when the sugarcane-cutting season reaches a peak. Private doctors, numbering about 10 in this village make a good deal of money. Canal irrigation was introduced in these villages some 15 or 20 years ago and it has brought rapid prosperity to many farming households in this region. However, the ratio of cultivable land to grassland is quite low. Bargaon Nandur and Digraj villages have no worthwhile grassland at all. This does cause a great deal of hardship to the poorer households in obtaining fodder for their cattle.

In the study region, the rural poor can be classified into two groups: (i) the local and (ii) the outsiders or the migrants. The locals are the longtime residents or natives of Kasbe Digraj and Tung from Miraj Taluka of Sangli district. The outsiders or the migrants are those who have migrated to these villages in recent times, mostly during the last 10–15 years. There are further two sub-groups among the migrants. These are (i) the early migrants, but now settled, *i.e.*, those who have some permanent dwelling in a new village and have regular occupational relations with the local farming households; and (ii) seasonal migrants, *i.e.*, those who move in and out of the village at regular intervals in correspondence with the agricultural season (mostly staying for six-eight months between October and June).

The Hindus are in overwhelming majority among the local poor households (91%). The Muslim household constitute about 8 percent. The rural poor are predominantly from the lower castes, comprising the artisan or service castes, the Scheduled Castes and the Scheduled Tribes, including the nomadic tribes. Over 92 percent of local poor households are landless. Some 8 percent have agricultural holding of less than one acre. The principal occupation of the head of the household is agricultural labour. Their other occupational activities are: non-agricultural, manual labour; service in the sugar factory or at a public works project; artisan work; petty trade; etc. Most of them are daily-wage labourers. They lack security of employment (Breman, 1985; Joshi, 1996; Katre, 1987). Only a Handful of them have got jobs in relatively better-paid occupations like loaders and unloaders in a sugar factory, tractor drivers or as peons in a cooperative society. They get monthly wages with paid leave and holidays. They enjoy some status and respectability because they are a little more educated, and earn monthly wages or salary. This is a particularly evident in village Kasbe Digraj and Tung, both from Miraj taluka (Maharashtra), and village Vankaner from Bardoli taluka (Gujarat).

Often the boys and girls of 10–12 years assist their parents in petty trade and even in agricultural labour. An early engagement of younger children in the above-mentioned activities serves a definite purpose of the poor households. For the families living below the poverty line, education is 'expensive'' though formally free. Educational data amply reveal this situation. Nearly half of the respondents (heads of households) are totally illiterate, some 9 percent have reached the 11th standard and some have reached an even higher level of education.

Out of 411 households, 32 (8 percent) have less than one acre of land. The rest are landless. Out of these, 24 households cultivate their land. The rest do not cultivate it. Of these 24 cultivating households, 21 have irrigation facilities. The major source of irrigation is river water. Only five out of 32 landowning farmers have canal irrigation facility. This is despite the fact that all eight villages are well endowed with irrigation resources. A majority of the local poor households are without electricity (64%), though all the eight villages are electrified. Also, a majority get drinking water from the water taps owned by others (32%) or from the public well (37%) Only 16 percent of the households have their own water taps. It was alarming to note that nearly half of the local poor households experience starvation on some days during the year. Some 42 households, *i.e.,* 10 percent (13 from Gujarat and 29 from Maharashtra) have to face starvation for more than 30 days during the year. This is despite the fact the some get 'cooked food, from their farmer-employers on various occasions. Pardhis who are nomadic tribals collect left-over food on marriage occasions in the well-off families. Yet, starvation stalks in the their face.

All the study villages have Primary Health Centres (PHCs). These are wholly government-run institutions. Even then, more than two-thirds of the local poor households go to private doctors for their medical treatment (276 out of 411 households). Experience suggests that the PHC and other such public health systems are not yet widely utilised by the local poor households despite the fact that over one-fourth of them faced acute difficulties in health matters, and needed help and assistance. A majority of them (59%) still do not utilise the PHC or hospitals for the deliveries of babies. Child birth takes place at home at the hands of the local *dai* or midwife who is experienced but 'untrained.' Modern facilities including health systems are still 'miles away' both socially and culturally for these households. Why do the public health institutions remain unutilised by the marginal sections of rural society? This question underlying the interface between the poor and health institutions is indeed a complex one and needs deeper investigations to get at the circumstances behind inaccessibility. Dominant reasons seem to be: poor facility structures at these PHCs as well as the apathy and indifference of the medical and paramedical staff towards the members of poor households.

Since the introduction of cash crops and especially sugarcane production, there has been considerable influx of migrant labour in this region. From drought-prone, dry regions like Dharampur, Dangs, Songadh, Uchchal, Nizar, etc. in Gujarat state; and Beed, Latur, Osmanabad, Paradhabi, Sholapur, Bijapur, Parner, etc., in Maharashtra state. As mentioned earlier, some neighbouring drought-prone talukas of Karnataka state also contribute to the supply of migrant labour to neighbouring irrigated villages in Maharashtra. As regards distance between the native place of the migrants and their destination point, *i.e.,* the villages where they work; it varies from 35–40 kms, to over 250 kms. Sugarcane Cutters (SCCs) constitute as sizable section of this migrant poor. The SCCs are mostly drawn from the dry and arid region adjoining this lush, green region such as our study villages. The SCCs come from nearby and also from far-off places. As mentioned earlier, the acute drought conditions prevailing recurrently in these areas compel many households to move out of their villages with cart, cattle and children. They seek employment through the contractors for sugarcane cutting or as daily-wage earners on public works. In the latter, they join individually in a gang which is provided work for road, nallah, or dam-building activities. Some join the labour co-operative societies which are 'co-operative' in name only.

The situation among the sugarcane cutters is worth examining (Katre, 1987; Breman, 1978). As mentioned earlier, the SCCs comprise more than 90 percent of the migrant labour in this region. In Sangli district alone, some 20–30,000 SCCs are employed during the crop-cutting season from October to May. Rahuri,

Kopargaon and Srirampur talukas comprising a sugar belt in Ahmednagar district, employ over 40,000 sugarcane labourers. According to Jan Breman, some 50,000 men, women and children from Maharashtra work in the sugarcane fields of South Gujarat especially in the Chalthan, Palsana and Bardoli areas. He further writes: But what marks them out even more definitely as outsiders is the way they live and work, bonded together. The cane cutters are put up in temporary camps close to the field in which they are working.The camps can be seen from the road-rows of little makeshift huts, consisting of a couple of mats which are held aloft with a few sticks. These camps are regularly shifted and the seasonal labour force thus works its way throughout the area to be harvested separated and apart from the village population. (Breman, 1978:1317).

Employing the migrants labour for sugarcane harvesting operations has been the permanent feature of this region. This practice seems to be beneficial to the sugar factory management (SFM). The SFM relies on the contractors or labour brokers called *Mukadams* in local parlance. Jan Breman has clearly established that labour recruitment through the *mukadams* is a clever move of the sugar factory management, He argues: The Mukadam system results in the seasonal migration taking place in a way which is controlled and which assures the sugar factories of a supply of the required number of the labourers at the right time for the least cost and without they themselves having to carry the risks attached to the process. In short, it is a cheap, reliable, efficient and workable system for making use of temporary labour on a grand scale (Breman, 1978: 1326).

These migrant labourers are 'strangers,' 'outsiders' to the village people. No one gives them cash loans. Even local private doctors do not give them medicines, if they do not have money. 'They are here in this village for 10–15 days. Soon they will go to other "Fads" (cane-field). How can we trust them?'—said one doctor in Sangli district. So when the question of medical treatment arises, the SCCs go to local doctors along with their contractors. The contractor pay or promise to pay the doctor.

Even shopkeepers in the village give grains on credit to the SCCs only after the contractor puts in a word. In some cases, the contractors settle their accounts with the doctors, shopkeepers and even liquor shop vendors. And later they deduct the money from the wage bills of the SCCs. 'We are mostly cheated in these transactions,' said one labourer with a deep sense of anguish.

The SCC settlement is known as *basti* in common parlance.These *bastis* have no electricity, water supply, and even approach road. The SCC families have to face scarcities in a variety of things including foodgrains and firewood. The local labourers also do not always view the SCCs in a favourable light. They consider them as 'outsiders', intruding into their work and livelihood. The *bastis* of the migrant labourers are usually on the roadside or on the cleared sugarcane fields. Their contacts with local village institutions are fleeting, to say the least. Some SCC families bring their children along with them, as there is nobody at the native place to look after them. These children spend their time in tending cattle, playing or assisting their parents. They do not attend village schools. Neither the village elders nor the school teachers are bothered about non-participation of migrants' children in school education.

Canal irrigation was introduced in our study villages some 15 or 20 years ago and it has brought rapid prosperity to many farming households. However, the ration of cultivable land to grassland is quite low and declining year after year. Bargaon Nandur and Digras have no worthwhile grassland at all. This caused a great deal of hardship to poorer households in obtaining fodder for their cattle. It is clear from the evidence that agricultural modernisation has not brought any noticeable relief to them. In all spheres such as health, housing and education, there appears to be little advancement in the conditions of the agricultural labourers, the lowest strata of rural society in Maharashtra and Gujarat (Desai, 1987; Jain, 1985; Lobo, 1993).

There are numerous attempts within and outside to organise them. But so far all mobilisation efforts seem to have achieved little success. The state, through its various programmatic interventions is attempting to provide some relief to this class. There are a variety of developmental schemes aimed at improving the lot of the landless and poor peasantry. And yet, there is very little impact of these schemes/programmes on their living conditions. The most urgent and immediate questions before them is survival; earning livelihood on a day-to-day basis. They are in constant search of strategies of survival at the individual or household level. For instance, entire labour input in some households is so apportioned that at least there will be a minimum living for each. Use of child labour at home or in the field; use of female labour for an amorphous range of duties (from one's own households to domestic service in landowner's household), the keeping of some goats, sheep, fowls at home; rearing of the sick calf of the Dhaniama at his home; seasonal migration to a nearby village or town, etc., exemplify some typical ways of the rural poor to cope with the problems of survival.

Why do the landless labourers remain the most neglected section of rural society? Why do they not come together and launch a collective struggle? These questions are significant, and to answer them, we need to closely examine the social, economic, and cultural contexts of their life including their work environment (Kurien, 1978; Punalekar, 1994). It is becoming increasingly clear that they essentially constitute a disaggregated mass which is fragmented into several caste groups with further divisions into religious sects and other primordial loyalties. There are no durable signs of their unity across class lines (Breman, 1978; P.M. Patel, 1981). They do not rise as a single, unified force in solidarity. And hence their demands do not get articulated with sufficient vigour and effectiveness. Also, there are occasions of mutual mistrust and misconceptions among the local and migrant workers about one another. Especially in seasonal, short-duration employment sectors like sugarcane cutting, mining, brick kilns, construction, or salt-pan work, such ill-will is distinctly surfacing. There are free-floating myths about the migrant labour in the minds of local villagers including the local landless labourers. The local labourers do not generally view the migrant labour in a positive way.

The local poor believe that the migrant labourers are much above them economically. 'They come from better off economic background; their staying power in the labour market is superior. They are cunning, shrewd and selfish. They are always for their own monetary gains and least concerned with the woes and discomforts of others working with them,'—such myths prevail. Their conditions at their native villages is not any better (Breman, 1985, Arjun Patel and Desai, 1992). Most of them barely manage to pull through the earnings they have gained while on migration. But even then, the local labourers are not able to see and get convinced about the real situation of the migrant labourers. Such notions or myths prevail among the local labourers and drive a wedge between the migrant labour and local labour; distancing them from one another. Howe are these myths floated and sustained? This is a question for separate enquiry. But we learn from our field experiences that some scrupulous elements like local contractors, Sarpanchs, sugar factory management officials, etc., concoct such stories and float these among the local population. One cannot also rule out the role of some disgruntled local labourers in spreading such myths.

The poor get divided, first in mutual perceptions and then in practice. The social and cultural distance between the two groups increases, and that further reduces the chance of their coming together and mobilising themselves as a united class. Seasonal employment, living separately in the camps (on fields or *gaothan/gauchar* lands, etc.), their concentration in a particular activity where there is hardly any chance to meet the local poor, and above all, the deliberate efforts of the contractors, *mukadams* and others from the employers' class are the known factors that are responsible for isolating and distancing the migrant labourers from the local labourers. Insecurities built into the work process also disengage the migrant labourers from interactions with the local or native labourers.

We observe that a small section of the cane cutters did speak well about their contractors. They felt a sense of gratitude towards them for providing them a chance to work and earn their livelihood.

This was a miniscule section mostly comprising older people and those without any formal educational background. But the majority spoke negatively about their *mukadams* or contractors in a hush-hush voice. Similar mixed reactions were visible when the SCCs talked about their co-workers, local farmers and labourers, and the village community at large. A few older people wisely chose to remain silent on these issues. But there were quite a few young, educated SCCs who did not wish to conceal their anger and fury. They were agitated about their own forced migration, about inhuman working conditions, low wages and insecurities of all kinds. 'We are living like our cattle; dumb and dependent,' said a labourer from Tasgaon taluka. 'These sugar factories are built on our sweat and blood. These sugar barons prosper and we languish after year. This is a miserable life indeed,' added another young migrant labourer from Valva taluka.

Thus, there were clear signs of protest and militancy (Katre, 1987; Breman, 1978; 1994). Especially they younger generation from the SCC households was unwilling to submit to the highhandedness of the farmers and the contractors. Tensions in work, life and relationships were getting projected onto the domestic front also. There were instances of conflict between husbands and wife, father and son on petty matters. There were physical fights also. All this was due to insecurity and instability built into the very mode of their migratory existence.

It is also evident that the situation of the ex-Untouchable castes has shown only marginal change in terms of social and cultural relations and behaviour of the village community. Even the members of the different Scheduled Castes (Mahars, Mangs, Chamars, Dhors, Vankars, Rohits, Meghwals, Bhangis, etc.) were not united among themselves socially and culturally. They believe in and uphold their separate identity based on social and occupational rankings. This fact of separation and disunity among the Scheduled Castes themselves: and between them and other lower Untouchable castes (Nhavi, Luhar, Suthar, Vanjari, etc.) demands deeper sociological attention. Though poverty was a common factor enveloping all or most of them and subjecting them to equally brutalising experiences, they were slow to learn the ways of closing their ranks and unite. As the present situation stands, both in Maharashtra and Gujarat, they seem to lack sense of social solidarity and unity of purpose. They seem to exhibit differential social consciousness. Why this is so is a big question; and we can ill afford to further postpone its investigation.

There is another set of questions which need to be directed towards the ground-level manifestations among the rural poor. These questions are: Why do the rural poor including women hesitate to join development activities or express doubts about the outcome of such projects? Why do they desist from displaying a forward-looking, future-oriented outlook? Why are they so much tied to the questions of mundane, day-to-day living? These questions are important.

What is significant to note is the experience and the perceptions of the rural poor. Their views matter a great deal in formulating strategies to initiate 'development' which can meet their needs and interests. Their doubts and fears, their anxieties and agitation are rooted in their own past encounters and interaction with local structures of power, authority and control. This can easily be discovered through the reactions of the Sugarcane Cutters (SCCs) to prevailing conditions.

Let us now focus our attention on Scheduled Tribes (STs). The STs constitute over 14 percent of Gujarat and 7 percent of Maharashtra population. Major tribes are Bhils, Varlis, Thakurs, Dublas, Dhodias, Katkaris and Chodhras. Other significant tribal groups are Gamits, Nayakas, Tadvis, Dhankas, etc. An over whelming majority of them live in rural areas, mostly in hills and forests. During the last 150 years, there have been substantial changes in the ecology and landscape of their habitat. Thanks to state planning and development efforts, tribals living in the command area or in villages having developed infrastructure are relatively better off. A few among them are getting closer to the mainstream peasant communities such as Marathas of Maharashtra and Patidars of Gujarat. Education has increased among some tribal groups like Dhodias, Chodhras. Gamits and Nayakas (STs) in southern Gujarat. Also, in Maharashtra, one observes a rise in the educational level of Thakurs and Mahadev Kolis (Shah, 1983, 1984; Punalekar, 1985a; 1985b).

The benefits of development including education have reached a small segment of this community. Only a few tribal households have advanced economically and socially. They have acquired a somewhat privileged position in their own social milieu and outside. A few of them have acquired a place in the mainstream political parties as well; giving them an opportunity to enjoy some share in political power too. They are the 'new' elites whose major attention is on improving their own socio-economic and political profile. Evidence suggests that they have achieved some measure of success in the present social system. However, the common tribals who constitute a majority and belong to the lower economic strata are outside the vortex of these' developments (Desai and Chaudhry, 1977; Punalekar, 1996).

We must note that tribal societies were relatively homogeneous some decades ago. Now they are getting internally differentiated and stratified. There is a distinct upper strata of the literate and educated tribals (Bose, 1981; Punalekar, 1985b; Shah, 1984). They come from the landowning groups with better access to input markets including seeds, fertilisers, credit, labour etc. Their closer acquaintance with (as well as membership in) other resource structures including co-operatives, has also helped them to strengthen their position. Among them, the households which have a larger share of development and prosperity in tribal regions belong largely to Dhodia, Kokna, Chodhra, Gamit and Mahadeo Kolis. Other groups such as Varlis, Dubias, Rathwas, Katharis, etc., are socially and economically far behind. These backward groups live in relatively underdeveloped and sometimes inaccessible areas. Their struggle for existence is still very acute and sometimes grim. Their experience, with outsiders (be they contracts, traders, moneylenders, petty officials) is not altogether happy.

They are exploited in exchange and credit markets. They feel frustrated and agitated. This is evident in the transactions that take place in the *hats or hatwadas (i.e.,* weekly markets). And, as mentioned earlier, whenever a 'development' project was launched in their territory, they became the first victim. Their ecological milieu is severely disturbed and their forest resources depleted. Their social and cultural relations are dislocated (Joshi, 1987; Mankodi and Gangopadhyay, 1983; Arjun Patel, 1994). In some cases, the tribals became 'oustees' meaning those who have been displaced; and were forced to shift to other places and community milieus where it took them years to readjust and resettle.

The effects, of dislocation on tribal communities are now known (for example, Koyana, Likai, Jaikwadi, and other smaller dams in Maharashtra and Gujarat). Needless to aver that the emergence of Naxalites and similar militant outfits among the tribals is largely rooted in these exploitative relations which rend to destabilise their society, economy and culture (Lobo, 1992; Punalekar, 1996; Joshi, 1996). The answer then is nor to fight and persecute Naxalites or other militants who are spearheading the movement; but to urgently address and resolve the basic socio-economic issues confronting the tribal masses.

In recent years, there has emerged a distinct group from among the tribals of Maharashtra and Gujarat, and that is of seasonal migrants. They live away from their village and family for over six months in a year. In Maharashtra, this trend is visible since the severe droughts in the state in the early 1970s. In Gujarat also, such migration has become a regular future since the mid-1970s. Not only do these tribals migrate to irrigated villages for agricultural labour, but they have begun to migrate to towns and cities in search of their livelihood. In major towns and cities of Gujarat, the large congregation of such tribal migrant labour is seen in the city squares, vegetable market yards, railway stations, goods transport depots, etc. In Gujarat these markets are known as *chakla* a market and the persons who assemble there to sell their labour are known as *chakla* workers. Infact, their labour share in urban services like loading, unloading, rass-cutting, construction of roads, buildings, etc., is considerable.

This is a distinctly post-Independence phenomenon.

Bhils of Dhulia district work as casual labourers in Surat city; and Bhils of Panchmahals are seen in the urban labour markets at Ahmedabad, Anand, Nadiad, Baroda and Bharuch. Many of them migrate with their families. Obviously, their children's education suffers. But the question of survival precedes the question of education and other pursuits. What are their condition of living in the urban areas? Do they get fair wages for their output? Does the settled urban population help them in coping with the problem of housing, health, water, and other social and cultural amenities? These and related questions need to be explored.

There is another social group, namely the nomadic or renotified tribes. Some of them were labelled as criminals during the British regime. Their numbers is considerable, both in Maharashtra and Gujarat. They are: Berod, Kaikadi, Kanjar Bhat, Banjara, Vadar, Vaghari, Gosavi, Joshi, Kolhati, Bhoi and Raval. In a changing socio-economic order, their problems of survival are becoming increasingly acute. Their day-to-day problems are too complex. Their traditional skills of trade, earth-digging, entertainment, repair services, etc. do not enable them must now to compete with modern technology and the service sector. The basis of their social relations with traditional clients is also getting eroded due to 'new' forces of production. Until recently there was no awakening among them. Even now, all nomadic groups have not come together. Also, perceptions of the common people and legal authorities have not sufficiently altered. To cite just one example, Paradhis of Maharashtra are still suspect in the eyes of the police *patil* and village headman. Vaghris and Chharas of Gujarat are still perceived as 'unreliable and untrustworthy.' So also are Kaikadis of Maharashtra who suffer several such humiliation and indignities.

Laxman Mane, himself a Kaikadi, indeed did a great service to the cause of his community by writing an autobiography *Upra* (1992). The literature world outside cold then know the woes and travails of the nomadic group. This also tells us how effectively a sociological account can be written by a literate and sensitive member of an oppressed community. *Upra* is reflective essay on living conditions of nomadic tribals. So are the autobiographical novels like *Balut* by Daya Pawar, *Athavaniche Pakshi* by 'Sonkamble, *Taral Antaral* by Shankarrao Kharat, *Katyavarchi* Pot by Uttam Bandu Tupe and *Majhya Jalmachi Chittarkathe* by Shantabai Kamle. They depict the lives of ordinary men and women from lower social groups. Literature of this kind provides vital sociological insights into the agonies and aspirations of marginal groups and their wounded consciousness (Punalekar, 1994).

The SCs STs, nomads and others are now beginning to find their 'voice' and insist or rigorous implementation of constitutional safeguards, protective schemes, educational assistance, legal support and more vigorous monitoring of the existing schemes. Outside intervention including leadership can achieve but little in terms of political mobilisation. Internal awakening of the community itself can achieve a great deal, once they begin to reflect on their own conditions in the light of their relations and experiences with other relatively better-off, settled sections of the society.

This chapter outlines the rural situation in Maharashtra and Gujarat, the premier industrialising, fast-developing states in the Indian Union. Signs of growth and economic development are too clear to miss; they are distinctly visible. But this growth is lopsided, creating in its wake a series of contradictions and paradoxes. And that gives rise to another significant set of questions, namely those relating to social justice. Rural development as evidenced in the countryside has bifurcated and broken the region in two parts; on is better endowed with externalities of irrigation facilities and developed infrastructure in input markets. It is richer in terms of production levels and productivity, buttressed further by a vigorous network of co-operatives and other institutions. A larger share of state resources seem to be concentrated in this part of the region. Political leadership at the state level is more attentive to their demands; so also others including the bureaucrats seem to concentrate on these pockets. The results are therefore 'promising,' from their viewpoint.

On the other end of the spectrum are the villages in the

underdeveloped region. They are dry, unirrigated and facing recurring drought and famine. People there are faced with the perennial question of survival and search for dependable means of livelihood. They have lands, but no means to irrigate them with any certainty. So they have to migrate and join a swelling army of casual labourers in the irrigated fields in their own district or outside. This migration stream from the arid, dry villages to green villages is becoming a permanent feature in the rural economy of both Maharashtra and Gujarat.

This migration is seasonal for some, and as years pass by, becomes a step in a permanent severing of their social and cultural linkages with their native village. They then live in the far-off host villages or in the town or city. We have seen that their conditions of living are indeed critical; whether they live in the open fields or in the city slums. Also, their conditions of work are critical, leaving them no space for creative, productive enterprise. Both their work and domestic life are full of tensions and unease, often leading to violence or self-abuse.

The question of survival obliterates all chances of meaningful participation in creative, constructing activities. As migrants, they are denied help and support in the host environment. Even the local poor families do not confide in or trust them. Rather, they are hostile and indifferent to the migrant families. Many myths supporting such chasms are prevalent in these rural areas, which further dim the prospects of their unity or solidarity. Alienated from the bonds of sympathy from the local populations, the migrant poor are further pushed into the network of their contractors or *mukadams*, who often take maximum advantages of such critical situations. Thus, the migrant labourers are subject to endless miseries and hardship. Their womenfolk too suffer a great deal. They have to work along with their male counterpart, and share the family support burden amidst greater self-exploitation and abuse. The children suffer in their health and education.

The centenary year of B.R. Ambedkar has seen a plethora of publications, thus adding to the growing literature on Ambedkar, Dalit politics and the Dalit Movement. Among sociologists it is possible to discern a dominant ideological current that has bearings on the study of the Dalit Movement. There is a 'liberal' trend among a group of scholars, who believe that it is the ancient Hindu reactionary traditions and the deep-rooted prejudice of the upper-castes against Dalits, that has led to the protest of the latter. Thus, this trend views Dalit protest as a necessary outcome of an obscurantist Hindu tradition. This liberal view also has a strong tendency to assume that the Dalit Movement is limited to achieving a partial advance in the socio-economic, civic and political fields within the existing social order, thus hardly any thought is expended on radical transformation in other respects. It is due to this ideological position, that concepts like 'social mobility,' 'reference group' and 'relative deprivation' figure so prominently in their writings on the Dalit movement thus becoming a major frame of reference in studying the Dalit Movement.

Among those notable scholars who fall into this liberal category is M.S.A. Rao who has used similar concepts for understanding the emergence of the protest movement among the backward classes and the Dalits in India (1982:4). Rao, taking a cue from Merton and Runciman, has argued that social mobility forms the major basis of the theory of relative deprivation (1982:4). (Social conflict as a basis of relative deprivation finds mention in Rao's study but without much detailed discussion.) Rao further argues that the relative deprivation is connected with the moment of emulation of a positive reference group (1982:194). Other scholars too have tried to link the emergence of the Dalit Movement with the issue of relative deprivation, reference groups and social mobility (Joshi, 1987; Issac, 1964; Lynch, 1974; Silverberg, 1968; Singer and Cohen, 1968; Sachchidananda, 1978; Bhat, 1971; Ram, 1988; Patwardhan, 1973). It is obvious from the works of these scholars that terms like social mobility and relative deprivation form and major frame of reference in discussions of the emergence of reform, protest and movement among the Dalits.

In studying Dalit mobility it has been suggested by some scholars that the process of Sanskritisation could be a model, *i.e.*, certain Dalit groups or individuals try to adopt either ritually or culturally higher groups or individuals in order to achieve similar social position or to adopt the values that promote the aspirations of an atomised individual in a civil society. According to this view if the Dalits fail in their achievement of thus imitation of the Sanskritisation model of upper mobility, they then suffer from relative deprivation because at the social level their attempt to overcome relative deprivation is restricted by the upper-caste group whom they cite as a reference group existing mostly in a pre-civil social situation which is still dominant in some pars of the country. At another level, the articulation of relative deprivation among the educated Dalits might take place when compared to the Westernised high caste. Thus, in the Indian case, as Oommen has pointed out, the deprivation is multi-faceted (1990:225).

However, studies establishing a link between the emergence of the Dalit movement and relative deprivation, social mobility and reference group theory, though inadequate in understanding the Dalit movement, need to be supported on the following theoretical and strategic grounds. Both historically and dialectically, this concept of relative deprivation could capture social reality at a particular historical juncture when Indian society was trying to release itself from the feudal ethos which was facing an ever-increasing threat from the advancing civil society in India. In this transitional process, the Dalits who were aspiring towards mobility of various kinds but were unable to achieve it due to the restrictions imposed by the feudal as well as colonial vested interests felt deprived, a fact which time and again prompted the Dalit movement, for example in the 1930s in Maharashtra, to challenge feudal values through a process of emulation and Sanskritisation (see Omvedt, 1994). This attempt to imitate the upper-caste values particularly in the case of the Maharas of Maharashtra, certainly contributed to the development of a negative consciousness which according to Gramsci may not constitute a mature and fully evolved class consciousness, but certainly is the first glimmer of such consciousness constituting the basic negative, polemical attitude (see Guha, 1983: 20). Gramsci further argues that the lower classes, historically on the defensive, can only achieve self-awareness through the identity and class limits of their enemy (Guha, 1983).

The Blacks were first imported from Africa into Virginia in 1619 as plantation labour, though they have been stressing for a long time that they are part and parcel of American society. Initially called 'Negroes,' they were enslaved by the Whites. By about 1700, the growing demands of expanding plantation economy of the new world attracted slave traders to bring increasingly large cargoes of Black slaves from Africa. Soon after, slavery was institutionalised in American society. In this system, family members, even wives, husbands and their children could be separated easily. Negro children often derived their status from their mothers. Negroes were denied not only socio-economic, political, and legal rights, but even minimum civil rights. The Dalits on the other hand are the original inhabitants of India though they have been treated as 'Untouchables' under the fourfold division of they Varna system and the Caste system.

It has generally been held that the Untouchables are outside the hierarchy of the varna system, though they are considered to be the lowest in the Hindu caste system. Systems of slavery and serfdom also existed in India, for instance in the state of Kerala and some other parts of South India, but these were not as developed as in America. In Kerala, the Untouchable castes, especially the Pulayas, Cherumans and Panas (a tribe), were recruited as agricultural labour. They were considered to be the property of their high-caste Hindu masters, and were sold and bought like a commodity in the market. But their family members could not be separated form one another as in the case of Blacks in America. Instead, these slaves were assigned to particular farm sites of their masters and were obliged to live there and work for them. They also suffered from social, cultural and religious disabilities and educational, economic and political deprivations. They were not allowed to worship at the Hindu temples nor even to read the sacred Hindus scriptures. They not only suffered from 'touch pollution' but also from the extreme form of 'distance pollution.' Untouchable women were obliged to leave their breasts uncovered, and were even sexually exploited, the Yellamma cult in South India being one example of such exploitation. The numerous forms of exploitation, deprivation and disabilities were institutionalised and governed by certain rules and regulations, violation of which was punished in various ways. Thus, both the Indian Untouchables or Dalits and the American Blacks have suffered from cumulative deprivations and inequalities in their respective societies. The authority of castes and the supremacy of ascribed values as determinants of social status are highly typical characteristics of Indian society to which neighter individuals nor social groups are exceptions. Dalits, as a distinct group in Indian society by virtue of heritage could enjoy only the provision of the lowest rank of social status. As a consequence, they remained socially, economically, politically and culturally backward as compared to any other social category.

However, as a result of consistent efforts in several directions, the widening spread of education and consciousness of rights enshrined in the Indian Constitution, there has been a great change in the position of Dalits. In this paper I intend to deal with the problem of social protest movements with special reference to achievements of Dalit men and women in India and to compare them with those of Blacks in the United States of America.

Comparing caste and race, Cox (1948: 438–39) emphasizes that factors influencing the choice of occupation for both the races in the United States (Blacks and Whites) are fundamentally different from those which operate in the caste system in India. The questions asked by caste members in viewing the field of labour are different from those which confront Whites and Blacks. In estimating the possibility of an occupation, the caste-man wants to know primarily the attitude of his caste and the degree of purity of occupation in question for the upper mobility. However, in both societies, the dominance of the subordinate groups is upheld by a social ideology to which the subordinate groups must seem to subscribe in front stage interaction but which they may reject in backstage discourse among themselves, *i.e.*, both Blacks and Dalits do not subscribe to the racial and caste inequalities, though they may be victims of their respective race and caste ideologies. On this point Berreman (1979) is in agreement with other sociologists such as Simpson and Yinger (1953), and Cox (1948), that in the Western forms of inequality, in egalitarian practice confronts egalitarian ideology.

Theoretical Framework

Scholars in sociology and social anthropology adopted various theoretical approaches in studing issues related to caste, gender and social movements in India. However, some major theoretical concepts and approaches may be grouped as follows: (1) Structural approaches grounded on functional and dialectical models; (2) Historical approach; and (3) Conflict approach. In this paper I do not intend to review all these, but attempt to find common grounds for an inter-sectional theoretical approach and also to show the biases and limitations from which the different approaches suffer.

Towards an Intersectional Theoretical Approach

In evaluating the above theoretical approaches, I find that each has advantages of its own for the study of caste, gender and social movements in India, but that none of them provides a comprehensive enough perspective on these issues. Therefore, there is a need for a theoretical approach which reflects and focuses on all aspects.

An intersectional theoretical approach, in may view, interlocks various theoretical concepts in order to study a research problem. A series of concepts related to caste, gender and social movements in this approach, could be integrated into a viewpoint on the basis of theoretical formulations. It is my endeavour to find out the underlying theoretical and conceptual formulations of various approaches to study the issues of caste, gender and social movements, and then unite them into a viewpoint which would achieve a fair degree of conceptual analysis of a particular problem. A comparison of the given situation of caste, class and gender in India with race, class and gender in the USA, suggests that multiracial feminism provides similar integrated concepts in the study of all three. Multiracial feminism provides an analysis of the above intersections and asserts that gender is constructed by a range of interlocking inequalities; what Patricia Hill calls 'a matrix of domination.' The idea of a matrix is of several fundamental systems interacting with and through each other. A person experiences race, class, gender and sexuality differently depending upon his social location in the structure of race, class, gender and sexuality (Zinn and Dill, 1996:11). Multiracial feminism encapsulates all aspects of the problem under the intersectional theoretical approach. In the case of caste and gender in India, and individual or group may face a similar situation, and it might be very useful to adopt an intersectional approach in order to understand the crux of the issue. What is most important conceptually and analytically in this work is the articulation of multiple oppression (Brewer, 1993: 13). The intersectional theoretical approach is quite open to the development of a multidimensional paradigm and articulation of the basis issues from different dimensions. Further emphasising the importance of this approach, Brewer said that as theorists explicate the intersection of race, gender and class, our conceptualisation of racial inequality will change. The complexity of race, gender and class intersections suggests that scholarly work must accomplish a number of difficult theoretical tasks especially around interrelationship (Brewer, 1993: 18). Glenn stressed that 'a starting point for developing such a theory would appear to lie in those models which view race and gender stratification as a part of a larger system of institutionalised inequality' (Glenn, 1985: 87). Similarly, the intersectional theoretical understanding of caste and gender in India gives a more specific multidimensional picture of the problem. Understanding race and gender as a relational, interlocking, socially constructed system affects how we strategise for change and also alerts us to sources of inertia and resistance to change (Glenn, 1992: 35–36). In the case of India, the relationship between caste and gender depends upon the same situation as in the case of race and gender in USA.

Liberation Movements in Comparative Perspective

In order to ameliorate their socio-economic condition, as

well as their cultural, religious and other deprivations and disabilities, both the Dalits in India and Blacks in the United States of America have been engaged in struggles and protest movements of several types for a long time. For an adequate sociological analysis of these social protest movements for a new social identity based on de-stigmatised caste and racial considerations of their ideologies and their styles of assertion, it is essential to put both the Dalit and Black protest movements together into a common theoretical framework.

There have been two types of ideology among the Dalits and Blacks. The first is an *acquiescent* ideology in which one accepts his/her low status or position and avoids any confrontation with others, but may request the dominant group (oppressor) to allow access to education, employment, etc., in order to serve them better. Such a person is submissive and the dominant group grants him/her some of the facilities out of generosity. The other popular ideology is *protest* by the deprived sections of the society who organise themselves to resist innumerable types of exploitation and oppression by the dominant groups.

Both the Indian Dalits and American Blacks have organised assertive efforts for their respective societies. Their protest ideology involves resistance, opposition, confrontation and conflict with the dominant groups (oppressors). Dalits and Blacks alike have adapted these to achieve their desired goals of social equality, social dignity and de-stigmatised social identity.

Retrospectively, it can be seen that the identity achieved with the help of *acquiescent* ideology was a type of self-mortification since the identifier accepted the status of servitude. A movement based on such ideology could hardly be called a movement to achieve social mobility which might lead to the formation of a new social identity. It was a situation of *sponsored mobility* where the dominant groups granted access to modern education and employment opportunities out of generosity. Under the rubric of an acquiescent ideology, there was no enhancement of self-image, honour, dignity and esteem, as patronage was received for being obedient, humble and submissive. Sponsored mobility merely buttressed the superordinate-subordinate relationship (Rao, 1984:208). To support his argument, Rao has cited the movement of the Chambhars (Untouchables) in Maharashtra who did not challenge the superiority and hegemony of the caste-Hindus, accepting their status as leather-workers, and also following all the religious rituals and rites of caste-Hindus, as an example. The patronage given to them by the caste-Hindus enabled them to get modern education which, however, resulted in individual rather than group mobility (Rao, 1984:208).

Bookr T. Washington in the USA followed the same ideology (Wood, 1970: 88), asking his followers and supporters to accept their unequal status but to pursue business-oriented education so that they could serve their masters inta better way (Washington, 1915:113–14). Since this meant accepting a position of servitude, this movement did not raise the honour and self-respect of the the Blacks. Gunnar Myrdal stressed that 'Washington was an all-out accommodationist leader because he never relinquished full equality as the ultimate goal. Washington's main motive was "accommodation for a price." He was prepared to give up social and political equality if the Blacks were allowed to work undisturbed with their White friends for education and business' (Myrdal, 1944: 210).

In contrast, the protest movements of Dalits and Blacks asserted the demand for self-respect, social dignity and equity and gave a new direction to liberation struggles in their respective societies. These movements did not depend on any kind of patronage from the dominant groups; rather they sought confrontation. Basically, the protest ideology of both movement centred around socio-economic-cultural dimensions rather than economic and political disabilities.

Historically speaking, the Brahminical orthodoxy and legitimacy of caste in India were first challenged in the 6th century B.C. by Buddhism which preached equality, justice and the fraternity of all human beings. In the present century, the Untouchables have been drawn towards Buddhism ever since Dr. Ambedkar revived it as an emancipatory religion for the oppressed. Some

Indian Dalits and Black Americans rejected their parental religions, *i.e.,* Hinduism and Christianity, in order to escape from the trap of degraded social status. They either sought for reform in their parental religion or embraced another religion in protest. In either case, there were organised movements. In India, from the 13th century to the present day, reformist movements like the "Bhakti Movements,' which attracted Dalits, were led by Kabir, Ravidas, Shivanarayan, Chaitanya, Chokhamela and others, who attached the caste system and stressed equality of status. Oommen has emphasised that, all the Bhakti Movements shared the following characteristics: First, they were 'reformist' in that they only attempted to correct some of the evils of Hinduism, particularly the practice of untouchability, without questioning the caste system in general. Second, they were mostly initiated by caste Hindus... Third, once caste with differing ritual rank was associated with the movements, the participants developed a dual identity; a religious ideological identity with fellow participants of the movements, and a socio-cultural identity with social collectivities (caste) to which they traced their origin. Fourth, none of the Bhakti Movements had a programme of socio-economic status; the equality professed by them remained a mirage (Oommen, 1990:258).

A new style of protest was established by Swami Vivekananda and Dayananda Saraswati in the middle of the 19th century. Their movements, called the Neo-Vedantic movements, upheld the Varna system as an occupational division of society, though they certainly called for the removal of the practice of untouchability in Hinduism. Thus, these movements were reinterpretationist, talking of equality, self-respect, and the dignified social identity of all human beings but within the fold of the religion of their origin, *i.e.,* Hinduism.

Likewise, another important movements the S.N.D.P. movement of Kerala, led by Sri Narayana Guru Swami who established a new social identity for the Izhavas, a former Untouchable caste. This was also based on reinterpretation of orthodox Hinduism. The Izhavas constitute about 26 percent of Kerala's population and have suffered from educational, religious, economic and political disabilities. Sri Narayana Guru Swami gave them a new religion of one God, one religion, and one caste which changed their lifestyle and social outlook. He also established a set of religious institutions, like temples, priests, monks and monasteries which are parallel to that of Brahminical Hinduism and facilitated their protest and challenge against the religious, economic, educational and political supremacy of the upper-castes.

The same type of protest ideology of reinterpretation of faith was adopted by Blacks in the USA. For instance, in the second and third decades of the 20th century, Marcus Garvey launched such a movement to establish a new social identity of the Blacks. He created a new religious faith, New Christianity, characterised by Christ as a god of Blacks only, since they considered themselves as oppressed and the oppressed are always blessed with God. Garvey also made a move to prepare a separate Black Bible which contained the pictures of their holy saints and angels. In addition, he established the Black Theology which emerged as the theology of liberation by identifying the Blacks as the oppressed and the Whites as oppressors (Garvey, 1971:90). According to Rao, the Black Christian theology which ran parallel to white Christian theology, 'gave them a new basis of identity, legitimising, their efforts towards self-determination and their efforts to gain honour and prestige' (Rao, 1981: 210–211). Altogether, Black theology was a package of revolt against the supremacy and hegemony of the Whites in American society.

Another set of protest movements was launched on the basis of the ideology of rejection. This, for both Blacks and the Dalits, meant rejecting their parental religion and embracing another which advocated equality and self-respect and also satisfied their human dignity. The main pioneers of this ideology in India were Jotiba Phule (1873), E.V. Ramaswami Naicker Periyar (1930), and Dr. B.R. Ambedkar (1957). They not only rejected the Brahminical supremacy of the Hindu caste system, but also advocated a new social order based on social justice. Ambedkar, who kindled this fire of 'Social revolution' among the Dalit Indians, stated that 'religion must recognise the fundamental tenets of liberty, equality and fraternity. Unless a religion recognises these three fundamental principles of social life, religion will be doomed' (see Ahir, 1991: 302). Certainly Ambedkar was a Hindu till a few months before his death, but he was anguished at the iniquity of the caste system. 'To untouchables' he said, 'Hinduism is a veritable chamber of horrors. The iron law of caste, the heartless law of *Karma* and senseless law of status by birth are veritable instruments of torture which Hinduism has forged against the untouchables' (see Ahir, 1991: 293). Hence, in October 1956, he subsequently rejected Hinduism and embraced Buddhism which satisfied his conscience and his understanding of the concepts of equality and justice.

Ambedkar's embracing of Buddhism, along with thousands of his followers in 1956 at Nagpur in Maharashtra has been popularly known as his religious conversion movement. However, Zelliot has pointed out that 'conversion as a way out of the untouchables status was not new in India. Islam, and more especially Christianity, drew large numbers of their converts from the lower castes, and Sikhism in the twentieth century actively encouraged untouchables' conversion' (Zelliot, 1992: 191).

Similarly, in 1925, E.V. Periyar Ramaswami Naicker, the founder leader of the Dravida Kazhagam (D.K. Movement) in South India, and in 1873 Jotiba Phule in Maharashtra organised anti-Brahmin movements and emphasised the creation of a just social order without any caste hierarchy. Naicker rejected all types of myths of the Aryan religion and culture and organised his protest movements against Sanskritic culture of the Brahmins and self-respect movements among the Dravidians. Phule too emphasised the building of a social system free from social inequalities, Brahminical hegemony and orthodoxy, and the caste system. Naicker's movement played an important instrumental role in changing the political power structure in Tamil Nadu while the movements organised by Phule and Ambedkar made a powerful impact towards changing the social system.

As stated above, the ideology of rejection was also adopted by Black Americans in several protest movements launched for evolving a just society and achieving a dignified social identity. Through such movements, a large number of Black Americans rejected the parental religion and converted to another which preached equality, justice and fraternity to all. Though Christianity advocated brotherhood and equality in principle, the situation was one of utter frustration in which Blacks were given the impression of living in the same religion yet were denied equality and justice. They identified Christianity with Whites, therefore, and embraced Islam, thus protesting against multiple forms of oppression but also against the domination of Whites in Americans society. The first such Black protest movement was launched by Elijah Muhammad who rejected Christianity and embraced Islam, and also started the Black Muslim protest movement in the United States.

In 1960, the nationalist phenomenon in USA reasserted itself and the Black protest movement ran parallel to the Civil Rights Movement (Draper, 1969: 544–55). During this period, the important Black leader was Malcolm X, who was also actively involved in the Black Muslim protest movement. He linked the Black Muslim ideology with African nationalism and Black-African civilisation and insisted on rejection of the White Western civilisation. A new identity was formed on the basis of claims to the African heritage and civilisation. The ideology of the African heritage was also adopted by Marcus Garvey and Du Bois, both of whom emphasised the superiority of their race and culture. Infact, Garvey's protest movement may be seen as a synthesis of two ideologies of protest: (a) a reinterpretation of Christianity, and (b) a rejection of American cultural values.

Both Dalit Indians and Black Americans strove to achieve their desired goals of equality and laid stress on the civil rights of the oppressed as a counter to atrocities perpetrated on them. In Maharashtra, the Mahar movement under the leadership of Ambedkar adopted the civil rights ideology while in Agra, a city in Uttar Pradesh, a self-respect movement was launched by some Jatav youths. These movements generated a sense of self-respect and an awareness of their basic rights as enshrined in the Constitution of India. From 'Mahad March in 1927 to Yeola Conference in 1936' Ambedkar adopted the ideology and means of civil rights to protest against the socio-economic, cultural-religious, and political disabilities and oppression of the Dalits. He not only protested and fought against the practice of untouchability and the tenets of Hinduism but also demanded basic civil rights for Untouchables. However, recently, the social awareness among Dalits is being manifested in conflict, especially in rural areas where atrocities on Dalits have increased tremendously in comparison to the past. This indicates that there is a need to generate still more awareness among them of their legal and constitutional rights so that they can protect themselves under the law.

Inspired by Ambedkar's ideology, Ram Vilas Paswan, a Janata Dal Member of Parliament, also launched a self-respect movement in December 1991. This Movement was organised by the 'Dalit Sena' which he headed from Tusundur, Andhra Pradesh where 22 Dalits had been massacred by caste-Hindus. During the course of his movement between 6 December 1991 and 14 April 1992, Paswan highlighted the issues and problems faced by the Dalits and also drew the attention of the whole nation towards the increasing atrocities on them. By mobilising the Dalits to fight for their self-respect, honour and prestige in Indian society he not only demanded protection for them from atrocities but also made them aware of their socio-economic, political and legal rights.

In the 1950s, a new chapter in the history of Black protest movements was added in USA by Rev. Dr. Martin Luther King Jr who adopted the civil rights ideology as a strategy in the Black movement and organised the Southern Christian Leadership Conference (SCLC), and by Du Bois, who established the National Association for the Advancement of Coloured People (NAACP). King practised non-violent, direct action on the model established by M.K. Gandhi during India's independence struggle with Britain. He moved the Black struggle from the courtroom to the street and from law liberties to church pews. He also led several economic boycotts, desegregation and voter registration campaigns always adopting a non-violent ideology of civil rights. Similarly, Du Bois also organise movements demanding full civil rights, economic opportunities and education for all the Black youth. He was influenced by Marxism and had developed an interest in pan-Americanism though he always maintained that race was stronger than class. Du Bois 'vacillated between Marxism and a middle class ideology and the later eventually got the better of the former in him. This was the strategy that he adopted in fighting for basic civil rights, and he came to be regarded as the father of the civil rights movement' (Rao, 1984: 201). Thus, both Du Bois and Martin Luther King Jr protested against the Whites' supremacy and the racial segregation which had subjected the Blacks to multiple types of deprivation.

A new ideological phase started in the history of social protest movements with the formation of the Black Panther Party in the USA, and the Dalit Panther Movement in India. While the immediate cause of the formation of the Black Panthers was the increasing brutality by the White police, the increasing atrocities perpetrated by the caste-Hindus on the Dalits were responsible for the formation of the Dalit Panthers.

The Black Panther Party was organised in the US in October 1966, at Oakland in California, with the aim of protecting the Blacks from police brutality and other harassment by the Whites. Bobby Seal and Huey P. Newton organised this movement for self-defense by carrying arms. It was an extremist development in the protest movement of Black Americans which held that war could be stopped only by war and not by any soft means. The Panthers emphasised revolutionary nationalism rather than cultural nationalism (Jones, 1988: 416–41). They were very radical and militant, and were able to penetrate into the poor working class of the urban ghettos in the USA.

The Dalit Panthers in India, for their part, organised themselves to attack the upper-caste Hindu capitalists and those who committed atrocities on Dalits. On 9 July, the Dalit Panther movement was formed under the leadership of Raja Dhale as president, Namdev Dhasal as defence minister, and J.V. Pavar as its general secretary.

To protect their fellow Dalits from violence and atrocities, they were prepared, if necessary, to adopt violent strategies. Thus, both the Black Panthers and the Dalit Panthers accepted the ideology of class-conflict and chose to directly confront the oppressors by adopting radical and violent means.

The Dalit Panthers, embellishing the concept of Dalits' emancipation in their 'Manifesto' emphasised that a complete revolution was needed. 'We do not want a little place in the *Brahmin Alley*. We want the rule of the whole land, we are not looking at persons but at systems and change of heart, liberal education etc., will not end our state of exploitation. When we gather a revolutionary mass, rouse the people. out of the struggle, the giant mass will become tidal wave of revolution' (Dhasal, 1974: 28). However, the Dalit Panthers recognised only the contributions of Jotiba Phule and Dr. B.R. Ambedkar for their struggle. They drew the organisational structure and strategies from the Black Panther Party. They were also greatly influenced by Black literature.

This resume of the Black protest movements brings out the similarities and differences in the socio-cultural, political and economic aspects of their social life. American racism in many ways parallels Indian casteism and the condition of Dalits in India is very similar to that of Blacks in America. Though untouchability is not practised against the Blacks in the American social system, the practice of racial segregation is very much there. Historically, most of the Blacks were both psychologically and materially deprived by the presumption that they were racially inferior to the Whites. In a similar fashion, the Dalits were deprived by the caste system in India. They were denied educational, political, economic as well as other civil lights before the period of British rule in India. Thus, the major cause behind the social protest movements of both Blacks and Dalits was their centuries-old exploitation, oppression and repression in their respective societies.

Yet, the socio-cultural differences between India and America are so great that the various types of protest movements tend to be more different than alike. While the Dalits in India have always been inhabitants of the country, the Blacks were migrant labourers in the United States of America which led to their enslavement by the Whites. Whereas the discriminatory practices against the Blacks are racial, based on the colour of their skin, the Dalits are the victims of religious discrimination based on the theory of *chaturvarna* of Hindu religion and suffer from ritual disabilities. The caste system has been prevalent for centuries in Indian society, while racism in the USA is only 350 years old. The most important difference, sociologically speaking, between the Blacks and Dalits in the structural placement of the respective societies is that the Blacks, though they have several political opinions of factions among them, are not segmentally divided into numerous endogamous groups like Dalits. The Dalit Indians are heterogeneous castes based on different cultural and linguistic divisions, while this is not the case of American Blacks. Moreover, they also do not suffer from ritual disabilities, as do the Dalits. Class-based divisions among the Dalits are not as sharp as in the case of Blacks. It is only in urban society that a middle-class Dalit group has appeared in increasing numbers and their bourgeoisie is still comparatively radical in its thinking. In contrast to this, Black capitalists have promoted a cultural and national-integrational approach which is opposed to the revolutionary approach adopted by the lower strata among the Blacks.

Another important difference between the Blacks and Dalits is that the latter rare a social category which is broad enough to include even the poor and downtrodden of other sections of society while the Blacks maintain a racial category, and can easily be distinguished physically from the Whites and segregated because of their visible racial identity. Any social movement is an organised effort by an individual, group, or community to achieve a particular goal. Essentially, the social movements launched by Blacks and Dalits are based on the ethos of protest which has been directed against their socio-economic, religious-cultural, and legal oppression and exploitation.

5

Harijans and Social Status

The practice of caste changed no doubt and a section of the Hindus not only acquiesced in that change but actively helped it. The orthodox Hindus did not like the modifications that had come about owing to changed circumstances. The actually deprecated them, and it they had the power they would fain reinstate the old situation. The progressive elements, on the other hand, not only welcomed the changes but proposed further modifications.

Gandhi and Harijans Status

Mahatma Gandhi did not give us a complete programme by means of which he proposed to reinstate the four-fold orders. It is not quit clear whether persons would be assigned to one or the other of these classes on the ground of their birth in a particular caste or on the strength of the occupation they now follow. Yet as he laid great stress on birth and heredity and subscribed to the view "once born a Brahmin always a Brahmin", he would no doubt rather rearrange the other castes into their proper groups on the basis of birth. If this procedure were sought to be put into operation I do not hesitate to state that there would be great strife among the various castes. The Kshatriya, Vaishya and Shudra classes have not remained as distinct and intact as the Brahmins. There is much difference of opinion as to which of the castes should be included in one or the other of the a love three classes. Even if an amicable settlement on this point were possible, what about the untouchable classes? Gandhi was vehemently opposed to untouchability, and he would naturally propose some respectable status for these classes. Where are they to be provided for? Wherever it may be proposed to include them, there is bound to be a tremendous protest from that class. The criterion of birth in a caste for the purposes of the proposed four-fold classification is thus found to be quite unsatisfactory.

Untouchability in India, as the race and colour problems in the West, rested upon the idea of the superiority of one section of people over another on account of their birth. A Brahman might be as poor as the untouchable, but he was not ill-treated by our society on that account. Gandhi called these so-called religious sanctions as a serious stigma on the fair name of a society which have deep-rooted culture and historical traditions to support its identity.

The disease of untouchability is fairly old in our society. It generated social hatred and discriminatory feeling of high and low, and as a result the later category suffered for centuries in the hands of the former. Time and again, ceaseless efforts were made by social reformers to alleviate the status of down-trodden and bring them to a level by which they could breathe and subsist with some confidence in the society. This was, however, a most complex problem, the complete or satisfactory solution of which could not be evolved in spite of efforts by prominent personalities including social reformers, educationists and political leaders of our society. For example, Buddha, Mahavira, Kabir, Nanak, Dayanand and others played their social and religious role at one time or the other. Besides numerous socio-religious reform movements had deep linkage with the cause of the untouchables who were labelled as a serious stigma on the fair name of Hinduism. The idea of social discrimination dawned on Gandhi in South Africa where he engaged himself against the discriminatory attitude of the South African Government against Indians.

The problem was akin to that of untouchability as the

migrants were treated as inferior to the local population which enjoyed numerous basic rights legally denied to Indians. As a youngman Gandhi began to realise how much hellish was their life which had weakened their social and moral fabric essential for the growth of physical and economic faculties of human being. In India, too, he was confronted with this problem when he came back to his motherland in 1915, during the second year of the First World War. For him the reconstruction of the life of the nation was of utmost significance. This could be achieved by alleviating the social status of the untouchables. He always called untouchablility as a cruel and inhuman institution. It violated human dignity. He did not believe that the imperial ambitions of Britain were alone responsible for our slavery, but it was the neglect of our national duty which was primarily responsible for it.

A reformed India, he stated, would be a free India. Untouchability in its extreme form always caused him so much pain, because he considered himself to be a Hindu of Hindus saturated with the spirit of Hinduism. As he always regarded it *at an* excrescence in Hinduism, he had even no hesitation in renouncing Hinduism itself. To remove untouchability was a penance that caste Hindus owed to Hinduism and to themselves. Thus the purification required was not of untouchables, but of the so-called superior castes.

The apathy of the high-caste Hindus worried him much. He, however, dealt with them as best as he could. During his discussion with Harijans, at Ahmedabad, he opined, 'This is a movement for the purification of Hinduism. Think what contribution you can make to it. If you bestir yourselves, if you shed your unclean habits, if you reform your way of living, irrespective of what the high-caste Hindus do, I assure you their superiority of birth will automatically disappear, Superiority consists in clean and pure living and I assure you that in spite of your unclean occupations you can live cleaner and purer lives than the rest of us. Yours is a service without which the community cannot do. I want you to be conscious of the dignity of your profession, to learn to practise it in a dean manner and I am sure you will be able to dictate your terms. Depend on yourself, stand on your own legs and work your own salvation.' Gandhi believed that the so-called caste Hindus had a personal obligation to fulfill towards the Harijans which they must do unconditionally and it was to be their atonement.

Whether in this world or the next, it is for each one to free oneself from bondage by one's own effort. Harijans should not look upon themselves as lowly, weak or crippled.' Time and again, Gandhi asked the Harijans to magnify their own faults so that they appeared to be as big as mountains and then make content efforts to overcome them. In it lay the key to obtaining the rights which they wanted. 'Never believe that since others have the same faults we need not mind our own. No matter what others do, it is your *dharma* to overcome the feelings which you find in yourselves...You will not be able, at the behest of others, to overcome what you yourselves do not look upon as failings. Hence, it should suffice to say that you should shake off whatever faults you can finding yourselves.'

In the process of regeneration of the nation, Gandhi waged an increasant and systematic war. 'If we are children of the same God how can there be any rank among us.' For him, there was only one *varna* in India—the Sudras. Indeed the *Sudras* are those who serve. He wished that all the hindus voluntarily call themselves *Sudras*. He was critical of any person who would claim superiority over fellow-men. In his opinion there was no such thing as inherited or acquired superiority. He was happy and felt satisfied to call himself a scavenger, a spinner, a weaver and favourer.

He wrote in the *Harijan*, 'I have intentionally described myself as a *Bhangi*.' In man made social ladder I want to be at the bottom. He indeed was much pained to see the appalling plight of untouchables in various regions of the country. Its eradication greatly agitated his mind and he devised ways and means, from time to time. Through his speeches and writings. He wrote in *Navajivan,* "By passing resolutions and talking about their problem we have raised hopes in them. It was absolutely necessary to do this. It was necessary also that hopes should be raised in them and to tell those *antyaja* friend that what has happened should be sufficient answer to them. Another answer can be that they lay the entire buden on me. I can understand the sting in their words. They accuse me of being satisfied with the more or less that I do myself and of being gullible enough to be taken in by others who only befool me. However, if I do something, there are others who may be doing less but still they do it.'

Gandhi called Harijans as men of God and believed that all the religions of the world describe God pre-eminently as the Friend of the friendless. Help of the helpless and Protector of the weak. He stated that there rest of the world apart, in India who could be more friendless, helpless or weaker than the forty millions or more Hindus of India who were classified as 'untouchables.' If, therefore, anybody of people could be fitly described as men of God, they were surely these helpless, friendless and despised people. He opined, "when Caste Hindus have of their own inner conviction and, therefore, voluntarily, got rid of the present day untouchability, we shall all be called Harijans; for according to my humble opinion, Caste Hindus will then have found favour with God and may, therefore, be fitly described as His men." Gandhi had the apprehension that "If we came into power with the stain of untouchability unaffected, I am positive that the 'untouchables' would be far worse under that Swaraj than they are now, for the simple reason that our weakness and our failings would then be buttressed up by the accession of power." Through his speeches in public and writings in *Young India* and *Harijan*, he emphasised the problem of untouchability and its removal from its roots. He hated untouchability with his entire soul. The Mahatma had the feeling that in Hinduism there was an sanction for treating a single human being as untouchable. The Bhagavad Gita has never taught that a *Chandala* was in any inferior to a Brahmana. "A Brahmana ceases to be a Brahmana, immediately be becomes insolvent and considers himself a superior being."

Gandhi regarded himself a Sanatani Hindu, because he

obeyed the eternal precepts of the faith as embodied in the Shastras as he understood them. He had no doubt that there are many interpolations in the Smritis and the other scriptural books. He rejected as interpolations everything in the Smritis or other writings that was inconsistent with Truth and Non-violence or other fundamental and universal principles of ethics. He opined, "The idea of superiority and inferiority is repugnant to the most elementary principles of morality. A Brahmana who considers himself superior to any single creature of God ceases to be a Brahmana. If we are children of superior the same God, how can there be any rank among us?... What will happen to the body, if these members begin to quarrel about rank? .... The verses in the Smritis about Sudras deserve to be summarily rejected as being contrary to the spirit of humanity."

Gandhi was quite sure in his mind that untouchability would not be removed by the force even of law. It could only be removed, he opined, when the majority of Hindus realised that it was a crime against god and man and were ashamed of it. In other words, it was a process of conversion, *i.e.,* purification, of the Hindu heart. The aid of law had to be invoked when it hindered or interfered with the progress of the reform as when, in spite of the willingness of the trustees and the temple-going public, the law prohibited the opening of a particular temple.

There are innumerable castes in India. They are a social institution... This institution has super added to it restrictions which, in my opinion, are undesirable and are bound to go in course of time. The difference, therefore, between the caste system and untouchability is not one of degree, but of kind. An "untouchable, is outside the pale of respectable society. he is hardly treated as a human being. He is an outcastes hurled into an abyss by his fellow-beings occupying the same platform. The difference, therefore, is somewhat analogue to the difference between heaven and hell.'

He assessed that social position of untouchables as follows: "Socially they are lepers. Economically they are worse than slaves. Religiously they are denied entrance to places we miscall 'houses of God.' They are denied the use, on the same terms as the Caste Hindus, of pubic roads, public schools, public hospitals, public wells, public taps, public parks and the like. . . . The wonder is that they are at all able to eke out an existence or that they still remain within the Hindu fold. They are too downtrodden to rise in revolt against their suppressors. . . . It is only ceaseless effort that can raise these downtrodden fellow beings from degradation, purify Hinduism and raise the whole Hindu society and with it the whole of India."

Regarding inter-dining and inter-marriage, the Mahatma opined that marrying and dining were matters of individual concern and no one had a right to ask to choose a girl for wife or to dine with anybody against his will. He, however, elaborated his point thus: "But my answer is at the same time 'yes' because if a person refused to take food touched by another person on the ground of untouchability or inferiority, he is observing untouchability. In other words, untouchability cannot constitute any ground for restraint on interdining or marriage."

An important organisation, known as the Harijan Sevak which was not a part of the Congress, was the outcome of the fast, the Mahatma undertook in 1932 when he was in jail. G.D. Birla was its President and Thakkar Bapa its Secretary... "it is the duty of Harijan workers and Caste Hindus to do sweepers' work themselves. . . . These reforms do not cost much. They require intelligence, hard work and love of an ideal. We may not relegate sleepers' work to one particular class. Therefore all should learn it in the same way as cooking. Each person should be his own sweeper. If this ideal were to be put into practice in society, the miserable condition of sweepers would at once be rectified."

The system of forced labour exacted by petty landowners from Harijans and other classes called backward is almost universal in India. The petty landlords are mostly Hindus. "It is the privilege of Harijan Sevaks, no matter to what organisation they belong to befriend Harijans, to study their condition in detail, to approach Savarna Hindus and show them as gently as possible what their duty is towards those whom they have treated as outcastes of society and depraved even of legal rights."

He always preached to the Harijans cleanliness, abstention from carrion-eating and intoxicating drinks and drugs, necessity of taking education themselves and giving it to their children, also abstention from eating the leavings from Caste Hindus' plates. He stated, 'On the contrary, I suggest to Caste Hindus that the shortcomings are not inherent to Harijans but that they are due to our criminal neglect of—even deliberate suppression of—these brethren of ours. . . . We must approach harijans as penitents or debtors, not as their patrons or creditors extending generosity to the undeserving."

Besides Gandhi recommended that common schools and wells should be opened where the existing ones were to available for Harijans either owing to the violent and successful opposition of the neighbours or some other unavoidable cause: Harijans, he opined, could not be left uncared for in matters of necessary services till public opinion had ripped. 'National schools, to be worth the name in terms of Swaraj for the attainment of which they have been brought into existence, must be conducted with a view to advancing the national programme in so far as it is applicable to educational institutions. Thus, for instance, national schools must be the most potent means of educating the 'untouchables' and abolishing the curse of untouchability from the schools. Whilst in theory the (present national) schools are open to the 'untouchables' very few, as a matter of fact, have untouchable children in therm. . . . I have no hesitation in advising that teachers should run the risk of closing down their schools if the condition of running them requires the exclusion of untouchables.

Thus, the Mahatma emphasised the fact that preliminary training should consist in teaching Harijan children manners, good speech and good conduct. "A Harijan child sits anyhow; dresses anyhow; his eyes, ears, teeth, hair, nails, nose are often full of dirt; many never know what it is to have a wash . . . their lesson should begin for the first three months with teaching them cleanliness. They should be taught also how to eat properly.

. . . If this preliminary training is to be given in all Harijan schools, pamphlets giving detailed instructions for teachers in their languages should be prepared and distributed, and inspectors of schools be required during their inspection to examine teachers and pupils on this head and to send full reports of the progress made in this direction."

Infact, Gandhi never reconciled himself to untouchability. He always regarded it as an excrescence in Hinduism. He stated emphatically that a religion that established the worship of the cow could not possibly countenance or warrant a cruel and Indian boycott of human beings. . . . I should be context to be torn to pieces rather than disown the suppressed classes. Hindus will certainly never deserve freedom nor get it if they allow their noble religion to be disgraced by the retention of the taint of untouchability.

He warned the Hindu brethren against the tendency which he saw of exploiting the suppresses classes for a political end. He stated that to remove untouchability was a penance that Caste Hindus owned to Hinduism and to themselves. The purification required was not of "untouchability" but of the so-called superior castes. There was no vice that was special to the "untouchables," not even dirt and in sanitation. It is our arrogance which blinds us, superior Hindus, to our own blemishes and which magnifies those of our downtrodden brethren whom we have suppressed and whom we keep under suppression . . . . That religion and that nation will be blotted out of the face of the earth which pins its faith to injustice, untruth or violence. God is light, not darkness. God is Love, not hate, God is truth, not untruth. God alone is great. We His creatures are but dust. Let us be humble and recognise the place of the lowliest of His creatures. Krishna honoured Sudama in his rags as he honoured no one else. Love is the root of religion."

For the opening of the roads was not the final but the firs step in the ladder of reform. Temples in general, public wells, public schools must be open to the untouchables, equally with the Caste Hindus.

"I want my Harijan brother, if he wishes, to share this temple worship with the millions of his co-religionists the so-called Caste men. It is the latter's duty to throw open their temples to their Harijan brethren.

Temple worship supplies the felt spiritual want of the human race. It admits of reform. But it will live as long as man lives." The Mahatma regarded untouchability as the greatest blot on Hinduism. He developed this feeling when he was a child. He described how he did not like numerous Hindu customs which promoted the feelings of high and low in Indian society. He regretted that Hinduism had sinned in giving sanction to untouchability, and Indian society had suppressed "our brethren."[8] I regret untouchability as the greatest blot on Hinduism. This idea was not brought home to me by my bitter experience during the South African struggle is not due to the fact that I was once an agnostic.

It is equally wrong to think—as some people do that I have taken my views from my study of Christian religious literature. These views date as far back as the time when I was neither enamoured of, nor was acquainted with the Bible or the followers of the Bible. While at school I would often happen to touch the 'untouchables,' and as I never would conceal the fact from my parents, my mother would tell me that the shortest cut to purification after the unholy touch was to cancel the touch by touching any Mussalman passing by. And simply out of reverence and regard for my mother I often did so, but never did so believing it to be a religious obligation. After some- time we shifted to Porbandar, where I made my first acquaintance with Sanskrit. I was not yet put into an English school, and my brother and I were placed in charge of a Brahamin, who taught us *Ramaraksha* and *Vishnu Puja*. The text *"Jate Vishnuh Sthale Vishnuh"* (there is the Lord present in water, there is the Lord present in earth) has never gone out of my memory. A motherly old dame used to live close by. Now it happened that I was very timid then, and would conjure up ghosts and goblins whenever the lights went out and it was dark. The old order, to disabuse me of fears, suggested that I should mutter the *Ramaraksha* texts whenever I was afraid, and all evil spirits would fly away. This I did and as I thought, with good effect. I could never believe then that there was any text in the *Ramaraksha* socriting to the contact of the untouchables as a sin. I did not understand its meaning then, or understood it very imperfectly. But I was confident that *Ramaraksha*, which could destroy all fear of ghosts, could not be countenancing any such thing as fear of contact with the untouchables.

The *Ramayana* used to be regularly read in our family. As Brahmin called Ladha Majaraj used to read it. He was stricken with leprosy, and was confident that a regular reading of the *Ramayana* would cure him of leprosy, and indeed, he was cured of it. 'How can the *Ramayana,*' I thought it myself, 'in which one who is regarded now-a-days as an untouchable took Rama across the Ganges in his boat, countenance the idea of any human beings being untouchable on the ground that they were polluted souls?" The fact that we address God as the 'purifier of the polluted' and by similar appellations, shows that it is a sin to regard anyone born in Hinduism as polluted or untouchable—that it is Satanic to do so. I have hence been never tired of repeating that is a great sin. I do not pretend that this thing had crystallised as a conviction in me at the age of twelve, but I do say that I did then regard untouchability as a sin. I narrate this story for the information of the Vaishnavasas and orthodox Hindus.

I have always claimed to be a Sanatani Hindu. It is not that I am quite innocent of the scriptures. I am not a profound scholar of Sanskrit. I have read the *Vedas* and the *Upanishads* only in translation. Naturally therefore, mine is not a scholarly study of them. My knowledge of them is in no way profound, but I have studied them as I should do as a Hindu and I claim to have grasped their true spirit. By the time I had reached the age of 21, I had studied other religions also.

There was a time when I was wavering between Hinduism and Christianity. When I recovered my balance of mind, I felt that to me salvation was possible only through the Hindu religion and my faith in Hinduism great deeper and more enlightened.

But even then I believed that untouchability was no part of Hinduism; and that if it was, such Hinduism was not for me.

True Hinduism does not regard untouchability as a sin. I do not want to enter into any controversy regarding the interpretation of the *Shastras*. It might be difficult for me to establish my point by quoting authorities from the *Bhagavat* or *Manusmriti*. But I claim to have understood the spirit of Hinduism. Hinduism has sinned in giving sanction to untouchability. It has degraded us, made us the pariahs of the Empire. Even the Musalmans caught the sinful contagion from us, and in South Africa, in East Africa and in Canada, the Musalmans no less than Hindus came to be regarded as pariahs. All this evil has resulted from the sin of untouchability.

I may here recall my proposition, which is this: So long as the Hindus willfully regard untouchability as part of their religion, as long as the mass of Hindus consider it a sin to touch a section of their brethren, Swaraj is impossible of attainment. Yudhistra would not enter heaven without his dog. How can, then the descendants of that Yudhistra expect to obtain Swaraj without the untouchables? What crimes for which we condemn the Government as Satanaic have not we been guilty of towards our untouchable brethren?

We are guilty of having suppressed our brethren; we make them crawl on their bellies; we have made them rub their noses on the ground; with eyes red with rage, we push them out of railway compartments—what more than this has British rule done? What charge that we bring against Dyer and O'Dwyer may not others, and even our own people, lay at our door? We ought to purge ourselves of this pollution. It is idle to talk of Swaraj so long as we do not protect the weak and the helpless, or so long as it is possible for a single Swarajist to injure the feelings of any individual. Swaraj means that not a single Hindu or Muslim shall for a moment arrogantly think that he can crush with impunity meet Hindus or Muslins. Unless this condition fulfilled we will gain Swaraj only to lose it the next movement.

We are no better than the brutes until we have purged ourselves of the sins we have committed against our weaker brethren.

But I have faith in me still. In the course of my peregrinations in India I have realised that the spirit of kindness of which the poet Tulsidas sings so eloquently, which forms the cornerstone of the Jain and Vaishnava religions, which is the quintessence of the *Bhagavat*, and which every verse of the *Gita* is saturated with—this kindness, this love, this clarity, is slowly but steadily gaining ground in the hearts of the masses of this country.

Many a fracas between Hindus and Musalmans is stilt heard of. There are still many of those who do not scruple to wrong one another. But as to the net result, I feel that kindness and charity have increased. The Hindus and Mohammedans have become god fearing. We have shaken ourselves free from the hypnotism of law courts and Government schools and no longer labour under any other hallucination. I have also realised that those whom we regard as illiterate and ignorant are the very people who deserve to be called educated. They are more cultured than we, their lives are more righteous than ours. A little study of the present day mentality of the people will show that according to the popular conception, Swaraj is synonymous with Ramarajya—the establishment of the Kingdom of Righteousness on earth. If it can bring any comfort to you, my untouchable brethren, I would say that your question does not cause so much stir, as it used to do formerly. That does not mean that I expect you to cease to have misgivings about the Hindus. How can they deserve to be not mistrusted having wronged you so much? Swami Vivekanand used to say that the untouchables were not depressed, they were suppressed by the Hindus who in turn had suppressed themselves by suppressing them.

I suppose I was at Nellore on the 6th of April. I met the untouchables there and I prayed that day as I have done today. I do want to attain *moksha*. I do not want to be reborn. But if I have to be reborn, I should be born an untouchable, so that I may share their sorrows, suffering and the affronts levelled at them, in order that I may endeavour to free myself and them from that miserable condition. I, therefore, prayed that if I should be born again, I should do so not as a Brahmin, Kshatriya, Vaishya or Sudras, but as an Atisudra.

Today is much more solemn than the sixth. It is hallowed by the memory of the massacre of thousands of innocents. And I prayed, therefore, also today that if I should die with any of my desires unfructified, with my service of the untouchables unfinished, with my Hinduism unfulfilled, I may be born again amongst the untouchables to bring my Hinduism to its fulfillment.

I love scavenging. In my Ashram, an eighteen-year-old Brahmin lad is doing the scavenger's work in order to teach the Ashram scavenger cleanliness. The lad is no reformer. He was born and bread in orthodoxy. He is a regular reader of the *Gita* and faithfully performs *sandhyavandana*. His pronunciation of Sanskrit verses is more faultless than mine. When he conducts the prayer, his soft, sweet melodies melt one into love. But the felt that his accomplishments were incomplete until he had become also a perfect sweeper, and that if he wanted the Ashram sweeper to do his work well, he must do it himself and set an example.

You should realise that you are cleaning Hindu society. You have therefore to purify your lives. You should cultivate the habit of cleanliness, so that no one may point this finger at you. Use alkali ash or earth if you cannot afford to use soap to keep yourselves clean. Some of you are given to drinking and gambling which you must get rid of. You will point your finger at the Brahmins and say that even they are given to these vices. But they are not looked upon polluted as you are. You must not ask the Hindus to emancipate you as a matter of favour. Hindus must do so, if they want, in their own interests. You should, therefore, make them feel ashamed by your own purity and cleanliness. I believe that we shall have purified ourselves within the next five months. If my expectations are not fulfilled, I will think that although may proposition was fundamentally correct, yet I was wrong in my calculation; and I will again say that I had erred in my calculation.

You claim to be Hindus; you read the *Bhagavat*. If, therefore, the Hindus oppress you then you should understand that the fault does not lie in the Hindu religion but in those who profess it. In order to emancipate yourselves you shall have to purify yourselves.You shall have to get rid of evil habits like drinking.

If you want to ameliorate your conditions if you want to obtain *Swaraj,* you should be self-reliant. I was told in Bombay that some of you are opposed to N.C.O. and believe that salvation is only possible through the British Government. Let me tell you that you will never be able to obtain redress by discarding Hindu religion and courting the favour of a third party. Your emancipation lies in your own hands.

I have come in contact with the untouchables all over the country; and I have observed that immense possibilities lie latent in them of which neighter they nor the rest of the Hindus seem to be aware. Their intellect is of original purity. I ask you to learn spinning and weaving and if you take them up as a profession, you will keep poverty from your doors. as regards your attitude towards the *Bhangis* I will repeat what I said at Godhra. I cannot understand why you should yourselves countenance the distinction between *Dheds* and *Bhangis*. There is no difference between them. Evening normal times their occupation is as honourable as that of lawyers or Government servants.

You should now cease to accept leavings from plates, however clean they may be represented to be. Receive grain only—good, sound grain, not rotten grain—and that too only if it is courteously offered. If you are able to do all I have asked you to do, you will secure your emancipation, not in four or five months, but in so many days. The Hindus are not sinful by nature—they are sunk in ignorance. Untouchability must be extinct in this very year. Two of the strongest desires that keep me in flesh and bone are the emancipation of the untouchables and the protection of the cow. When these two desires are fulfilled, there is Swaraj, and therein lies my own *moksha*. May God give you strength to work out your salvation.

In a huge assembly of students at Nagpur on 9 November, 1933, the Mahatma stated that he was not confined to Hinduism, and if untouchability was removed from the Hindu heart, he expected far-reaching consequences and a great change in Indian society. The barrier of untouchability, he said, was a great hindrance towards achievement of any kind of unity. He was, however, not sure if his dream about the removal of untouchability would be achieved during his life.

I know this tussle between English and Hindi is almost an external tussle. Whenever I have addressed student audiences, I have been surprised by the demand for English. You know, or ought to know, that I am a lover of the English language. But I do believe that the students of India, who are expected to throw in their lot with the teeming millions and to serve them, will be better qualified if they pay more attention to Hindi than to English. I do not say that you should not learn English; learn it by all means. But, so far as I can sec, it cannot be the language of the millions of Indian homes. It will be confined to thousands or tens of thousands, but it will not reach the millions.

Therefore, I am delighted when the students ask me to speak in Hindi. You, both the speakers, have spoken of me in terms, which if I believed to be true of myself, I do not know where I would be. But I know my place. I am a humble servant of India, and is trying to serve India, I serve humanity at large. I discovered in may early days that the service of India is not inconsistent with the service of humanity. As I grew older in years, and I hope also in wisdom, I saw that the discovery was well made, and after nearly 50 years of public life, I am able to say today that my faith in the doctrine, that the service of one's nation is not inconsistent with the service of the world, has grown. It is a good doctrine. Its acceptance alone will ease the situation in the world and stop the mutual jealousies between nations inhabiting this globe of ours. You have said truly that, in taking up this war against untouchability, I have not confined myself to Hinduism. I have said more than once that if untouchability is removed in its fullness from the Hindu heart, it will have far-reaching consequences, in as much as it touches millions of human beings. As I said last night to the great meeting in Nagpur, if untouchability is really removed from the Hindu heart, that is, if the high caste Hindus purge themselves of this terrible taint, we shall soon discover that we are all one and not different peoples. Hindus, Muslims. Christians, Parsis, whatever we may call ourselves. We shall feel the unity, once the barrier of untouchability is removed. As I have often said, untouchability is a hydra-headed monster, appearing in many shapes. Some of them are very subtle. If I have jealousy for any human being, that also is a species of untouchability. I do not know if my dream about the removal of untouchability will be fully realised while I am living. All those who are religiously inclined, those who believe not in formal religion but in the essence of religion, cannot but believe in the removal of a subtle type of untouchability that affects the lives of a vast mass of humanity. If Hindu hearts can be purged of this evil, our eyes of understanding will be more and more opend. It not possible to estimate the gain to humanity when untouchability is really removed. You can now have no difficulty in understanding why I have staked any life for this one thing.

If you, the students who have assembled here, have followed me so far and understood the implications of this mission of mine, you will soon extend the help I want from you. Many students have written to me asking what part they can take in helping this movement. It is a surprise to me that students are obliged to ask this question. The field is so vast and near you that you need not task the question as to what you may do and what you may not. It is not a political question. It may become one, but for you and me, for the time being, it is not connected with politics. My life is governed by religion. I never lost sight of the principle that governs my life when I began dabbling in politics. As this is a humanitarian campaign, students must devote a part of their spare time, if not the whole, to the service of thousands of Harijans. By giving me this magnificent purse you have certainly equalled the brightest records of students' meetings which I have addressed in my many perreginations throughout the length and breadth of India. But I want much more from you.

I have found that, if I get many helpers who can give their spare time, much work can be down. This work cannot be done by hired labour. With hired labour we cannot go to Harijan quarters and sweep their roads, enter their houses and wash their children. I have described in the columns of the *Harijan* what students can do. A Harijan teacher has shown what a Herculean task it is for him to tackle. Even wild children are better than Harijan children. Wild children are not sunk in utter degradations, as the Harijan children are, nor do they live in such filthy surroundings. This problem cannot be tackled by hired labur. No amount of money can enable me to do this. It must be your prerogative. It is an acid test of the education received by you in schools and colleges. Your world will not be measured by your ability to make faultless English speeches. Your worth will be measured by the service your render to the poor and not by Government posts worth Rs. 60 or Rs. 600 that you may have got. I wish you would do this work in the spirit I suggest. I have not met a single student who has said that he cannot spare one hour per day. If you write your diary from day to day, you will find that you waste many a precious hour in the 365 days of the year. If you ant to turn your education to good account, you will turn your attention to this work while this hurricane campaign lasts. Erstwhile students are serving Harijans within a radius of 5 miles round about Wardha. They are doing good silent work; therefore, you do not know them. I invite you to see their work. It is hard but pleasurable. It will give you joy, greater than your cricket or tennis. I have repeatedly said that money will come if I have real, intelligent, honest workers. As a boy of 18 I began my education in begging I have seen that money can be found easily if we have the right kind of workers. Money alone will never satisfy me. I would ask you to pledge yourselves to devote a definite number of spare hours to Harijan service. As you, Mr. President, have said, I am a dreamer. I am indeed a practical dreamer. My dreams are not airy nothings. I want to convert dreams into realities as far as possible. Therefore, I must hasten to auction the gifts I have received from you.

There was much difficulty in running schools for Harijan

boys. In spite of allurements of fee-concessions and scholarships to them, their attendance in the schools was not up to the mark. The Mahatma suggested ways and means for the improvement of their lot by devising novel schemes by the teachers attached to these schools. One who is responsible for the management of over twenty-five Harijan schools writes a long letter stating the difficulties experienced in the management of the schools and ask how I would conduct them if I had the direct management thereof. I need not recount his difficulties which he has described carefully. What I am about to say is an attempt to answer them.

While we are bound to give scholarships and other help to those Harijan boys and girls who attend the established schools, there is no reason whatever slavishly to reproduce the mode and methods of those schools in the ones under our own management. We have to recognise that we get Harijan children with great difficulty to attend any school at all. We cannot expect any degree of regularity in them and, thanks to our past criminal neglect, they are so unkept that we have, in the beginning stages, to handle them in a manner wholly different from the ordinary.

On first admission their bodies have to be minutely examined and thoroughly cleaned. Their clothes might have to be cleaned and patched. The first daily lesson, therefore, will for sometime consist of applied hygiene and sanitation and simple needle-work. I should use no books probably for the whole of the first year. I should talk to them about things with which they are familiar and, doing so, correct their pronunciation and grammar and teach them new words. I should note all the new words they may learn from day to day so as to enable me to use them frequently till they have them fixed in their minds regularly. The teacher will not give discourses but adopt the conversational method. Through conversations he will give his pupils progressive instruction in history, geography and arithmetic. History will begin with that of our own times, and then, too, of events and of persons nearest us, and geography will begin with that of the neighbourhood of the school Arithmetic will begin with the sums applicability the pupil's houses. Having tried the method myself, I know that infinitely more knowledge can be given to the pupils through it, and without strain on them, than can be given through the orthodox methods, within a given time. Knowledge of the alphabet should be treated as a separate subject altogether. The letters should be treated as pictures which the children will first be taught to recognise and name. Writing will follow as part of the drawing lesson. Instead of making daubs of their letters, pupils should be able to make perfect copies of the models placed before them. They would not, therefore, be called upon to draw the letters till they had acquired control over their fingers and the pen. It is criminal to stunt the mental growth of a child by letting him know as much only as he can get through a book he can incoherently read in a year. We do not realise that, if a Child was cut off from the home life and was merely doomed to the school, he would be a perfect dumee for several years. He picks up information and language unconsciously through his home, no in the schoolroom. Hence do we experience the immense difference between pupils belonging to cultured homes and those belonging to uncouth homes, which are no homes unreality. In the scheme I have adumbrated, the schoolmaster is expected to treat his occupation seriously and feel one with his pupils. I know that, in putting the scheme into operation, the want of schoolmasters of the right type is the greatest difficulty. But we shall not get the right type till we have made the right beginning.

The various representations made by caste organisations, before the Government of India Act of 1935 emerged from the anvil of the British Parliament, clamoured for all kinds of special attention to vociferous caste-groups.

Buddhism and the Concept of Religion

It is notable that in books published within the 'religion' genre one rarely, if ever, finds any analysis of the rituals of untouchability or bonded labour. Instead, one finds idealised accounts of Gods and Goddesses, Varnasrama-*dharma,* the various theological schools, the great high-caste Hindu reformers, and of course the *satyagraha* and *vegetarianism* of Gandhi. I have never seen a religious studies book which gave a proper account of why Untouchables generally despise the paternalistic Gandhian word "Harijan,' nor an account of Ambedkar's detailed critique of Gandhi's high-caste reformism. Generally speaking, religious books give the high-caste view of the ecumenical construct Hinduism, and it is a view which facilitates a rapprochement between the elites of the colonisers and the colonised.

In this article I have two aims. The first is to discuss the different concepts of religion found in Ambedkar's writings. The second is to suggest why, for the researcher, 'religion' has become a fairly useless concept. These aims are connected. Ambedkar was a highly educated and intellectually brilliant man, who mastered the law to such an extent that he was able to chair the constitutional committee of the new Republic. He was also able to write penetrating analyses of Indian society which reflected a sophisticated anthropological understanding. But the centre of his life was his devotion to the liberation of the backward classes, and he struggled to find a satisfactory ideological expression for that liberation. Though he talked a great deal about 'religion,' I believe he really went beyond that concept (see Ambedkar, 1957:225). His evolving ideas about religion suggested to me why we could abandon the word without any real loss.

I will try to place different concepts of religion found in Ambedkar's writings in a theoretical context which illustrates wider social and cultural issues affecting the Scheduled Castes. I have in mind particularly the modern coexistence in India of an egalitarian Constitution (for which Ambedkar was largely responsible) and caste hierarchy. Ambedkar himself offers a striking example of the subjective aspect of this institutional dichotomy by his identity as a middle-class barrister and political activist on the one hand, and a member of an Untouchable caste on the other. We seem to have a direct conflict of fundamental principles or values, and passages in the *Annihilation of Caste* (Ambedkar, 1936: 123–28) suggest that for Ambedkar this conflict could be expressed as being between different 'religion.' He referred to these respectively as 'the Religion of Rules' (by which he meant essentially caste hierarchy) and 'the Religion of Principles' (by which he meant essentially democratic egalitarianism, though not the extreme individualism of the West). Ambedkar has the insight here that principles or values which are normally referred to as 'secular' are as sacred as those conventionally referred to as 'religious,' for example, those found in Hindu texts like *Manusmriti*. Furthermore, the so-called 'secular' values—unlike those found in *Manusmriti*—are universal, and thus make possible what he calls a 'True Religion' (1936:126). But I will show that in other texts such as *The Buddha and the Future of His Religion* (Ambedkar, 1950) his concept of 'religion' changes again, until eventually in *The Buddha and His Dhamma* he concludes that it is 'an indefinite word with no fixed meaning' (Ambedkar, 1957:225).

Though Ambedkar certainly believed in the liberation of the individual, he saw clearly that in the modern world the priority must be *institutional* liberation. The struggle for liberation, traditionally symbolised by the solitary renouncer in the forest, or by Gautama Buddha sitting alone beneath the *bodhi* tree, had to retransformed into a struggle against *institutionalised* bondage. I use the word 'bondage' here deliberately, because even today there is bonded labour in parts of Maharashtra such as Marathawada (Pandit, 1990; Fitzgerald, 1994). Thus, for Ambedkar, 'fetters' were not only those karmic hindrances which conditioned the individual's consciousness from one lifetime to another. They were also institutionalised realities which required a political solution.

Ambedkar studied Anthropology at Colombia University in New York, where he received a Ph.D. in 1916. He also qualified as a barrister in the Inns of Court in London. But though a great scholar, his main goal in life was to help create a peaceful revolution in India which would liberate the Untouchables and the backward classes generally from caste oppression. Much of his writing is therefore polemical. It is not surprising, therefore, if his uses of the word 'religion' should be as varied and imprecise as that of many other scholars. But infact as with so much in his writing, Ambedkar had insights into the nature of 'religion' which help us to disentangle some of the different meanings which make it an inherently confused concept. In his desire to formulate a new consciousness for people who are now called Dalits and Buddhists, he raised many important issues which we can try to develop.

Rules' and Principles of Religion

In some of his most famous writings, such as *Annihilation of Casts* (1936). *The Buddha and the Future of His Religion* (1950), and *The Buddha and His Dharma* (1957), Ambedkar tried to develop a coherent account of the nature of religion and its relation to politics and power. In *Annihilation of Caste* he argues that Hinduism is a religion of rules, a compendium of ritual regulations which are based on the caste ideology of hierarchy and untouchability. For him, caste is the central fact of Hinduism, and untouchability is a defining characteristic of caste. He argues that you cannot reform caste because untouchability is an inherent feature. This was one fundamental unreason why he strongly opposed Gandhi's reformism.

Annihilation of Caste was originally written as a speech which he had been invited to deliver by the Jat Pat Todak Mandal of Lahore, a high-caste reform group. When they read it they found it too dangerous so they cancelled the speech. Consequently, Ambedkar published it as a pamphlet instead. The second edition includes a preface, a prologue including the correspondence between him and the Mandal, and two appendices, which include Gandhi's review and Ambedkar's reply to Gandhi.

The published correspondence makes it clear that the reason the Mandal cancelled the speech was that Ambedkar refused to cut what he considered to be the essential point of his argument, but which they variously found to be either irrelevant or too dangerous, that 'the real method of breaking up the Caste System was not to bring about inter-caste dinners and inter-caste marriages but to destroy the religious notions on which caste is founded' (1936:49).

The 'religious' notions he was referring to were of course the traditions Hindu ideology of rank based on purity and untouchability, and which manifested itself in caste, in ritualism, and in the suppression of autonomous individuality. He was not thinking primarily of the tradition of renunciation, of *Sannyas*. On the contrary, in a footnote he suggested that the Upanishads contain ideas about equality and freedom.[2] At this stage Ambedkar's focus was the pervasive hierarchical ritualism which was given its most potent codification in the 'religious' principles in *Manusmriti*, a text of fundamental importance in orthodox thinking which he burnt in public protest at the Mahad Satyagraha, 25 December, 1927 (see Ahir, 1990: 15).

A Summary of Ambedkar's Argument

Political and constitutional reform cannot succeed unless it is preceded by social reform aimed at the eradication of untouchability. But social reform can only mean abolition of caste, because untouchability is a *defining feature* of caste. In reality, caste cannot be *reformed* (contrary to Gandhi's hope) only annihilated. And the annihilation of caste implies the abolition of Hindu ideology particularly as it is formulated in the Shastras and Smritis. Caste is fundamentally 'a state of mind' (he meant this both collectively and individually) which is systematised in these scriptures; and while endogamy is what he calls the 'mechanism' of caste, it is religious dogma that prohibits intermarriage, and therefore ultimately it is the religious values that must be destroyed:'.... it must be recognised that the Hindus observed caste not because they are inhuman or wrong headed. They observe caste because they are deeply religious...the enemy you must grapple with is not the people who observe caste, but the Shastras that teach them this religion of caste' (1936:111).

Ambedkar's insistence that political reform could not succeed unless preceded by social reform (and therefore by a revolution in the sphere of values) may, in retrospect, appear to contradict his own achievement as India's first law minister in piloting through the Constitution which made untouchability illegal. More likely though, it will prove his point, since making untouchability unconstitutional has not in fact abolished it. This demonstrated something which Ambedkar was painfully aware of: that modern law (which implies equality, and which was introduced by the British) is subordinated infact to ritual hierarchy.[3] In contrast, at around this time Gandhi did not want to abolish caste as such, but to reform it according to an ideal model. True, his views changed over the years (Zeliot, 1972; 6*ff*.). But Ambedkar severely criticised Gandhi for his view that caste was essentially a division of labour and that inequality and untouchability were extraneous distortions.

Ambedkar wished to replaced the religion of rules with true religion, the religion of principles, which is the basis for civic government. These principles, liberty, equality and fraternity (1936:9, 128) are true religion. He says, 'True Religion is the foundation of society.' For Ambedkar, these principles were religious principles. He was perfectly well aware that these were the principles of the American and French revolutions. However, he wanted to bring this alternative (non-Indian) tradition into line with traditional Indian ways of thinking, which in effect meant identifying a strand of his own indigenous culture which could legitimately be presented as a critique of Hindu ritual orthodoxy. This was the connection with the *sannyasi* tradition mentioned before; near the end of the *Annihilation of Caste* he suggested in a footnote that this ideology of liberty, equality and fraternity could be found in the Upanishads, though he does not pursue this tantalising statement. Later, he found it in Buddhism. In both cases, it is the religion of the renouncer where he identifies the universal values which can replace that Hindu ritual system. However, though there is a sense in which renunciation remained important in Ambedkar's thinking about religion, his modernising tendency transforms the renouncer into a socially engaged and politically committed individual. I return to this point later.

Putting the issue of renunciation on one side for the moment, so far we have identified two concepts of religion, one, a religion essentially characterised by caste hierarchy and the other a religion essentially characterised by individual freedom an equality. The religion of cast hierarchy described by Ambedkar reveals and opposition between Brahmin purity and dominance, on the one hand, and Untouchable impurity and subservience on the other. These ritual values permeate traditional Hindu society and are most clearly codified in texts such as the *Manusmriti*. The other concept of religion is similar to, and perhaps initially derived from, Western democratic principles and institutions, based on the belief in the formal equality of all individuals, equal rights under the law, the abolition of hereditary status, personal freedom to choose one's own occupation and to develop one's own individual talents. These were the principles which he was to built into the Constitution. These sacred principles are what Westerners generally like to think of as the secular, the non-religious but which Ambedkar suggests are the basis for a concept of 'True Religion' (1936:126). This is one reason why Ambedkar's view of religion is interesting. For him, the bases of religion are *values*, the values which hold a society together. Concepts of the supernatural were not the essentially important point of Ambedkar. Indeed, he came to see supernaturalism as irrational and irrelevant to true religion.

Thus, the concept of religion implied in this kind of analysis is not essentially about supernatural beings, transcendental worlds or spiritual salvation in a life after death. It is about the fundamental values which make possible different kinds of social institutions, in one case the institution of caste which is based on the sacred Brahminical principles codified in the Smritis, and in the other case the institutions of democracy which are based on the sacred principles of liberty, equality and fraternity.

However, one significant way in which these sets of values differ from each other is that for Ambedkar, the democratic values are universalist in the sense that they apply equality to everyone in principle, for all humans are individuals and all humans have equal rights and obligations, and all humans deserve the opportunity to discover their own true talents. In contrast, the Hindu values are particularistic. There is one set of rules for Brahmins, one for Marathas, one for Mahars and one for Mangs.

In a democratic world, anybody can in principle become president, get a good education, marry the partner of their choice regardless of caste (and presumably of nationality), live in their preferred neighbourhood, be respected for what they are or do rather than for their inherited status. But in the case of the caste system in India, rules apply to particular people in particular situations. Different categories of people must marry only into a specific sub-caste, must have different occupations, must live in different parts of the village, must weal different clothes, and so on.

In a democratic kind of society, freedom of the individual implies a new kind of freedom, the freedom to choose one's religion. But here we have a different concept of religion emerging. Here religion is conceived as a body of doctrines about salvation which the individual can choose to adhere to because he finds it the best, the most rational, the most suitable for his or her personal needs. The religious principles of equality, liberty and fraternity make possible (paradoxically) a secular' society in which religion becomes a matter of personal commitment and choice. This different concept of religion is implied in Ambedkar's *The Buddha and the Future of His Religion*, where he does a comparative analysis of the rationality and ethical principles of Buddhism. I do not want to claim that the distinction between these different concepts of religion is clearly and consciously demarcated, but I believe it is there. Indeed, I would argue that it is inevitably there, because the emergence of what in the West and elsewhere is referred to as secular society, but which Ambedkar (in my view very perceptively) calls a religion, has historically also produced a concept of religion which is a private affair, a matter of personal choice and commitment, something one gets converted to. In a caste society, you do not get converted to Brahminical hierarchy. It is not something which anybody chooses.

According to Ambedkar's understanding, *Buddha Dhamma* is essentially *morality*. By morality he means compassion, earing for one's fellow human being and for the natural world, feeling a sense of responsibility and commitment, being actively committed to the well being of the world. Morality, unlike ritual obligation, springs from the heart of the individual and is based on a sense of brotherhood and sisterhood. Thus Buddhism, on this line of reasoning becomes the basis of the new egalitarian society, the structural equivalent of hierarchy as the basis of Hindu society. For this is not a traditional sectarian dispute about which is the true path to liberation—a disputation which takes for granted a whole structure of shared assumptions. This is a questioning of the basis of the structure itself.

One the other hand, this very notion that one can change one's religion, that one can move from one religion to another, that one can look around for a more suitable religion than the one which one has at present, it itself a modern idea. On this concept, Buddhism is one of a number of religions which, in *Buddha and the Future of His Religion* Ambedkar compares with Christianity, Islam and Hinduism Buddhism is the-best of these because it is the most rational, the most scientific in its principles, the most moral. It is therefore, the religion which Ambedkar advocates and which he seeks to persuade others to adopt.

But this concept of religion as being a matter of private choice itself involves another political principle, the Freedom of Religion which is guaranteed by the Constitution. Buddhism is thus intended both as the fundamental basis of the new social order and as the most rational choice of the individual. So his Buddhism is a highly rational blend of individualism with socio-political commitment, a Buddhist modernism with a crucial element of liberation theology, but intended to be the basis of the new social order.

Ambedkar's own analysis of Hindu ideology sometimes sounds more like a kind of Marxist revolutionary sociology when he says "The problem of Untouchability is a matter of class struggle' (B.R. Ambedkar, quoted in Ahir, 1990: 21). But this surely is as much an appeal for class-consciousness as an analysis, a revolutionary desire to transform the traditional inertia of untouchability into a politically conscious movement cutting across caste lines. Infact, Ambedkar was not a Marxist in one sense because he did not believe in violent revolution. But he seems to have believed that the emergence of politically conscious classes might act as an agent for fundamental change in Indian society. He was also a socialist in the sense that he believed that the redistribution of wealth and opportunity in a society needed some direct government intervention, such as the nationalisation of key industries. He also wanted separate electorates as a way around the problem of electoral intimidation and a guaranteed number of seats for backward classes; and the wanted an employment and educational policy which actively countered the discriminatory tendencies of traditional caste loyalties. But his long-term aim was the creation of a society of morally free and responsible individuals.

From as early as 1935, Ambedkar indicated the fundamental importance of religion by publicly declaring untouchability to be an inseparable part of Hinduism, and his own intention to convert to Buddhism (Ahir, 1990:20*ff*.). There is no doubt that Ambedkar was an intensely religious man, in the sense of a deep commitment to values and principles such as compassion, justice and equality. But he needed a religion which made a difference in this world, a religion which could change society and empower the backward classes. Therefore, his interpretation of Buddhism has some modernist natures. As a *soteriology* (doctrine of salvation), Buddhism has always been concerned with the fate of the individual, but in the sense of release (*nirvana*) from this world (*Samsara*) through the self-discipline of the four noble truths and the eightfold path. Ambedkar was critical of the Theravada Sangha of South and South-East Asia for its tendency towards detachment from the world. For Ambedkar, soteriology has a strong social and political component. Bhikshus should be socially and politically committed to justice. He was more attracted by the Mahayana concept of the Bodhisattava who delays his own liberation out of compassion for less fortunate or less advanced beings. Furthermore, the Bodhisattva ideal lends itself more easily to modern concepts of democracy, human rights and social justice, for it can easily be seen as a compassionate activity in favour of the oppressed and the fight against social and political injustice. Salvation is conceived in terms of the struggle for emancipation and dignity of the oppressed classes of Hindu society. And the individual is in *some* respects more like the autonomous individual of Protestant Christianity, committed to rational action in this world, than the renouncer who turns his back on the world.

In this sense I find it illuminating that on all Buddhist shrines in Maharashtra one finds two pictures. One is of the Buddha sitting cross-legged in the rags of the renouncer meditating beneath the *bodhi* tree and achieving enlightenment. In the other one sees Ambedkar, dressed in a modern blue business suit, wearing heavy-rimmed glasses, and holding a large book which represents literacy, education, and also perhaps the egalitarian Constitution of India, which he wrote and which is reputed to be one of the most advanced constitutions in the world. These are the ancient and modern conceptions of liberation side-by-side (see Tartakov, 1990).

In his posthumously published *The Buddha and His Dhamma* (1957), Ambedkar wanted to revive what he took to be the main principles of original Buddhism. In this book he says that 'dharma' and 'religion' are entirely different (1957:225), which is another shift of meaning. His interpretation of Buddhism here is strongly favoured with 'scientific' materialism. It has to be remembered that this book was not completed before he died, he had written some notes while he was ill, and the editors had the task of putting it together afterwards. The end results a book which tends to emphasize an interpretation of Buddhist liberation as a social and political liberation, rather than as traditional enlightenment. For example, he equates *nirvana* (the Buddhist concept of the transcendent) to the eightfold path (which in traditional Buddhism is the way,the practice, by which to obtain *nirvana*). He said '*Nibbana* is naught but that 8-Fold Path' (1957:228); and the eightfold path's most important aspect, 'right outlook,' is in turn defined as the recognition of cause and effect (1957:281). Logically, therefore, this is almost like saying that nirvana is equivalent to scientific rationality. In this way, Ambedkar attempts to present traditional Indian Buddhism as fully consistent with materialism, with scientific rationality, with parliamentary democracy, with the principles of equality, fraternity, liberty. To do this he asserts that Buddhism has no place for belief in the supernatural; that the doctrine of karma is a theory of causation only; that *prajna* (wisdom) means the ability to think rationally and without superstition; that *karuna* (compassion) means the ability to love one's fellow men and to work for social justice; that the *Bhikshu* (monk) is not (or should not be) merely an ascetic intent on this own enlightenment but a social worker dedicated to the betterment of human welfare. In his account, enlightenment seems much closer to the enlightenment of the French philosophies of the 18th century than to the *nirvana* of the Buddha. In short, he has almost nothing to say about the central Buddhist soteriology concerning nirvana, meditation, and the ending of karma and rebirth. This does not mean that he was not concerned about the traditional concept of *pratitya samutpada* (conditioned origination), only that his goal was conceived in terms of *institutional* liberation (liberation from the institution of untouchability and ritual pollution) as a necessary precondition to any personal freedom.

Ritual, Politics and Steriology

I have suggested that Ambedkar uses religion in different ways to mean (i) the system of caste hierarchy; (ii) traditional asceticism, that is, release from this world through meditation and self-discipline, as found in the Upanishads and traditional forms of Buddhism; (iii) democratic society (usually referred to as secular society in the West) based on the sacred values of liberty, equality and fraternity; (iv) the religions such as Christianity, Islam, Hinduism and Buddhism, which in a free society the individual should choose on a personal basis. One point to note is that so much is included inches different uses that one might as well abandon the word altogether and find different terms which make more precise distinctions.

This idea in fact coincides with my own research on Buddhism in Maharashtra. I have not found the concept of religion very useful as an analytical concept for understanding the situation of the Ambedkar Buddhists. If I were a 'comparative religionist,' meaning someone who believes that there are many religions in the world, and all one has to do is go out and find them, probably the first thing I would notice if I visited the communities at all would be their temples, and their *puja* performed to pictures of Gautma Buddha and Ambedkar side-by-side on the Shrine. And there is no doubt that may Buddhists conceive Buddha and Amebdkar (who is considered a Bodhisattva) as supernatural beings who can bring benefits. In this sense they fulfill the same function as some Hindu deities.

The concept of Ambedkar as a Bodhisattva or enlightened being who brings liberation to all backward classes is widespread among Buddhists. However, Ambedkar himself was entirely against supernaturalism, seeing it as a form of dependency induced by the traditional oppression of Hindu caste culture. And the dominant understanding of present-day Buddhists, especially more educated Buddhists, is explicitly against the idea that Ambedkar is a supernatural being. Some Buddhists believe Ambedkar was enlightened or partially enlightened in a way similar to traditional Theravada interpretations of Gautama Buddha's enlightenment, which stresses his humanity and refrains from turning them into a god. Indeed, in the traditional stories the god Brahma is depicted as asking Buddha to show him the way to liberation. When such Buddhists perform *puja*, they are recalling Gautma Buddha's and Ambedkar's outstanding life and example. Many educated Buddhists interpret Ambedkar's enlightenment not in a transcendental way but as the product of education and the full realisation of his potential

This is true even though transcendentalist or supernaturalist aspects of the movement exist. And when one realises that the vast majority of Buddhists are members of the same Untouchable caste, then it becomes obvious that caste hierarchy must be a fundamental part of the analysis. This reflects Ambedkar's focus on liberation as an *institutional* problem in the first place.

I have developed a topology *of ritual, politics* and *soteriology* to make sense of my fieldwork. Here I can do not more than summarise my published research in order to clarify why the concept of 'religion' is in my view analytically redundant.

It seems to me that Amebdkar's analysis of Indian (Hindu) society was that it is fundamentally a ritualistic (rather than moral) system, "and that caste, untouchability and supernaturalism were its main institutional expressions. Though he did advocate some simple Buddhist rituals such as *puja* and simple Buddhist wedding and funeral rites, he believed that these should be cheap (to avoid dowry problems), transparent and non-mystifying. The *ritual* referred to in this category is the whole spectrum of ritualistic practices which Ambedkar condemned, ranging from worship of the supernatural, exorcism, possession states, caste ritualism such as endogamy and dowry, or rituals of purity and pollution. This would include the ritual location of the Untouchable quarter in the villages (previously called Maharwada, now Buddhawada), and the ritually defined duties of scavenging and night-soil removal. As I have shown above, Ambedkar himself analysed "Hinduism' as a ritual system encoded in texts such as the *Manusmiti* which gave ideological justification form untouchability. Ideologically, when we identify the for of life indicated by ritual, we are not really talking about Buddhism here (certainly not Ambedkar's understanding of Buddhism), but about *a de* facto lifestyle which many people who are proud to identify themselves as Buddhists do (by default) practice. For example, sub-caste endogamy is widespread among all categories of Buddhists, at least in certain areas such as Nagpur and Marathwada, including highly educated academics with a sophisticated understanding of Ambedkar's teaching. It is therefore part and parcel of contemporary Buddhist identity, even though Buddhists themselves deplore it. Another example is that Buddhists who have proved their commitment and courage by exposing themselves to the dangers of high-caste anger by refusing to perform some ritual services such as scavenging may still be themselves practicing untouchability against other Untouchable castes like Mang and Holar, or be involved in the worship of the goddess Mariai, or may be worshiping Buddha and Ambedkar as though they were Hindu gods. The importance of this element of *ritual* is that, though logically it is incompatible with Ambedkar's teaching, it is to some variable degree part of the actual situation and identity of Buddhists, and consequently has to be investigated as such.

Politics

It seems to me that 'secular' rationalism and social democracy are central to Ambedkar's understanding of Buddhism, and that against this kind of interpretation is to some variable extent identifiable in the thanking of most Buddhist groups in Maharashtra, whether they be Dalits, academics, village teachers, community spokesmen, local urban activists who sometimes lead *puja* in the local temple, or even monks and dharmacharis. I believe that 'polities' in the sense of social activism directed towards the exercise of political power for the purpose of peaceful social revolution my be the best, single world to encapsulate this element of Ambedkar's Buddhism. This notion of politics is not arbitrary, for it is closely linked with the fundamental principles of a democratic Constitution (largely written by Ambedkar himself as India's first law minister, and astounding achievement for a man who carried the stigma of untouchability throughout his life), a modern judicial system based on the value of equality before the law, and the legitimate pursuit of power through constitutional means.

Soteriology is traditionally a doctrine of spiritual salvation or liberation from the world of suffering and evil. Traditional Theravada Buddhism is a soteriology par excellence, for it provides the analysis of suffering, the means for its eradication and the transcendental goal. It is particularly a doctrine concerned with the individual, for it is the individual consciousness which is put together through the karmic factors of suffering and it is the individual who practises moral restraint, social concern and meditation along the path to enlightenment. However, in Ambedkar's writings, social concern is given a distinctively political emphasis. The institution of caste hierarchy and its ritualistic mechanism are particularly identified as major causes of suffering. The concept of individual liberation is very closely linked with socio-political liberation, and the factors of suffering are identified more broadly with institutiona-lised exploitation, particularly caste and untouchability. Therefore, in Ambedkar's writings, soteriology and politics are closely identified, politics being understood as the pursuit of power within the jurisdiction of a democratic constitution, and soteriology as liberation from inequality and exploitation.

Nevertheless, many Buddhists hold strongly that soteriology is not *only* political and social activism in Ambedkar's thinking, but has an important spiritual or transcendental element as well, which is pursued through reading Buddhist texts, practising mediation and going on retreats. Socio-political activism and a more 'spiritual' understanding of liberation are often (through not always)[7] seen as complementary and even dialectically implicated. One highly organised expression of this idea of soteriology is the Trilokya Buddha Mahasangha (TBMS), which has developed a sophisticated interpretation of Buddhist soteriological doctrine based on both Ambedkar's teaching and the scholarly writing of the Venerable Sangharakshita. This teaching holds social revolutionary and transcendental goals as complementary.

To what degree any particular Buddhist group in Maharashtra does or does not exemplify these elements is an empirical issue. My point is that, when we talk about Buddhism in Maharashtra, we are talking about different combinations of, and oppositions between, these qualities. Buddhists want liberation from their ritual status as Untouchables, but the dilemma is that they are defined by that status in the predominant caste ideology. I suppose ritual, politics and soteriology could all be refined as 'religion,' but then I cannot sec that the world picks out anything distinctive.

My own ethnography of Buddhism is based on three broadly distinctive categories within the Buddhist community: (i) Buddhists living in villages, in this case in Marathawada, a remote and backward area of Maharashtra; (ii) Middle-class Buddhists, in this case academics living in Nagpur; (ii) Buddhists who have actually renounced ordinary lay life and become monks, or something equivalent, in a community which is explicitly concerned with traditional Buddhist practices such as meditation, in this case the Trilokya Buddha Mahasangha (TBMSG) in Pune, which is arguably the most effective of the agencies for propagating soteriological Buddhism of a transcendentalist kind. However, this agency is deeply committed to social work and thought it is non-poitical it certainly sees individual liberation as being strongly connected with peaceful social revolution. It would not do justice to the reality of the situation to present one of these emphases out of context.

This is not an exhaustive classification of tall the varied occupations and lifestyles of Buddhists. Many Buddhists are poor urban factory workers. There is a strong element of political activism both in the formal political parties such as the Republican Party (founded by Ambedkar, but now factionalied), and also in the Dalit movement, which is a generally backward classes militant movement dominated by the Buddhists. There are Buddhist novelists and poets writing in Marathi (see Zelliot, 1992). Nevertheless, the groups that I have interviewed do in fact tend to reveal the predominance in one way or another of these different factors.

What is notable about all these different categories of Buddhists is the high degree of consciousness that exists of Ambedkar's writings, his political and soteriological goals, in short, of the meaning of Ambedkar's Buddhism. In my view, the fundamental value of Ambedkar's Buddhism is egalitarianism understood as the ethical autonomy of the individual but. with the political realism to realise that dominant institutions such as caste can only be changed through the agency of alternative institutions, such as courts of law and anti-discrimination policies of governments. Ambedkar is sometimes described as a socialist and he certainly wanted to use the power of the state to bring about social reform and redistribute wealth, for example through nationalisation.

But his concept of liberation through social revolution is based to a significant extent on an appeal ultimately to the ethical autonomy of individuals and their ability to transform themselves and their society through collective action. And this understanding is widely understood among present-day Buddhists. This is true despite the fact that the Buddhist is movements almost completely confined to one Untouchable caste of about four million people.[9] Though Buddhists apparently continue to practice untouchability against other Untouchable castes, there is also simultaneously, widespread conscious and bitter rejection of these notions. Buddhists are thus caught in a contradiction, much as a committed British Communist is caught in a contradiction when he puts his house on the marked and tries to get the best price. If one is living within a system, one is to some degree forced to conform to it unless alternative institutions grow strong enough to legitimate an alternative lifestyle.

REFERENCES

Ambedkar, B.R., 1916 (19136). "Castes in India: Their Mechanism, Genesis and Development' in *B.R. Ambedkar, Annihilation of Caste*, Jallandhar City: bee ma Patrick Publications.

Bheema, 1950. *The Buddha and the Future of His Religion*, Jallandhar City: Bheema Patrika Publication.

Fitzgerald, T. 1994. "*Buddhism in Maharashtra: A Tripartite Analysis*", in A.K. Narain and D.C. Ahir (eds.), *Dr Ambedkar, Buddhism and Social Change*, Delhi; B.R.Publishing Corporation.

Guru, Gopal, 1991. 'The Hinduisation of Ambedkar,' *Economic and Political Weekly* XXVI (7) 339–41.

Narain, A.K. and D.C. Ahir (eds). *Dr. Ambedkar, Buddhism and Social Change*, Delhi, B.R. Publishing Corporation.

6

Economic Policy of Dalits

There was a time, before the collapse of communism in Soviet Union, debates on economic policy had a clear 'left-right', progressive-conservative line-up. Socialists and progressives pushed for more role for the state, if not in building socialism then at least in assuring welfare where markets failed, while rightists hailed the market. Those days are gone. Today the most notorious reactionaries on social issues, from Pat Buchanan to Zhirinovsky, join with old leftists and trade unionists in calling for protectionism. The former socialist countries are forging a path towards capitalism, the Asian ones are under the leadership of their communist parties. On the other hand, fervent free-marketers such as the 'Freshmen Republicans' of New Gingrich in the USA have discovered the virtues of at least some subsidies. In India, the BJP and CPI(M) alike have opposed 'Dunkel' tooth and nail while in opposition, but have promised that 'reforms will not stop' while in power; the effective debate now is only over the speed and type of reforms. Socialism is seemingly dead, but the market has hardly triumphed, welfare survives and people everywhere behold the doings of their political classes and intellectual leaders with scorn and puzzlement. Rethinking is clearly necessary.

Bhimrao Ramji Ambedkar, 'Babasaheb' to his Dalit followers, received his degree in economics from Columbia University. In spite of an event-filled political life, he found time to write numerous books, many dealing directly or indirectly with economic theory. In these days of intellectual confusion, can we find any guidance in the Dalit tradition, as compared to the Marxist one? This article takes a brief look at Ambedkar's theorising.

Ambedkar—even more than Marx—was primarily a political activist, though with a Ph.D. in economics. He had little time for deep academic research, but was immersed in the turmoil of his times. This is reflected in his economic thinking, which broadly went through three stages. The first was in his early, more academic economic writings of the 1920s (especially *The Problem of the Rupee and the Evolution of Provincial Finance in British India* [Moon, 1990c] which gave strong anti-imperialist but fairly orthodox liberal economic a assessments of British rule.[4] The second was in the 1930s and 1940s when as a central figure in the social and national movements of the period he was heavily influenced by traditional Marxism in the field of economics, a period that climaxed with the slogans of 'state socialism.' During this period Ambedkar used a kind of 'dual systems' approach in which Brahmanism and capitalism were seen as parallel systems of exploitation. The third period was towards the end of his life, marked by his historical researches on caste, Hinduism and Buddhism, when he sought a total alternative in Buddhist philosophy.

In the 1920s, employed as a professor at Sydenham College, Ambedkar spent his time reading and working and preparing the base for a surging Dalit movement. This included the organisation of the Bahishkrut Hitakarni Sabha and the first great campaign (later to be memorialised as 'Untouchable Liberation Day') for water in the Mahad tank satyagraha. This organising of Mahad tank satyagraha in the Konkan region, it might be noted, was in an area that was later to become a centre for a united Mahar-Kunbi movement against the Khoti Landlord System. But, with a pace somewhat lower than that of later years, Ambedkar found time for two major economic treatises. Both followed fairly conventional economic thinking, and both also had important similarities with the Indian economic nationalists—with the Evolution of Finances taking a harsh stand against much of British, policy.

The *Problem of the Rupee* was the book that justified Narendra Jadhav's contention that Ambedkar would have supported devaluation. In the final sections of the book, Ambedkar dealt with the devaluation controversy of his day. Strikingly, at that time it was the Indian bourgeoise who wanted a low rupee against the pound, while the British bureaucracy wanted a high rupee—the first, undoubtedly because they were primarily in an industry which had been a world leader from the very beginning (the textile industry), the second at least partly because of personal interests which would have preferred to be able to buy more pounds from their rupee salaries when they retired.

Ambedkar's own position was to argue for a moderately low rupee. In the course of his discussion, however, he did something which few in the devaluation debate of the 1990s had done; he gave a class analysis of the (at least temporary) effects of devaluation—arguing that entrepreneurs and the self-employed (from businessmen and farmers) would benefit from a low rupee, while wage and salary owners (from bureaucrats to daily labourers) would benefit from a high one which would keep consumer goods cheaper.[5] Ambedkar's recommendation was therefore one which he consciously saw as a compromise between workers and capitalists—a devalued rupee but not quite as much as the Indian bourgeoisie would have liked.

Ambedkar did not remain a 'conventional economist' for long. In the 1930s and 1940s, under the impact of a mass upsurge, the pressure of the Great Depression and the evidently successful economic progress of the USSR and the working-class radicalism, this gave birth to, he turned to the left. This was the period when his Dalit-based Independent Labour Party joined with communists to organise peasants and workers and he formulated the struggle as being against both 'capitalism' and Brahmanism.' In the largest peasant March of the 1930s, organised to demand abolition of the Khoti landlord system in the Konkan, he had told the rally that 'in regard to the toiler's class struggle, I feel the Communist philosophy to be closer to as (*Janata*, 15 January, 1938). Later that year at a conference of Dalit railroad workers, he said. There are in my view two enemies which the workers of this country have to deal with. The two enemies are Brahmanism and Capitalism. . . . By Brahmanism I do not mean the power, privileges and interests of the Brahmins as a community. By Brahmanism I mean the negation of the spirit of Liberty, Equality and Fraternity. In that sense it is rampant in all classes and is not confined to the Brahmins alone though they have been the originators of it' (reported in *The Times of India*, 14 February, 1938).

These were years in which the pages of *Janata*, Ambedkar's weekly, were filled with reports of the struggles of workers and peasants against 'capitalists and landlords' as well as the fights of Dalits against atrocities. Ambedkar did not have much time for theoretical writing in this period of tumultuous organising, but his programmes and speeches indicate that he accepted broadly the Marxist analysis of class struggle so far as economic issues were concerned. What this led to, though, was a kind of *dual systems theory* which saw capitalism and Brahmanism (casteism) as separate systems of exploitation, the one to be fought by class struggle, the other by caste struggle.

The climax of this approach in many ways came with the writing of *States and Minorities* (Moon, 1990a), proposed to be a draft of sections of the Constitution. Here Ambedkar gave a severe critique of capitalism and called for the nationalisation of land and basic industries, explicitly calling this 'state socialism.' In a sense the term 'state socialism' indicated his difference with the communists, in that in contrast to a revolution under 'working class leadership, ' state ownership was to be written into a democratic constitution. At another level, the phrase simply made the assumption of a mechanical Marxism that 'socialism' or collective ownership of the means of production was equivalent to state ownership.

There were, however, many problems with the 'dual systems' of Brahmanism and capitalism. These became clear in *State and Minorities* itself, which seemed to contain two rather disparate sections, one advocating land nationalisation and state socialism, the other calling for separate village settlements of Dalits. The connection between the two was not clear. The problems of any' dual systems theory remained seeing separate systems of class and caste exploitation left unchallenged by the Marxist assumptions of a class analysis accepted the idea that 'class' dealt with the economic issues while the 'caste' system of exploitation was at a cultural and ideological (superstructural) level. The dual systems of 'capitalism' and 'Brahmanism provided useful rhetoric and a rule of thumb for analysis, but this left the question of the connection between the two systems completely unresolved. And if other systems of oppression (for instance 'patriarchy' and 'national oppression) were also included, then such an approach simply would yield to an unwieldy amalgam of many disparate 'system's of exploitation. In other words, the dual systems theory could not give an integrated, holistic explanation. It reflected Ambedkar's initial grappling with Marxism, when he insisted that 'caste' be added to a class approach (and even that it should have priority) but did not develop an overall alternative theory.

Buddhism *Versus* Marxism

If 'Capitalism and Brahmanism' were the themes of the 1930s and 1940s, the last years of Ambedkar's life were preoccupied with Buddhism, and from time to time with the question of Buddhism and Marxism. But the framework of thinking was different. Whereas in the 1930s and 1940s Ambedkar had tended to see dual systems of exploitation, increasingly he came to give weight to caste and Brahmanism, and to try to theorise these in a way that would provide a unifying theme for the entire society. In the process, he also came to question his earlier acceptance of a mechanical class approach and of 'state socialism' as the solution to economic exploitation. In his search for a 'single system' theory, Ambedkar began to look towards Buddhism as the solution not only to problems of caste but also to economic exploitation.

We do not have to seek far for the reasons for this change.

One was 'internal:' that is, the logic of a dual systems theory was inadequate in the sense that it gave no idea of the connection between Brahmanism and capitalism. Making 'class' the economic base and 'caste' a political-ideological superstructure tended to give legitimacy to the mechanical Marxist position that the base was primary and that caste was a secondary issue. This was unacceptable to Ambedkar and other Dalit-Bahujan activists.

But the other reason for disillusionment with the existing theory of Marxism was *eternal*, the result of historical experience. On the one hand, Ambedkar had an ongoing struggle with the Indian communists, who saw him only as a party bourgeois misleader. On the other hand, the world context was changing. In the 1930s and 1940s the revolutionary claims of mechanical Marxism appeared justified by world wents depression, war and revolution abounded and the Soviet Union seemed to be able to achieve both equality and impressive economic growth. By the 1950s these conditions had reversed themselves. Capitalist growth in the West was showing a few dynamism, and its proletariat was becoming integrated into the system. And, the Soviet 'model' was beginning to tarnish; the state was not withering away, it was showing its dictatorial face in a way clear to all. In this context, Ambedkar began to define himself not so much as a socialist but as an equalitarian who was equally devoted to freedom and a moral community life. His earlier definition of 'Brahmanism' had seen it as the negation of the ideals of liberty, equality and fraternity; now he returned to this theme. As his conclusion to a draft essay on Buddha and Marx says: Society has been aiming to lay a new foundation as was summarised by the French revolution in three words, fraternity, liberty and equality. The French revolution was welcomed because of this slogan. It failed to produce equality. We welcome the Russian revolution because it aims to produce equality. But it cannot be too much emphasised that in producing equality society cannot afford to sacrifice fraternity or liberty. Equality will be of no value without fraternity or liberty. It seems that the three can coexist only if one follows the way of the Buddha. Communism can give one but not all (Moon, 1990b: 462).

What did Ambedkar mean by 'the way of Buddha'? He couldn't finish the book he proposed on this, but the essay on 'Buddha or Karl Marx' gives some indications of his thinking. The essay begins with an outline of Marxist propositions and states that most of these have been historically invalidated: the proletariat has not become increasingly immiserated and revolutionary; the state has not withered away after revolutions. Marx's assertions of private property as the origin of exploitation and of class conflict remain, in Ambedkar's words, 'a residue of fire, small but still very important' (Moon, 1990b: 444)), but now he sees the way to overcome the exploitation of private property in a radically different way. In other words, with this Ambedkar rejects state socialism, nationalisation and the dictatorship of the proletariat as solutions to the problem of exploitation and turns to Buddhism for an alternative. And here he comes up with what may be called a "moral economy' solution to the problems of exploitation. This was not simply a matter of a stress on non-violence as opposed to violence.

Ambedkar had never rejected Marxism simply because of the role of force in its philosophy; unlike. Gandhi he did not see non-voilence as an absolute or religiously based principle. In this essay he expands on what he feels is a more practical Buddhist attitude towards violence. His argument is that we cannot (and Buddha did not) renounce force when it is necessary to obtain justice. '[Buddha] certainly would not have exempted property owners from force if force was the only means for that end,' Ambedkar writes (Moon, 1990b: 451). But this kind of force was not necessary, he argues first because equality and the abolition of private property was achieved in the Bhikku Sangha through voluntary means, and second because morality and a welfare state could ensure that private accumulation of wealth did not lead to impoverishment.

Thus, a long Buddhist parable in the essay describes how the rule of 'righteousness' rather than the 'rule of law (force)' is necessary to maintain the prosperity of the kingdom. The role of the state (as symbolised by the righteous king) seems to be twofold: one is the *guarantee of property and protection to all in the kingdom*, and the second is *direct action to remove property by 'providing wealth to the destitute.'* The second is crucial; in fact it is the failure to remove poverty which leads (in the parable) to the downfall of the society.

But Ambedkar assumes here that property and wealth accumulation will continuous though under state regulation. In regard to this, Ambedkar makes an important contrast between Buddhism and Christianity. Christianity gives a high value to poverty and other worldliness, Buddhism does not—and Ambedkar believes he was superior precisely for this reason: "There is no Sermon on the Mount to be found in the Buddha's teachings. His teaching is to acquire wealth' (Moon, 1990b: 460). For householders, lawful and moral accumulation of wealth is praised: Thus to acquire wealth legitimately and justly, earned by great industry, amassed by strength of the arm and gained by the sweat of the brow is a great blessing. The householder makes himself happy and cheerful and preserves himself full happiness; also makes his parents, wife and children, servants and labourers, friends and companions happy and cheerful, and preserves them full of happiness (Moon, 1990b: 461).

Ambedkar in this essay thus talks of equality but not of 'socialism. 'Similarly, in his speech introducing the Indian Constitution, he refers to 'social democracy' rather than 'socialism (Moon, 1993: 1216). Was he having doubts about the value of socialism as defined in terms of collective ownership of the means of production? Or were these response only due to the situation: after all, a summing up of the debate on the Constitution was not a place to talk of socialist ideals since no one had, at that time, seriously proposed that independent India define itself as socialist.

But, if Ambedkar maintained a socialist ideal, it must have been in a very different form than the traditional understanding of socialism at the time. Socialism was defined in terms of 'collective ownership' and Ambedkar's identification of this as 'state ownership' was similar to the confusion shown by all the

Marxists of his day. Soviet developments (and the continual communist defense of the 'dictatorship of the proletariat') identified this, in turn, with dictatorship or the use of force. This is perhaps why in this essay, Ambedkar continues to emphasise equality but does not use the word socialism and explicitly rejects the abolition of property by force. 'Equality' is to be maintained by voluntary communism in the Bhikku Sangha, and poverty is to be remedied by the redistributive activities of the state. Thus, by the end this life Ambedkar can be called a 'socialist' only if socialism is defined in terms of the value of equality, and not as equivalent to the collective ownership of the means of production.

Ambedkar and the Moral Economy

Today, provoked by the failures of 'state socialism' and by the resurgence of issues of identity, culture and spirituality, many socialist activists and theorists are centring their attack on the immorality of commercial capitalism and writing about the need for a 'moral economy.' Ambedkar would have agreed, and the need for morality' in the economic and political ordering of society was one of the crucial points of his criticism of the Marxism of his day.

At the same time, Ambedkar's 'moral economy' differed crucially from the version being put forword by many in India (and other countries) today. Today, most of the progressives arguing for a 'moral economy' in the abstract, do so basing themselves on a criticism of the 'immorality' of the 'market economy,' and the meaninglessness and destructiveness of 'economic growth for its own sake,' also avoid this issue. But the guiding theme for their 'moral economy' is a neo-Gandhian Hinduism, in which 'Indian (Hindu) spirituality' and the 'limitation of needs' are praised. On these points Ambedkar would have thoroughly disagreed. Morality in economic life required, according to him, a firm rejection of the pseudo-morality of traditional 'Hinduism,' it had to be grounded in the three revolutionary values of 'liberty, equality and fraternity,' and it presumed the overcoming of poverty through the development of human productive forces. Ambedkar sees these as (not Western but) universal ideals and as necessary for the welfare of the Bahujan Samaj.

This is clear in an early essay of Ambedkar, a review of a book by Bertrand Russell. In contrast to the Gandhian notion 'of limitation of needs.' Ambedkar never accepted the equation of morality with suffering, poverty, asceticism or renunciation of money and consumption. As he wrote, This time-honoured complaint of the moralists against 'love of money' is only a part of their general complaint against the goods of the world and finds in justification in the economic circumstances which gave rise to this particular belief...At a time when the whole world was living in 'pain economy' as did the ancient world and when the productivity of human labour was extrement low and when no efforts could augment its return, in short when the whole world was living in poverty, it is but natural that moralists should have preached the gospel of poverty and renunciation of worldly pleasures on because they were not to be had (Moon, 1990a: 489).

Ambedkar's moral economy, then, was to be one of abundance and wealth accumulation. His rejection, in *Buddha or Karl Marx*, of the Christian glorification poverty is consistent with this. It seems at the end of his life he returned to history insight, 'the trouble..is not with property but with the unequal distribution (ibid.: p. 491).

It has three basic elements: (1) the role of the state was seen to be in providing 'protection' and the removal of poverty; (2) the role of the market was to be in the production and accumulation of wealth by individual householders (modified by moral concerns); and (3) the role of community which would give equality was seen in the development of a voluntaristic equalitarian communism in the Bhikku Sangha.

Ambedkar's Economic Theory

One should not make too much of *Buddha or Karl Marx*; it provides at most a direction of economic thinking but by no means provides a fully developed economic theory. Would Ambedkar have opposed privatisation or supported liberalisation? Statements at this level remain to a large degrees speculation. But it seems clear that a large part of his approach, finally, would have been pragmatic , looking for the most effective combination of state, market and community roles; that he would have been clearly for the kind of globalization that would aid the Dalits and other sections of the poor to establish their full place in a world heritage; that he would have been concerned both with all-round economic growth and its impact on the poorest and most deprived sections of the community.

REFERENCES

Chaudhuri, Nagesh, 1994. 'What Policy Should We Take Towards Dunkel?, *Bahujan Sangharsh*, 30 April, Editorial.

Kamble, Siddharth, 1994. 'What is the Dunkel Draft?, *Bahujan Sangharsh*, 30 April.

Moon, Vasant (compiler). 1990a. *Dr. Babasaheb Ambedkar: Writings and Speeches. Vol. I. Mr. Russel and the Reconstruction of Society*, Bombay: Education Department, Government of Maharashtra.

Moon, Vasant (compiler), 1990c. *Dr. Babasaheb Ambedkar: Writings and Speeches. Vol. 6, The Problem of the Rupee and the Evolution of Provincial Finance in British India*. Bombay: Education Department Government of Maharashtra.

7

Social Justice to Dalits and Other Weaker Sections of the Society

We shall confine largely to urban Indians in what may be described as modern occupations, leaving aside, except for occasional comments, the large majority of Indians who inhabit the rural areas and derive d their livelihood from agriculture and related occupations. This does not mean that my argument does not have some implications for the latter, but those implications are not as yet fully clear. We do not wish to circumscribe too narrowly the class or section of society on which we seek to focus attention. It may be referred to loosely as the 'urban middle class' or even the 'urban middle classes'. More recently, the terms 'intelligentsia', 'professionals' and 'service class' have been employed to refer to roughly the safe category of person. These terms are useful, not because they are accurate, but because they draw attention to the growing importance of this class or stratum in contemporary India. Here numbers are important but not recessionaly decisive. If we adopt a narrow definition and take into account only civil servants, managers and higher professionals, we will still be dealing with a population that runs into hundreds of thousands.

If we extend the conception to include school teachers, clerks and other white-collar workers, as some are inclined to do, we will have a much larger category numbering 50-70 million persons or more. There is a reason why it is necessary to have some sense of the numbers involved even when it is not possible to give precise numbers. It is sometimes said that the underlying structure of caste remains what it was, and that if there are changes in caste practice, they are superficial and confined to a handful of urban or educated, or Westernised individuals who are in any caste not truly representative of Indian society and culture.

Social Justice, vague and vagarious in its semantics, is the vogue word in the Ambedkar Centenary Year. It has been constitutional claptrap since January 26, 1950 and whenever the downtrodden have sought justice on the basis of equality in the context of terrible deprivations in the past, this chameleon chant 'social justice' has played hide and seek with the victim sector of Indian humanity known popularly as the Scheduled Castes and Scheduled Tribes. They are large groups which suffer adversities, social and educational, economic and cultural, struggling to join the mainstream. They too have so far not succeeded in securing for themselves what the great Preamble to the Constitution has pledged to the people of India. While it is assumed that the pariahs, the melchchas and the antyajas of Bharat have constitutional title to the blessings of socio-economic justice, equality of status and opportunity as well as fraternity assuring basic dignity, the actualisation of these fruits of freedom has been but paper-togged illusions emanating from State Secretariats and Planning Commissions. Far too long have the political echelons of various hues hidden the truth of their lies regarding social justice, and now, during the Ambedkar Centenary Year, militancy in the demand for right and Justice has catalysed these deprived and desperate sections of society. The rhetoric of social justice been the opium of the suppressed people all these decades. A new hope will rise from the ashes of the past, a power from the social proletariat to claim back their just rights. I recently came across some lines quoted by a young tribal intellectual:

"One day, the fields will stay green and the earth black, sweet and wet.
Our children will grow tall on that earth and our children's children.
And they will be free as the mountain trees and birds. They will walk each day. happy to be alive knowing the land was conquered once more, for them.
Oneday...
Now we plought dry fields each furrow wet with blood."

— *Zamora*

But the ceremonial revival of homage to that human thunderbolt called Dr. B.R. Ambedkar has inevitably awakened into action those who have suffered silently till now. As the bonded labour of the status quo, no longer are they in a mood to continue. As the eternal tenants of an extortionate order they will not submit any more. Statesmanship, legislative, administrative and judicial, must sharpen our perspective of history, and with dynamic sensitivity conscientise the democratic process into becoming a radical locomotive of social transformation. These weakest sections of society, sometimes described as harijans and girijans, are many millions strong and their unheard cries and unseen tears have given place to clenched fists and angry eyes. True, even to-day their voice is muffled, their wails ignored and their lives are but long nights.

Once the wielders of power show the will to liberate these categories of Indian society there will be a great upsurge of equality, a new awareness of dignity and an out-pouring of untapped energies as a new human resource at the service of the Nation. Only then can there be true *fraternity*, homogenising the suppressed sector with the upper classes. Mere legislative prescriptions cannot abolish deeply entrenched social abuses and economic bondages. A radical rupture with the status quo ante involves not merely legislative mandates and administrative directives but activist cadres with a passion for the cause and able to mobilise the victims of injustices into liberating themselves. This Operation Freedom of the *Panchama* Proletariat is itself a struggle and constitutes the current phase of the battle for swaraj of the suppressed human sector.

The Statute Book of Indian contains many legislations designed to lift the dalits, to abolish their disabilities and to give them special opportunities for advancement in education and employment. Bonded labour is by law abolished. Untouchability, by Constitution, is forbidden. The Civil Rights Act goes a long way to eliminate injustice inflicted on the dalits. Specially stern punishments are prescribed for commission of offences against Scheduled Castes and Tribes, but these magic remedies sleep as paper tigers. The social evils continue. The economic wrongs go on. The law is dead, vis a vis these unfortunates. There are plans and sub-plans, schemes and projects worked out by the Administration at the Central and State levels. There are special reservations for employment and education and these facilities look like reverse discrimination. But what are the raw realities?

Even to-day discrimination against the Scheduled Castes and the practice of untouchability persist tho'only in certain parts of the country. Even today, serfdom and bonded labour implicating dalit families continues. All the laws and constitutional prescriptions notwithstanding, enforcement is a flop, a fraud. Investigation into offences against the Scheduled Castes and Tribes is often done by hostile policemen. Gang rapes of these backward women rarely reach the court and if they do they hardly survive to end in conviction. The truth is that neither the Police nor the Court has any emotional involvement or sufficient social commitment where, on the one side, is the feudal order and, on the other side, is the dalit brother or sister. What is of moment and accounts for the law's betrayal is the implicit hostility of the dominant classes to legislative measures which are merely the skin-deep homage paid to social justice.

The situation is no different even regarding the special provisions made for lifting the lot of the SC/ST sections at the educational and employment levels. Whatever the quantum of reservation in official orders, the fact remains that in actual figures only flimsy percentages get the benefit. How many IAS or IPS officers are there among the SC/ST? How many Chief Ministers and Chief Justices are there from among these backward-most groups? Indeed, how many Attorneys General, Solicitors General, Advocates General or other high Law Officers or Judicial echelons in the High Court and Supreme Court have ever been appointed from the SC/ST? How many SC/ST cadres occupy the highest posts in the various professions in the country? How many great artists, singers and dangers and professors and scientists, have been drawn from the SC/ST? It is clear that the alleged special advantages extended to the Scheduled Castes and Tribes are a hoax or gross exaggeration. I will cite two examples to illustrate how one can practice deception through reservations on paper, the dalits getting absolutely little or nothing in actual fact. Suppose you reserve 75 percent of the judgeships in the Supreme for the SC/ST categories. It is well-known that ordinarily recruitment to the Supreme Court Judgeships is made from among High Court Judges. If there are no SC/ST judges in the High Courts the mere fact of reservation of a high percentage does not secure a single seat on the bench in the Supreme Court for the SC/ST. Similarly, you rarely come across a judge from these 'untouchables' on the High Court benches because there are few Advocates belonging to these categories. Similarly, by attaching certain qualifications which cannot be fulfilled by the SC/ST one may successfully defeat reservation percentages. It happened in Kerala that there was reservation for the tribals in the matter of appointment as mahouts employed by Government in trapping and training of elephants in centres maintained by the Government; but since the minimum qualification of matriculation was prescribed no tribal could get even a mahout's post altho' they were traditionally living in forests where the elephants roamed wild. One can multiply instances to demonstrate that in the higher categories of posts where State Power can be exercised the SC/ST are successfully kept out even while making it appear that 22.5 percent is reserved for them right through.

The grievance against the SC/ST whose population bears

a proportion of 22.5 percent even in high posts. The truth is that they are getting reservation of 22.5 percent is that they are getting reservation of 22.5 percent even in high posts. The truth is that is 1979 the SC got 4.75 percent and the ST. 0.94 percent in Class I services. In 1981 in Class 1. The SC got 4.62 percent and the ST 0.97 percent. Out of the total of 370 High Court judges as on March 16, 1982 only 4 were from amongst SC and none from the ST. It is thus clear that in the bureaucracy and the Judiciary not to speak even the Ministry from time to time, the SC and ST have been suffering great discrimination in actual facts. Untouchability is still writ large.

In the field of higher education also, the actuals fall far less than the formal percentages of reservation. Mahatma Phule whom Dr. Ambedkar Admired stressed that adisudras suffered because of lack of education. Dr. Baba Saheb Ambedkar himself argued: "I firmly believe in the efficacy of education as a panacea for our social evils. The problem of lower order in this country is not only economic but also cultural. It is not enough to house them, feed them and then to leave them to serve the higher classes as was the ancient ideal of this country. It is even more necessary to remove from them that feeling of inferiority which has shunted their growth and made them slaves of others and to create in them a consciousness of significance of life for themselves and for their country of which they have been cruelly robbed by the current social order of this country. I am convinced that nothing can achieve this except the spread of higher education."

Therefore reservation in access to higher education is a *sine qua non* of Dalit uplift. The illiteracy rate of the SC/ST is abysmal and therefore attracting them into attractive high standard, even English medium schools is a compulsive need if abolition of backwardness is the desideratum. Unfortunately the State has done little to *actualise* admissions without dropouts of the SC/ST children into Convent School, English Medium Schools, or any schools for that matter. Special concessions and financial attractions to bring in Dalit children on a massive basis is the desideratum if the *mlecha* masses are to awake and arise. In the matter of higher education, mere reservations liberalising age restrictions and minimum marks could not do. More must be done. Special training and coaching, tuition geared to overcoming handicaps should be a first priority if reservation in education is to bear fruit. In scientific and technological fields preferential treatment should be extended to the SC/ST. Until these minimum steps are taken educational untouchability and invisible *Chathurvarna* will survive the Constitution. What we need is a social revolution, an educational revolution and a public services revolution through crash programmes and mass line methodology. Navodaya schools, from this angle are a new hoaxes. *Antyodaya* in the "widest commonality spread" is the "consummation devoutly to be wished."

There is the question of merit urged against them altho' the truth is that given better environment, better opportunities, better training and special coaching, they can more than successfully compete with the so-called upper classes. Give them education in the LKG, UKG and the Doon Schools, the St. Stephens College or Miranda House or other high class colleges with sophistications woven into the courses and the careers; they will beat the best. Do you know that the wisest Indian of ancient India, *Thiruvalluvar*, was a dalit by birth? The most devout composers in ancient Tamil countries like Alwars were of dalit origin. The retort by Dr. Ambedkar on this point deserves to be quoted here:

"The Hindus wanted the Vedas, and they sent for Veda Vyasa who was not a caste Hindu. The Hindus wanted an epic, and they sent for Valmiki who was an untouchable. The Hindus wanted a Constitution and they sent for me."

There is no genetic discrimination inflicted by Divinity on the SC/ST humanity. It is society, the disabling environment, the penurious privations and the long disease from intellectual, industrial, educational and cultural opportunities and social suppressions for sinful centuries which have kept these millions of Indian humans in dark and depressed serdom. What an irony that the culpable classes charge the victims with the guilt of 'reservations' which are a paltry part of history's reparations!

All the Mandal fury, with blood in the streets, against evolving an egalitarian synthesis out of competing inequalities is based upon a misunderstanding of the actual facts. It is a terrible pity that people do not look beneath the reservation' percentages. They will then realise, once they lift the veil, and see 'the petty done and the undone vast' that we have miles to go and promises to keep if equal justice to the handicapped social groups is the goal. What is more, when a few members of the SC/ST get a little education, they forsake the lower layers in their own communities and engage themselves in selfish pursuits of promoting their own families. Dr. Amedkar way back in 1956 bitingly observed: 'The educated—highly educated class (from Dalit-Shoshit Samaj) have betrayed me. I had expected that after acquiring education—higher education, they will serve the society. But I see here a crowd of clerks who—are engaged in feeding their own stomach!"

What we find as a fact is that even when some benefit accrues to some members of the SC/ST they are cornered by a few families, the pariahs being always the panths and the desperate dalits at the dismal bottom layers of the SC/ST segment continuing for ever as the dreg.

The general development of the masses of these mlecha sections—a categorical imperative if fraternity is the condition of social stability—can be achieved *only* by massive economic programmes which can make dynamic impact. While jobs and education are extremely important, as Baba Saheb Ambedkar emphasised, equality and homogeneity are a far cry if the landless dalit is not given land, the penniless pariah is not given opportunities to start small factories, the bonded woman is not liberated from servitude so as to enable her to pursuea vocation and the dalit youth, now illiterate and disorganised and drawn into delinquent and destitute situations, are given effective opportunities to enter the professions and public services in large numbers through short courses and on-going education. Do not the rich and the powerful *to-day* bypass merit thro' cavitation fees, graft, nepotism

---

* Dr. Babasaheb Ambedkar—March 18, 1956 of Ramlila Ground, Agra

and buying marks? More than all, the humblest levels of th harijans and girijans must be reached and raised by specia projects, and other backward classes should not permitted to rob these Least Developed Castes of their hope of standing up an entering offices of State to exercise power.

It is fallacious to imagine that because there are reserve seats in legislatures for the SC and ST they wield political powe They are divided among the political parties and, with the thre line whip, act according to the directives of the dominant classe in the Parties. This causes disunity and debility in political action The remedy for this malady is Dr. Ambedkar's exhortations "Political power is the master key by which you can open eacl and every lock." His message to the Panchama proletariat stil holds good: "Educate! Unite! and Agitate!" India can never b truly free until the last Indian segment of SC/ST is free.

The Weaker Sections of Society

The Scheduled Castes, one of the Weaker Sections. Th term Scheduled Castes given currency in 1930s is a blanket terr including within itself hundreds of castes and sub-castes whicl constitute a hierarchy among themselves and in relation to th Hindu castes. The regional, linguistic and cultural differences adc to make the picture more complex and complicated. The worlc of caste and practice of untouchability have been subjects o serious thinking and research over the past few decades. They have also provided opportunity for reformists and revolutionary social movements historically. In post-Independence India and also during the British regime, untouchability in particular has made the Government to assume the role of social workers.

The origin of untouchability remains obscure even in a society like ours with vast literacy traditions. In the Vedic period Varna-Ashrama Dharma no doubt carried occupational attributes though much less rigorously and these get themselves crystallised in due course. The post-Vedic period, the Epics, Puranas and Upanishadic times in particular, laid the firm foundation for the

Indian social structure. The several law givers also contributed their mite, in particular the writings of Manu stands out as a beacon light on the horizons of Indian caste system.

Birth became the decisive criterion of membership in the caste. Occupational attributes of cate became more pronounced and carried values of rank and status. Some occupations were of high status and rank, others carried low rank and status. Groups following particular occupations came to enjoy social position commensurate with caste occupations. For instance, priesthood and scholarship in sacred literature carried higher values thus enjoining superior position to the Brahmins. Scavenging and leather work correspondingly carried low social status. Multiplication and classification of castes and sub-castes as well as occupations continued unchecked since then resulting in a social hierarchy.

The caste system with its social hierarchy and implicit inequality of status and rank, in religious, educational economic political and juridical relationships among caste groups has been in existence from the earliest known historical times. At the top of the hierarchy are the Brahmins, untouchables come at the bottom end. Ritual purity and pollution as part of Hinduism have pervaded all the walks of life. A gradation or hierarchy of values obtains in most mundane things as well. Food, cloth, metals, in a word, everything that surrounds human life carry values, not necessarily always based on their utility. High rank is usually associated with economically costly items like silk cloth, precious metals like gold and silver which at least in the past only higher castes could possess.

Practices, which were initiated with such elaborate value system associated with them, in the course of time, ceased to be voluntary. They became part of the tradition, customarily enforced and later supported by public opinion and ruling powers. In all, this, higher the status of caste, greater were the rank and privileges, in ritual, educational, economic, political and juridical powers. The lower castes were reduced to utter subordination devoid of many privileges and occupied the lower rungs of the hierarchical ladder.

Hinduism and the Caste System are so much intertwined with one another that together they cover all the temporal and spiritual aspects of life. The educational, economic and political aspects of life belong to secular sphere and are associated with achieved status. In the Indian context, these areas of life have been subjected to and controlled by the religious and caste values to such an extent and are so loaded with notions of Dharma and Karma that people are generally afraid of transgressing the boundaries. A poor Brahmin and a rich untouchable are hardly comparable in terms of status and rank even under the present changed circumstances.

The supremacy of the religious values and Brahmins as the only authority being supposed to have mastery to interpret their religious implications gave them a definite edge over everybody else as custodians of all knowledge. Life on the earth and life after death, as developed in the theory of Karma and transmigration of soul coloured all secular and spiritual activities.

By and large, one sees the ascendancy of Brahmanical values throughout the centuries ad these are held against all odds. Infact, the legendary attribute of the curse of the Brahmin, the worst that could be invited by anybody, seem to have held the sway. No one really tried to seriously challenge his spiritual authority and power. All the protest and reform attempts made from time to time historically amount to 'rituals of rebellious' which hardly meant a serious threat. The various political powers themselves were dependent on the advice, blessings and good offices of the Brahmins. Hence the Brahmins as a class and the Brahmanical values as a category have enveloped all aspects of life and continue to persist.

In all this the most deprived and depraved class of people rare the Untouchable group with a conglomeration of castes and sub-castes within it. In ancient India it was just an emerging category which got crystallised with the passage of time. In medieval period, even under the impact of Muslim rule, their position was by no means better off. Conversion to Islam in some ways ushered in changes but hardly brought about structural changes.

The British who succeeded the Muslim rulers took time to realise the intricacies of the Indian social structure. Since they were interested in the political consolidation of their position, their openly declared policy was one of 'non-interference' in the social and religious matters of the people of India. Christianity which came to India, like Islam, from outside, added another dimension to the existing social categories. Conversion to Christianity by lower castes and upper castes for several reasons did not help to bridge the gulf between them. The pro-conversion caste status, rank and values continued and loomed large influencing all kinds of social intercourse.

The indigenous reform movements starting from Buddhism, Jainism, Sikhism, Brahmo Samaj, Arya Samaj, including Veerasaivism in the South, rebelled against caste rigidities and other social evils. The founders of most of these movements themselves came from upper castes and as one could glean, the results of these attempts to reform Hinduism could not really succeed. Preaching against caste differences and discriminations, aspiration to establish social equality and justice at best helped the middle range caste-groups and not really the down-trodden to raise their status.

Ritual purity and pollution, the barrier which separates the untouchable groups from others in India meant that these people could not be incorporated into the mainstream in Hinduism and largely remained so even under the impact of foreign and indigenous movements including that of Ambedkar's neo-Buddhism. It is noteworthy, how all these attempts were conceived and covered with religious ideology. There is hardly a movement which attempted to influence the minds of the people minus the religious idiom. In this sense religion—old and new—provide and act as opiate to masses. People are generally susceptible to religious ideologies.

It is far more easier to win over people by giving a religious appeal and character to a movement than merely trying to introduce changes in the economic and political arenas.

The Scheduled Castes and Tribes, their problems, have assumed new dimensions in the post-independence India. Historically, they have been an ever-growing menace to national an social integration. Each of the conscious and unconscious attempts made to eradicate the evils of caste system has made the system much more vulnerable and monstrous to the down-trodden groups. The situation can be compared only marginally with their counterparts, the Negroes of America and South Africa and similar groups elsewhere.

For the present, we will briefly touch upon the coming to lime light of the wees of the group, largely by the efforts made by the late Dr. Babasaheb Ambedkar and the controversy between Gandhi and Ambedkar that resulted in the Poona Pact. During the Post-Independence period, in contemporary India, under parliamentary democracy, these issues are of vital importance precisely because the problems continue unabated and are becoming sources of social unrest in spite of protectionist policy adopted by the Government.

During the Independence Movement the National Congress remained largely oblivious of the fact that there were social groups in the country which were scorned at and relegated to a position worse than of animals. The leadership in the Congress again was largely confined to upper castes and richer sections. They hardly perceived the sufferings of the lower and lowest groups. Social inequality and injustice at its worst afflicted the untouchable caste groups.

From among the neglected Sections there arose Ambedkar as a champion and spokesman of the millions of dumb human beings. When he made his demands on behalf of the untouchable groups the ruling British Government conceded political representation to them by the Communal Award. Gandhi and the ongress were quick to grasp the implications of the same. lready staggered by the demands of Muslims, the Hindu leaders ere not at all in favour of recognising the demands of untouchable paratism.

Gandhi promptly undertook fast unto death for the withdrawal the Communal Award. Ambedkar was finally coerced to sign Poona Pact to save the precious life of Mahatma by sacrificing cause of millions of untouchables. Though all this is a part history of the struggle of Indian untouchables under a leader o had sprung up from among them by chance coincidence, cause of untouchables was furthered in the hands of Ambedkar the Chairman of the Constitution Drafting Committee.

Ambedkar was forced to agree that untouchables were Hindus that their conditions had to be ameliorated from within the ial system. Personally he was bitter against Hinduism and the te system and became a Buddhist in the last days of his life. he made a fresh bid in the Constitution to provide measures the betterment of these communities. The lot of the millions literate poor untouchables needed a national awakening both ng the Untouchables and the caste Hindus. Therefore, the tion to the problems was visualised at national level and not at State levels.

A series of measures was provided to combat against social consequent upon social discrimination and the practice for uchability. Social discrimination is loaded with differential es, often supported and sanctioned by religious beliefs and ices. Provisions to eliminate discrimination, and to establish l equality have to be supported from other possible sources. al inequality and discrimination are inherent and therefore otive. It is hardly possible to alter ascriptive values by ation.

In the Constitution economic, political, educational facilities corporated for the upliftment of the secular position of the chables. Ambedkar seems to have believed that as the ss of modernisation sets in, acquired status and the values associated with it would gradually displace values and status based on ascription. The tensions which we are witnessing in contemporary India between the Scheduled Castes and non-Scheduled Castes may be rightly described as a clash between the traditional and emergent values.

The achievement oriented tradition still has to take its roots. But before it could become possible, the middle range clean upper castes which have emerged as dominant groups in all the States as a result of the linguistic reorganisation have come to believe, that if this transformation is allowed, they would be the loosers for good. Hence, fierce attempts are made to thwart all well-intentioned Government policies meant to uplift the Scheduled Castes.

Access to public places like temples, tea shops, drinking water places and places of essential services like hair-cutting saloons are fraught with extreme difficulty in contemporary India. The Scheduled Caste population is spread out and is essentially a minority in almost all the villages in India. These people can hardly hope to assert themselves to avail the constitutional benefits. That each one should know one's place in the hierarchy, has such as stronghold in the minds of people, that any attempts by the low caste people to break this barrier is resisted by all upper castes in addition to, sometimes, by other religious minorities in the village situation.

Political reservations are given from village panchayat to the parliament. The party leadership has vested interest in maintaining the same. Infact a good number of Indian political parties, national and regional, conform closely to the patterns of caste groups in the country. The Scheduled Caste members in political parties remain essentially subordinate to the party bosses. No Scheduled Caste leaders worth the name are allowed to grow within the political parties and they are all contained and curbed effectively.

Political reservation and representation is a constitutional obligation. It is also a vote catching mechanism for a successful political parties. The Scheduled Castes are lured to vote by promising them many returns. The Scheduled Caste Political leaders are bound and regulated by party interests overlooking sometimes interests of their castes. This has created two different situations. The Scheduled Caste politicians firstly do not wish to be identified as Scheduled Caste leaders, presumably on the same lines such as there are no Brahmin or other caste leaders. Secondly' there is a growing tendency among the scheduled Caste politicians to overlook and brush aside the problems of Scheduled Castes precisely because 'general' votes in 'reserved' constituencies outnumber the Scheduled Caste votes. As such the politicians from these caste groups need not be under ran obligation to the voters of their castes. The access to power enhances the secular status and rank of Scheduled Caste political leaders. So the class mass differences are inevitable amongst themselves.

Political reservation and representation minus the emergence of effective leadership among the Scheduled Castes is a tragedy. Given the political mechanisation, unscrupulous methods, bossism, exploitation, corruption and favouritism, it is an uphill task for a Scheduled Caste politician to emerge as an effective and generally accepted leader.

Social values die hard. An ambitious and aspiring Scheduled Caste politician can be cut underneath his feet. Rivalry and pitting one against another, exploiting sub-caste differences etc., can be used as political weapons to contain them externally by caste Hindu politicians. The political game is an important mechanism in democracy. The economics of politics is frightening an it is very difficult to visualise whether Scheduled Caste politicians can ever reach a bargaining position, get weaned of their dependence and have access to real power.

The various provisions made in the Constitution to bring about economic benefits have touched only the fringe. All kinds of economic assistance have roused the anti-Scheduled Caste feelings among the non-Scheduled Castes. The knowledge of availability of these benefits itself is limited to a small and negligible number in urban/town and rural areas. It is only the vocal and advanced sections among the Scheduled Castes who have availed themselves of most of the benefits. These are the people who have also acquired other forms of assets and influence and wield some power.

Since nearly ninety percent of the Scheduled Caste population is scattered in rural areas, they are the ones who are the worst hit and continue to suffer. The knowledge of the Constitutional benefits is known to about 10–15 percent of those in rural areas. Similarly economic benefits either in the form of and, house-site building material, loan and so forth have proved much more deterrent. The land reform-ceiling and distribution of surplus land among the Scheduled Castes has led to much ill-feeling among he non-Scheduled castes. One wonders whether this measure could succeed at all at any time. In many cases, it has let loose the anger and wrath of caste Hindus besides continued circumvention of the law itself.

Segregation based on caste lines in residential pattern in an age-old practise and very little could be done to curb this in rural India, thought in towns and cities it could be tackled and set right. Distribution of house-sites and construction of Janata Houses by the Government, though laudable, unfortunately have now thrown the Scheduled Caste people, further away from village location. This means again total segregation. Further, the new locations and their Scheduled Caste inhabitants can be easily held to ransom by irate villagers. Settlements can be set on fire, people beaten up and all kinds of atrocities directed without affecting the rest of the village community.

Dependent as they are economically, the Scheduled Caste population has to eke out their livelihood by selling their labour. That their economic vulnerability can be totally exploited by the villagers is born out by many instances of total boycott of the Scheduled Caste population in villages. In Karnataka this was reported recently from a remote village in the Bidar district. The police officials who went to the rescue of these people were humiliated and beaten up by the villagers. The State Government denied anything like that while the press and others who visited the village came out with stories of horrible woes and sufferings of the Scheduled Caste inhabitants living in constant fear of death.

Abolition of bonded labour and redeeming the borrowers from the clutches of local money-lenders, similarly have yet to produce the desired effects. Land distribution among the Scheduled Castes by Government has led to resentment and increase in physical violence and burning down of crops. Infact every effort made by the Government to create opportunities to make the Scheduled Castes economically viable and sound have led to increase jealousy and hatred among the non-Scheduled Castes. All these are conceived as a direct threat to undermine the upper castes. Slightest attempts on the part of the Scheduled Castes to assert themselves and their claims for constitutional privileges have led to clashes.

Actually the constitutional benefits have covered only a fraction of the Scheduled Caste population, while most of the deserving among them have not even the slightest ideas of these benefits. The publicity, bordering on propaganda, given by the Government agencies regarding the benefits in a way has been responsible to make the non-Scheduled Castes much more sensitive to the ideas of deprivation. People are keen that the protectionist policy should not be there. They think that such preferential discrimination is the antithesis of democracy.

The Government machinery by itself is inadequate and too slow to move even under emergent conditions. So when clashes occur, it is the weaker sections who are put to plight and often relieved of everything including life. Their womenfolk are wilfully subjected to ill treatment. Their modesty is meddled with. Denuding, raping and murdering women of all ages to frighten the aspiring Scheduled Castes, is one of the techniques evolved in recent years, while the Scheduled Caste menfolk are harassed and often axed to death for alleged theft or molestation of caste Hindu women.

Even if an army stands by, it is doubtful that such cases can be curbed in the immediate future. The awakening which has come about in certain pockets of the Scheduled Castes population, more particularly among the educated, no only resist caste Hindu assaults but are trying to organise the weaker sections to meet the eventualities. This is just making a beginning and they may not be a match to well organised, rich, influential and powerful caste Hindus who can both inflict innumerable miseries on the Scheduled Castes, and who also seek protection for themselves by using the Government machinery often against the Scheduled Castes themselves as law-breakers. Kilvanmani incident of Taniore district in Tamil Nadu is not an isolated event. Similar follow up cases have been fairly widespread throughout the country.

Next to political reservations, some significant advances have been made in educational concessions. This again is causing heart burning among the non-Scheduled Castes. Reservation of seats in colleges, technical and professional courses, and other facilities given to the Scheduled Caste students are severely criticised as wilful lowering of standards, at the cost of merit. This situation causes mental torture to the Scheduled Caste students and adversely affects their educational pursuits.

Demands of social justice and achievement oriented courses of action, although independent, can be made dependent variables. For even among the Scheduled Castes, increasing number of merited students are emerging. There is competition from among the Scheduled Castes themselves of the reserved seats. Effects of the denial of any opportunities for formal education for centuries cannot be set right overnight. What militates perhaps is the backlog of social heritage and unfavourable environmental surroundings. It is not at all correct to say that educational standards are lowering because of reservationist policy. The reasons for the lowering of standards have to be searched for elsewhere too.

Similarly reservation of jobs said to have corroded the

efficiency in administration. Barring class IV employment, in all other categories, the quota is never filled up. The Government departments themselves have paid lip service to reservation, while semi-Government and private organisations largely flout the rules. Yet by dint of hard work a class of officers among the Scheduled Castes has emerged, but they can hardly lead the Scheduled Caste masses. The official class is a small and self-contented group who can neither exploit nor help to further the cause of the Scheduled Caste masses except trying for their own chances of success—appointment, promotions—with which they are naturally concerned like everybody else.

In some ways it is only in Maharashtra, even after the exit of Ambedkar, attempts to organise the Scheduled Castes are continued. During the lifetime of Ambedkar, he tried to organise Labour Party, then the Scheduled Castes Federation and finally, the Republican Party of India. But these organisations did not have a smooth sailing. The Republican Party faction are too well-known and the party virtually could do nothing positive for the welfare of the Scheduled Castes.

Exasperated by the internal fights and factionalism among the elderly leaders of the Republican Party, younger generation sprang up in the name of Dalit Panthers, styled after the American 'Black Panthers,' in recent years. They made themselves felt by Government and others. Educated Scheduled Caste youths outside Maharashtra have also come under their influence to some extent. But in Maharashtra itself the Dalit Panthers movement was closed in from many sides. The ruling Congress Party lured some of the leaders of the Dalit Panthers and also helped to bridge the factional differences in the Republican Party. What could have become a major organisation working for the welfare of the Scheduled Castes was steadily undermined by a variety of forces. Only in literacy field some of them remain active today. Community-based political organisations, especially of the down-trodden, have little success. A very pathetic situation indeed.

The foresight with which Ambedkar established the educational institutions at Aurangabad and Bombay was commendable. They have played a positive role. Yet when the Neo-Buddhists and Scheduled Castes of Maharashtra wanted the Marathwada University to be named after Ambedkar, one of the illustrious son of Maharashtra, there was bitter opposition from the caste Hindus. It is strange and painful to dub Ambedkar as a narrow communal leader. The downtrodden, who number several millions in the country, are as much indebted to Ambedkar for focusing the world attention on the plight of India's untouchables, as should be the Hindus for the services rendered by him.

The Government as a reform agent can achieve only limited objectives. While it has championed the cause of weaker sections, minorities and backward classes, it cannot cope up with the colossal tasks ahead. Reservations if continued indefinitely will convert themselves into vested interests. The political patronage will lead to social estrangement among the people and politicians as big brothers trying to increase the area of their influence have succeeded in floating and heading a plethora of communal organisations in recent years.

Whatever changes might have occurred, one thing is certain that there is very little sharing of political power between upper and lower caste politicians both in the parties and in the Government. Andhra, Bihar and Rajasthan which have had Scheduled Caste chief ministers may be exceptions and such things could happen under exigencies and peculiar circumstances. The ameliorative measures—Constitutional provisions—under democracy will take a very long time to solve the pressing problems of the Scheduled Castes. Further structural changes, if any, cannot be simply assumed. The Caste System has a notoriety about it, incorporating and absorbing everything within itself including contradictions and conflicts.

Historically Caste System has withstood all attempts made to modify or destroy it. It has absorbed various shocks. Adsorptions of Buddhism, Jainism, Sikhism, Christianity, Islam are but few cases providing elasticity of the system. Unless there are structural changes, values will not alter. So long as old values continues, snobberies of caste and also untouchability will continue, perhaps in different ways and shades. Government efforts are not matched by voluntary organisations in India. For bringing about large scale awakening among the Scheduled Castes and non-Scheduled Castes, it is necessary that they are made aware of the human problems. The Scheduled Castes and Scheduled Castes sympathisers can organise and exert pressure on the Government. For it is only under pressure that the Government machinery will move at some speed. Gradually Scheduled Caste problems should converge with those of other weaker sections. Equality, justice and fair play have to be achieved by mobilising all those who are denied the same. Social mobility cannot be achieved when other groups are not willing to concede. This is exactly what is happening with new converts to Buddhism. When the secular position of the people remain unchanged, change of religion hardly matters. Lot of tensions build up when one group wishes to push itself while other groups do not concede to its claim.

The history of the Backward Class Movement in Tamil Nadu and elsewhere highlight's how the forward groups among some of the backward communities seized the opportunity to lead the movement. In this process they tried to consolidate their positions which was often detrimental to the aspirations and development of other backward classes. These lessons should provide guidelines. Both communal organisations and continued categorisation and patronage extended by the government to some caste groups will add to the existing divisive forces. Even when the Government wants to single our communities and groups for preferential treatment, the programme should be made time bound. Instead of giving doles, substantive assistance should be given to strengthen the group economically and educationally. Once certain level is achieved, the benefits should be gradually withdrawn.

Infact, it is a vicious circle within which the social problems of the scheduled castes are revolving. Doles are given to strengthen their secular position. In this process the concerned person has to constantly declare that he comes from such and such low caste. Such public demonstration of caste status for personal benefit can never help a man to psychologically rise above narrow loyalties or to free himself from feeling constantly inferior. It is necessary for the government to devise measures and initiate a policy to strengthen weaker sections in general and the scheduled castes in particular.

A number of new approaches may have to be devised. Scheduling or de-scheduling need not go by entire groups, but by families. Similarly the unnecessary propaganda regarding the benefits to the scheduled castes which adversely affects them may be stopped by the Government. Official records and discussions in the legislative assemblies and Parliament should serve the purpose. Economic diversification, increased educational facilities coupled with universal literacy perhaps would help to awaken the people.

Increased tensions and conflicts which the country-side witness today may be rightly viewed as leading to changes. unfortunately, they may demoralise the Scheduled Castes and make them victims of circumstances. The dominant upper caste groups with landed property have emerged so strong that they influence and control policies often twisting them for their own benefits. The Government should not play itself into the hands of vested interests, but in a democracy ambition knows no scruples.

There are two ways in which the Scheduled Caste problems can be solved. Firstly within the existing system, hoping that constitutional benefits would continued, piecemeal development of the community will take place. This is a very slow process which is fraught with internal contradictions. Public opinion, as pointed out earlier, is already against the policy which is dubbed as reverse discrimination.

Only political and educational benefits are visibly used. Political reservations have catered to individual families, which in turn perhaps have helped their kith and kin. In each state there have been a monopoly of some half a dozen families. In the Centre till recently except for one person no one could continue as a minister. From the entire scheduled caste political leadership, apart from its being manipulated by upper caste party bosses, no one is allowed or tolerated to emerge powerful. This kind of dependency restricts their role. They always are made to play second fiddle and there is no genuine leadership as for instance, of the type provided by Ambedkar. Keeping the Scheduled Caste political leaders as show-pieces, while perennially cutting at the roots to prevent them emerging strong, was not the purpose with which political reservations were given.

Political reservations should be tagged with responsibility to focus attention on the Scheduled Caste problems. Given this, the role of the Scheduled Caste politician will become more purposive and less subjective. They have to be social workers-cum-politicians and not the other way round. The handpicked scheduled caste politicians and the speed with which they are lured to change party affiliation, a general malady, make a mockery of reservations. As long as this continues only individual families will benefit themselves in the name of the community. This amounts to exploiting the community for personal benefits. Can this be prevented or set right within the framework of political processes in India?

Education and white-collar jobs are the well-known avenues leading to achieved status. Though in the case of scheduled castes it is not readily happening, but over a period of time it is bound to come about amongst themselves and in relation to others. The class structure which has always co-existed with the caste structure finds a favourable milieu with the Scheduled Caste educated groups. This is again a slow process and the status of the entire scheduled caste communities cannot be improved.

The conflict between the achieve status and ascribed status—class and caste—cannot be easily resolved in the case of scheduled Castes. What the Scheduled Castes desire is an honourable social position to the entire lot, no matter what kind of internal contradictions persist among themselves. The social hierarchy and gradation have always figured in public relation in the Indian context. So mere abolition of untouchability practices and making their observance a cognisable offense, involving the legal processes have made the situation more complex and complicated.

By and large the enlightened Hindu sympathisers of the scheduled castes are for reforms. They wish that the Scheduled Caste should get education, achieve economic betterment and come up in life. But when it comes to tackle traditional values, status and so forth they are not very keen or sure where it will lead. Equality of opportunity in secular life, and not achievement of social equality in absolute terms, seems to guide their thoughts and actions. They can rationalise that structural changes will come about, given the improvement in secular life. The Indian untouchable *vis-a-vis* the history of caste system unfortunately belies this.

The democratic form of government cannot interfere with social lives of the people and coerce them constantly. Both in public and in private matters, the Government has to carry the wishes of the majority with it. Given the existing machinery, form of government and policies, it will take a very long time and one can never be sure of the results. The Scheduled Caste problems will continue to persist and there will be more violence and tensions between the caste Hindus and aspiring scheduled castes.

If the existing system is not acceptable, then the Scheduled Castes should organise themselves and take more drastic steps. Revolutionary changes cannot occur when only a neglected section of people rise in revolt. This can be curbed with am iron hand both by the Government and public in general. The issues have to be focused internationally. By doing this once again the methodical slow process sets in. The Scheduled Caste alone cannot organise and successfully lead to he movement. All the deprived and down-trodden across the castes have to come together. Caste interests need cut across class interests.

There will be more violence and bloodshed, with determined efforts to resolve the problems afflicting the Scheduled Castes. A good number of scheduled caste people themselves may get eliminated in this process. Though it is often generalised that Indian soil and climate are not conducive to violence and revolution, pressure tactics are paying good dividends under democracy. Pressure could be brought to bear upon the Government to use extra legal measures to resolve the problems.

So far all the efforts made by the Government and the money used in the name of the Scheduled Castes have gone down the drain. Only few have been benefited. Exploitation of the Scheduled Castes continues. Apathy of the officials and the ambitions and unscrupulous men in public life has rendered the welfare measures a source of corruption and nepotism.

Punishing the guilty is one way of containing corruption and nepotism. Instead, if the measures themselves are made such that middle men will not have a role to play, they would prove to be useful. For all economic, educational and job matters, the government should have direct control and efficient machinery. For instance, land need not be distributed by cents and acres to individual scheduled caste families. Deserving scheduled caste and non-scheduled caste families can be settled on government farms and payment can be made on work point. Agro-industries and marketing facilities be promoted. Rights to property can be made secondary and not fundamental.

Food, shelter, clothing, a minimum standard of life have to be ensured to all. To this extent, rights to private property be limited and made secondary. Since people have never showed inclination to give up property rights voluntarily, beginning may be made with sections of people coming under direct control of the Government. Right to acquire and own only limited amount of property may be given to all people.

Awakening and organising the Scheduled Castes, voluntary organisations taking up the cause in right earnest, the government machinery gearing up its actions in addition to evolving new policies and approaches, to put it modestly can usher in changes over a period of time. There is no national consciousness with regard to the Scheduled Caste problem as is the case with religious minorities. While religious minorities can always project their image outside the country and politicise their issues, the scheduled castes have suffered for long, languishing for liberation. Betterment which is coming in the form of doles that are neither sufficient nor free from foul play. The entire process is anything but short of revolutionary changes.

Social Profiles of Scheduled Castes

The economic and social conditions of Scheduled Castes and Tribal population all over the country. The Government has taken many development programmes, but the programmes have not succeeded in making the desired impact which should have been perceptible in terms of life, development of human resources and distributive justice. Although the development process in itself was supported to create more earning opportunities to such sections of the society. Extensive educational facilities and reservation in jobs for Scheduled Castes and Tribes was also aimed to hasten their betterment. The present study aims to analyse the impact of development upon social conditions of Scheduled Castes of ten selected villages in Koran Block of Allahabad district, which has the highest percentage of Scheduled Castes population. But primary and secondary data has made use for the study. Purposive stratified sampling was used for selecting ten villages out of 193 villages of the Block, one from each *nyaya* panchayat, varying in caste and size composition. Total study comprises of 866 respondent households having a total population of 6404.

This region is entirely different from the rest of the district Allahabad. It geographically belongs to Bundelkhand or Mirzapur. Almost the surface of the ground of Koraon Block is broken by small hills and rocky outcrops but in the north of the Belan river there is fairly rich plain of alluvium. The region enjoys typical monsoon climate with seasonal variation in rainfall (85.6 mm annually) and temperature (winter 15°C and summer 35°C). On the whole its geographical setting provides a base for its agricultural economy which is the source of livelihood for nearly 93 percent of its total population. Industrially it is a backward area and also lacks an efficient transport networks as nearly 36 percent of its geographical area is inaccessible because of difficult terrain.

Social Structure

The Scheduled Castes of the Koraon Block, are socially less privileged as the vested interests of privileged upper castes work against their legitimate interests. Broadly speaking, social development of the Scheduled Castes has been hampered because of their educational backwardness, social alienation, poverty and economic deprivation. In most of the sample villages, there is a remarkable social alienation among themselves because of purity-pollution relationships. The Chamars do not accept water or food from the Dhobis, the Doms; the Dhobis do not wash the clothes of other Scheduled Castes and are more attuned to the traditional Jajmani system. They have no socio-ritual relationship to each other.

It has been observed that the elite-mass gap is much wider than that among the general population and consequently their susceptibility to social hierarchy is more pronounced. The common denominator of the Scheduled Castes often ignores this social reality which reflects multiplicity of their sub-division which are arrayed one against another and often resort to the same disguised practices of untouchability and discrimination which is accorded to them by the higher castes.

The impact of development programmes on social development of the Scheduled Castes is to be examined in the light of these social realities which often work as limiting factors. Education is the catalyst of development and is measured in terms of literacy levels. Next come health and housing conditions which are basic ingredients of social improvement for improving living conditions and quality of life of Scheduled Castes.

The Government has taken many steps for removal of mass illiteracy and ignorance among the Scheduled Castes, because literacy is a measure of socio-economic development and political consciousness of social group. However, the social inputs designed for improvement in the their literacy levels have been by and large wasted without desired result.

Table 7.1: Literacy Pattern in U.P. Allahabad District and Koraon Block (In percent 1981)

S.No. Region	Population Group	Persons	Male	Female
Uttar Pradesh	Total	27.40	38.90	14.42
	Rural	23.34	35.40	9.86
	Urban	45.91	54.44	35.82
Allahabad District	Total	27.99	41.51	12.81
	Rural	21.02	35.28	—
	Urban	55.24	64.76	43.66
Allahabad District	Total	12.11	20.59	2.91
S.C. Literacy	Rural	9.30	17.20	0.80
	Urban	32.06	43.75	18.49
Koraon Block's Total Literacy	Total	18.51	31.51	4.14
Koraon Block's S.C. Literacy	Total	6.28	11.90	0.57

Source: Census of India 1981, Part II–B.

It clearly shows that Koraon Block has a much lower literacy rate for the Scheduled Castes, than that of the State and District. The study region is almost rural area, therefore the literacy has been calculated for rural literacy. The total literacy of the Koraon Block is 18.51 percent (males 31.55 per-cent and females 4.14 per cent) whereas the Scheduled Castes literacy is 6.28 percent (males 11.90 percent and females 0.57 percent) of these literacy rates with the literacy rates given in 1981 census for the Scheduled Castes in rural area of the Koraon Block, surely indicates a perceptible change because of the various educational facilities provided by the Government. Table 6.2 also given the literacy structure according to age-groups. The age-group 15–44 carries the highest literacy (Total 13.02 per cent: males 23.85 percent and females 1.58 percent) followed by the age-group of 5–14 which has totalliteracy rate of 7.34 percent (boys 12.23 and girls 2.09 percent). The age group of 15.44 has been also benefited by the adult education programmes. But it indicates that the female response to both formal and non-formal educations very meagre. The female education in 5–14 age-group (2.39 percent as compared to the total females literates of 1.36 percent) shows a heartening position because if the female literacy goes up the overall literacy will improve as the females constitute nearly 50 percent of the total population.

In the age-group of 5–14 years 52.17 percent literates have primary school level, 34.06 percent of them have the middle school level and hardly 13.77 percent of literates could claim high school education. The proportion of the females in this education level is almost negligible because of their later entry and heavier drop-outs.

The age-group of 15–44 has representatives in all educational levels, but their high percentage in primary stage establishes that the Scheduled Castes children go for schooling at a much later stage. Their falling rate in Middle, High School/Intermediate/Graduate and Training levels of literacy presents their drop-out trend which is more spectacular in the case of females Scheduled Castes, who lose their share much faster than males. the age-groups of 45–59 and 60 + show that formerly educational levels of the Scheduled Castes were much lower but they have appreciably improved because of the increasing educational facilities provided by the Government during the successive Five Year Plans.

On the basis of foregoing discussion it may be hypothesised that the level of literacy varies directly with female literacy and the impact of urbanisation. Its policy implication is that unless the mass literacy of the Scheduled Castes population and more specifically of their females is increased, the educational levels will not rise as envisaged in the educational planning programmes. For the Scheduled Castes the school going age corresponds with the working age and their child labour, is common both, directly and in disguised form as their traditional occupations and poverty stand to their way and force them to become bread earners by direct participation in labour force or by doing odd jobs of fuel collection, tending cattle or baby sitting. That is why fewer Scheduled Castes children are studying in schools as compared to those belonging to the general population and the position is certainly the worst for the Scheduled Castes. It vividly reveals the pattern of drop-outs and the declining share of the Scheduled Castes children as they move from primary (Classes 1 to 5) to Middle (Classes 6 to 8) to High School/Intermediate/Degree Classes. The Scheduled Caste girls (1983–84) fare much worse than the Scheduled Castes boys in this vertical movement in literacy levels. The respective figures for boys and girls and 25.95 and 20.49 (Primary Stage), 15.38 and 13.10 (Middle School Stage), 13.67 and 8.60 (High School/Intermediate Stage) and 20.99 and 13.40 (Degree Stage).

TABLE 7.2: Trend of Schooling of Scheduled Caste Children in Koraon Block

Year	*Scheduled Castes Students As Percentage to Total Students*							
	Classes 1 – 5		*Classes 6 – 8*		*Classes 9 – 12*		*Degree Classes*	
	Boys	*Girls*	*Boys*	*Girls*	*Boys*	*Girls*	*Boys*	*Girls*
1980-81 (Total)	25.99	16.72	17.95	8.89	12.59	4.04	N.A.	N.A.
1982-83 (Total)	26.72	19.46	15.84	10.83	12.77	4.41	12.74	3.33
1983-84 (Total)	25.95	20.49	15.38	13.10	13.67	8.60	20.99	13.40

Source: Statistical Bulletin, Allahabad District.

In 1981–82 the percentage of Scheduled Castes girls in total girls enrollment was barely 16.72 percent which rose to 20.49 percent in 1983–84 in the Primary classes. In higher levels of literacy the change was more encouraging. Certainly it is a welcome change and bears an unmistakable impact of the educational facilities provided to the Scheduled Caste children by the Government. But these data must be accepted with caution because they are the result of target approach which is basically quantitative and leaves much scope for qualitative improvement. The enquiries reveal that the Scheduled Castes have not shared equitably the benefits of massive adult education programmes which has not clicked so far. In total reckoning these economically deprived castes remain at a lower level for educational achievement.

TABLE 7.3: Accommodation in Sample Villages of Karaon Block

Sample Village	*Number of Households*							*Total No. of House-holds*
	One Roomed	*Two Roomed*	*Three Roomed*	*Four Roomed*	*Five Roomed*	*Six Roomed*	*Seven Roomed*	
Khiri	39	36	17	5	3	1	2	103
Usari	6	4	5	3	1	—	—	19
Lendiari	17	29	30	18	6	3	1	104
Badokhar	36	57	18	7	2	1	—	121
Deoghat	21	27	15	8	4	2	—	77
Khajuri-Khurd	7	11	6	5	3	—	—	32
Sikaro	24	19	14	11	6	2	—	76
Koraon	60	38	18	8	2	1	1	128
Pasana	38	43	21	9	3	2	1	117
Semari-Baghrai	27	31	18	7	5	1	—	89
Total	275	295	162	81	35	13	5	866
Percentage	31.76	34.06	18.71	9.35	4.04	1.50	0.58	100.00

Housing Conditions

Their housing conditions remain hopelessly poor and consequently, adversely affect their health and living conditions. My survey shows that the vast majority of houses owned by the Scheduled Castes lack in essential physical and social requirements of a shelter. They are often over-crowded, structurally unsound, dingy, infested with vermin and lacking in facilities for cooking and storing food and often devoid of drinking water facilities. sitting, kitchen, store and domesticated animals. Only 23.33 percent households have separate rooms for sleeping and sitting purposes whereas 3.35 percent of households have separate rooms for sitting purposes only. 19.16 percent households have separate kitchen and only 16.52 percent of them have separate cattle-sheds gloomy picture of the living accommodation of the Scheduled castes households in the study region. 34.06 per cent of the sample Scheduled Castes households have double-roomed accommodation whereas 18.71 percent households have triple-roomed accommodation and 15.47 percent well to do households, have four or more rooms in their houses.

It shows that 87.30 percent of sample Scheduled Caste households live in thatched houses with mud walls whereas Harely 6.12 percent of the houses are made of tiled roofs with mud walls and hardly 1.50 percent houses are pucca ones. Of course, there are variations from village to village. Two out of ten sample villages have not a single pucca house which is the symbol of economic well-being and social status. Tiled roofs with mud walls are found in all sample villages and tin roofs with brick walls occur in barely 0.23 percent houses which are founding two villages. The thatched roofs with bamboo walls account 3.00 percent of households but their proportion varies from village to village.

The building material used in floor construction is a more critical measure of economic conditions and living styles. In my sample households as many as 98.38 percent houses have mud floors; some with a plaster of cowdung. Hardly 1.04 percent houses have floors made of brick, whereas 0.59 percent are plastered with cement, even though the Government have provided them bricks and cement on subsidised rates. Vary few Scheduled Castes households have opted for the subsidised houses built for the weaker sections as they neither suit their purpose nor pocket. Often their sites are unattractive. On the whole it can be stated that mud and dung floors are predominant. All the pucca houses with concrete roofs, tin roofs and tiled roofs do not share the credit of having pucca, that means brick laid and cement plastered floors.

The sources of drinking water available to the Scheduled Castes households in the Sample Villages have been analyse. The tap water is available to 6.81 percent of the Sample Scheduled Castes households and 12.59 percent of them have been provided with handpumps, but the remaining households and (88.02%) still depend upon wells. In the many of the sample villages except few households, who have a hand pumpfacility, many of them depend on open wells for drinking water. In few Sample Villages each of them has hardly one or two hand pumps. As the drinking water facilities are limited, public wells are crowded and quarrels are not uncommon for getting water supplies.

In the study region the water level of the lowlands and the plains is fairly high ranging from 20 to 35 feet below the surface; but the sub-soil is frequently unstable and unprotected well cannot be made. In the hilly country of the south the water level is very deep and the construction of wells is very difficult and costly if not impossible. In many parts there is great scarcity of water, even the drinking purposes and often the available supply is of a very inferior quality.

The refuse disposal methods of the Scheduled Castes also add to the insanitary conditions in their neighbourhoods. As a common practise they make use of nearby open spaces or fields for lavatory purposes. Our survey shows that as many as 13.09 of their households dump refuse just outside their houses, only 81.87 percent of them use dumping pits a little away from the residential neighbourhood. However, the households which are engaged in agriculture and rear livestock, nearly 2.54 percent of them make use of cowdung and other refuse for compost. As there is scarcity of fuel wood, most of the household use dung cakes for cooking their meals and waste cowdung, which is a valuable organic manure.

My sample survey reveals that the insanitary conditions of the Scheduled Castes households are made worse by their methods of water disposal. As many as 99.65 percent of households just let refuse water flow in open space in the courtyards and streets. Hardly 0.35 percent have soak pits. Only three sample households had soak pits out of 866 sample households. The problem of health and sanitation is aggravated due to lack of drainage facilities. Most of the houses have kuchha open drains overflowing with human excreta, refuse and dirty water.

Health Conditions

The study regions generally considered healthy. My survey also reveals that the health conditions of the sample Scheduled Castes population are far from being satisfactory. My enquiries show stark conditions of under-nutrition and malnutrition because of their poverty, low living standard and ignorance. Many workers who are engaged in physical labour hardly get an intake of 1700-2000 calories per day, when their requirements are of 2500– calories. The protein, vitamin and mineral requirements of a balanced diet are not available even to 19.5 percent of the Sample Scheduled Castes households. They suffer mostly from deficiency diseases, as their habits of cleanliness are bad and their residential houses are in imsanitary conditions. Their mortality and morbidity rates are also high. The infectious diseases like cholera, small pox/measles have more than usual tolls. The incidence of tuberculosis, penumonia, bronchitis, dysentary, hook worm and round worm is high. As their houses are as small and dingy the epedemics prove disastrous because of adverse environmental conditions and contamination of food and water. In the canal irrigated and water logged areas the incidence of malaria has particularly increased.

Among other diseases the most common are bowel complaints, pulmonary ailments and affections of the skin, eyes and ears. Mention should also be made of the peculiar form of the lacomotor paralysis which is very prevalent in the study region. It is undoubtedly due to the consumption of the small pea which is extensively grown in those areas. This paralysis appears to be permanent and is not cured by the discontinuance of the use of the grain, which affects animals as well as human beings. The sufferers naturally belong to the poorer class of cultivators.

My survey reveals that hardly 44.69 percent (vide Table 6.9) of the Sample Scheduled Castes households ever availed of the medical and health services provided by the Government. It appears that they have not been properly motivated for use of health and medical facilities provided by the Government. Their ignorance, illiteracy and superstitions come in their way and discourage them. The Integrated Child and Women Development Service Project was launched in 1975–76. It is certainly a well conceived plan for taking the health and nutritional problems of the children and women of weaker sections of the society, particularly the Scheduled Castes and Schedules Tribes. However, my Sample survey reveals that hardly 4.27 percent Scheduled Castes households have been benefitted by aforesaid programme. Six out of ten Sample Villages are still not covered by the programme. The impact of the programme is noticeable in the villages which lies in the close vicinity of the Block Headquarter. During my field survey I have noted that the Scheduled Caste children and women do not get equitable share among the beneficiaries selected under the programme. Now it is very necessary to bring out the co-ordination in the policy and implementation of various programmes relating to health and nutrition, and to create awareness about improving the food habits amongst the rural masses. Nutrition education is the best way by which the route of under the malnutrition can be changed, and this education must relate with their local environment and food availability as well as their respective traditions.

REFERENCES

Barnabas, A.P., and Mehta, S., *Caste in Changing India*, 1993, (New Delhi, Indian Institute of Public Administration).

Census of India, *Census of India*, 1971, Uttar Pradesh, Part II–C,

(II), Social and Cultural Tables.

Census of India, *District Census Hand Book*, 1971, Allahabad Part-XIII A, B and C.

Kamble, N.D., *The Scheduled Castes*, 1982, (Ashish Publishing House, New Delhi).

Malik, S., *Social Integration of Scheduled Castes*, 1979 (New Delhi, Abhinav Publishers).

Mukherjee, A.B., *The Chamars of U.P., A Study of Social Geography*. (New Delhi, Inter-India Publication).

Singh, L.R., *Impact of Development Programmes on Socio-economic Conditions of Scheduled Castes in Rae Bareli District*, U.P. (Research Project), 1986.

8

Chamars as a Leading Force of North Indian Politics

BSP's Upper-caste Fling does not worry Dalits—Mayawati came third behind Meira Kumar AND Ram VILAs Paswan the first time she fought a Parliamentary by-election in 1985 from Binor. She was barely 27. In the 1989 assembly election, the BSP fielded candidates in all seven segments of Binor, winning three and coming second in the remaining four. One could say that both Mayawati and BSP were born in Bijnor," said O.P Gupta, political watcher and former principal of the Vardhaman PG College. In the beginning, the political base of the first woman only Muslims and Dalits. Now more than two decades later she is adding a third dimension, the upper castes. In these elections, she has fielded 86 candidates from them. Bijinor has two BSP upper caste candidates—Ashok Rana Thankur (dhampur) and Thakur Yaspal Sing. But will the BSP's new caste alliance work? In the villages around Bijinor, it seems clear that dalit votes are likely to go to Mayawati. Villagers are evasive, saying the contests would be triangular. But the common factor in variably is the "hathi", the BSP symbol. Be it Harpool from Timarpur village or Mukesh from Dharmanagri, the refrain were either, "Congress, BJP and BSP" or the "RLD, SP and the BSP.

The fact that Mayawati was attempting to woo upper castes seemingly did not matter to BSP supporters in villages, locally known as 'harijan bastis." We have been with the BSP for many years. People here feel that even if an upper caste member wins from the BSP, the party will take care of our needs," said Take hand of Timapur village. Among the Muslims too, Mayawati hold away because of the candidate and not the party. In Bijnor, the BSP has put up Shahnawaz Rana, who has a clean reputation and also has hold over the Muslim domanated villages because of family connections.

Kanshi Ram, a leader of the North India-based Bahujan Samaj Party (BSP), has become one of the most controversial political leaders in India today. Citing slogans such as "Brahman Bania Thakur Chor, Baki Sab DS-4," most progressives and leftists characterise the movement as "casteist." Reacting to the extreme leader-centered functioning of the BSP and to literature which itself presents Kanshi Ram as the "New Messiah," some would go even further and stamp it as "fascist." Yet aside from the fact that Kanshi Ram is becoming the hero of large sections of the most oppressed castes in India, it is clear that politically the main effect of the new party has been to call into question for the first time in decades the secure hold of the Congress over the "Harijan vote Bank" in North India. In an interview, the Rashtriya Swayamsevak Sangh (RSS) leader Balasabeb Deoras named the BSP (along with Mahendra Singh Tikait) as one of the real problems for the RSS in North India (*Illustrated Weekly*, August 14, 1988).

Surely, a political force that can strike fear both into the Congress and the RSS cannot simply be stamped as reactionary. Nor, for that matter can a *dalit* (depressed) political leader who characterises Shivaji as "ours" and claims to represent the constituencies not only of Babu Jagjivan Ram but also of Chaudhary Charan Singh and to so some extent, Syed Shahabuddin (*Illustrated Weekly*, March 8, 1977) be easily characterised as casteist?

Infact, Kanshi Ram's Bahujan Samaj Party represents one of the celebrated examples of a new political assertion by *dalits,* coming after decades of fragmentation and absorption/

co-operation by the Congress-ruled establishment. The other good example, of course, is Prakash Ambedkar's Bharatiya Republican Party. But rather than making a detailed comparison, this paper will focus on some aspects of the BSP and of its North Indian base.

Politics of the Ambedkarite Movement

Ambedkar's political direction was clear and consistent throughout his life, although changing circumstances and constraints led to different political formations. The direction was to maintain the autonomy and leadership of *dalits*, but at the same time to seek a broader alliance coalition which would include peasants and workers (in class terms) and all middle castes—non-Brahmins/ backward castes (in caste terms). Throughout, the Congress as the representative of Brahmins and capitalists, was viewed as the most dangerous political enemy of the exploited and oppressed.

In the 1930s, Ambedkar formed the Independent Labour Party (ILP) which came out with a bold peasant-worker action programme in the mid 1930s, a period of tumultuous mass movements. The ILP fought not only for *dalit* interests, but also organised joint struggles of Mahar and Kunbi tenants against the *khoti* landlord system in the Konkan as well as participated fully in the major textile workers' struggle of 1938. At the same time, Ambedkar sought to convince non-Brahmin leaders in Maharashtra not to join the Congress, and urged the Bihar *kisan* leader Swami Sahajanand to pull his movement out of the Congress orbit. Although the ILP had some respectable success in Maharashtra, at an all-India level the middle castes and the peasant movement were getting fairly firmly drawn under the Congress hegemony and were helped considerably by the illusory leftism of the Congress Socialists and by the Communist policy of seeing Congress as a "national united front."

Thus, in 1942, the Scheduled Castes Federation (SCF) was formed as a party of *dalit* though on an all-India level. Although this was seemingly a surrender of efforts to develop a broader movement, Ambedkar's political aspirations did not change the 1951 election manifesto of the SCF and declared that it would like to work with backward castes and scheduled tribes and would be willing to change the name to Backward Castes Federation. To make this possible, it also declared a willingness to accept a merger into a federal party like the Socialists, the Justice Party and the Kisan Mazdur Party (the latter mainly represented peasants castes), without jeopardising its autonomy. Finally, before his death, Ambedkar gave a call to form a formally open party to represent all exploited groups which resulted in the creation of the Republican Party.

This broad political thrust towards forming an alliance/ coalition with middle castes and non-Brahmins and often Muslim peasants was shared by other sections of the pre-independence *dalit* movement, in spite of the tensions that continued to exist between middle caste Hindus and *dalits*, between peasants and agricultural labourers. In Bengal, in the 1930s, Nomasudras had a sporadic alliance with the Muslim peasant-based Krishak Praja Party. In Punjab, Mangoo Ram's Ad-Dharma joined the Muslim-Hindu-Jat peasant-based Unionist Party. Both the parties had the broader anti-Brahmin, anti-Bania, anti-Bhadralok rhetoric and tenor thrust.

However, the extraordinary absorptive power of the Congress managed to stifle such attempts at an alliance from below. In a way, this was spearheaded by Gandhi with his various Harijan programmes and his very strong assertion of not a national, but a Hindu unity. However, it has to be clearly recognised that Gandhi was not the only factor, that the Congress elite very consistently and over a long period of time had developed a capacity and willingness to appeal to Harijans and scheduled castes whenever they were threatened by the non-Brahmin peasantry. Put in other terms the Congress capitalists tried to use agricultural labourers against peasants and the Congress Brahmins tried to use dalits against the non-Brahmin middle castes, and they were quite successful in doing so. Gandhi's Harijan Sevak Sangh was not the only (or even main) effort in 1930s to appeal to *dalits*. Perhaps just as significant, though overlooked, was the role of Jagjivan Ram. He founded an agricultural labours organisation to split the Bihar Kisan Sabha, and Depressed Classes League as a counter to Ambedkar's ILP and Depressed Classes Federation—both in the same year 1936.

Thus, Indira Gandhi's rhetoric of *garibi hatao* and appeals to the rural poor and Harijans was no new political creation. Coming in the late 1960s after the massive political alienation of middle caste peasants which had shaken Congress strongholds in North India, it was simply the perfection of many decades-long Congress strategy. Pro-Congress progressives (needless to say, invariably urban, salaried Brahmins) described "Kulaks" and the "Rich and middle peasantry" as the sole beneficiaries of agricultural progress and the main exploiters of agricultural labourers and *dalits*. Indira Gandhi and Congress leaders perfected "KHAM" alliance in many states referring to Kshatriyas, Harijans, Adivasis and Muslims (where as Kshatriyas referred to various backward castes in Gujarat)—but the bidden, unnamed term of the KHAM alliance was the Bramins. It was really a renewed effort to unite the upper castes with the lowest castes against the politically assertive middle castes.

In the face of this political strategy, the *dalit* movement by and large wilted. Even in Ambedkar's own time, of course, large sections of the scheduled castes were entrapped enough in their Hindu identity and traditional subordination and they were pulled into organisations like Congress and even Hindu Mahasabha. The appeal to *dalit* poor peasants/agricultural labourers to see the village dominant peasants/middle castes as their main enemies and exploiters did of course have a base in the day-to-day forms of subordination and exploitation—and the power of this appeal and the ideology of the "rural poor" took on even more force when backed up by the very substantive political/economic benefits which Congress had to offer (at least to *dalit* leaders). Congress did manage to capture the Harijan vote hank in most states, and most of the various factions of the RPI were pulled eventually into some kind of open or indirect alliance with the Congress. *Dalit* interests got expressed only in sectional lobbying. Even the explosion of the "Dalit panthers" in the early 1970s got dissipated into factionalism, with a good proportion of the leadership getting reabsorbed into Congress.

In this background, the rise, from the early 1980s, of an independent, largely anti-Congress political force, firmly based on *dalits* but with a broader appeal to all backwards and exploited, can in fact be seen as a renewal of the earlier political thrust of the Ambedkarite movement. Kanshi Ram's Bahujan Samaj Party and Prakash Ambedkar's Bharatiya Republican Party have numerous differences in strategy and rhetoric, but they both represent the new political assertion, in which *dalits* seek to emerge as leaders in a wider coalition of the exploited and marginalised. A comparison here can even be made with the phenomenon of Jesse Jackson and his "rainbow coalition" in the U.S., where perhaps for the first time in history a black leader emerged with an impressive degree of success. In this sense, whatever the differences and limitations, the harbingers of a new era seem to be with us.

Charmars and the North Indian Politics

However, it is necessary to see political phenomena in their another specific socio-historical and geographical contexts. Though Kanshi Ram has an all-India appeal to *dalits*, and though his root organisation, BAMCEF, is all-India in scope, so far the political base of the BSP has been limited to Northern India, North-West India, to be more accurate. In spite of the genuine ability to appeal to other backward and minority communities, the main social base has been the large Chamar Caste-group just as that of Ambedkar and the Republican Party today whose social base is the Mahars of Maharashtra.

The *dalit* movement throughout India has tended to be based among the largest (and relatively most advanced) *dalit* caste of a particular region—Namasudras in Bengal, Malas in

Andhra, Mahars in Maharashtra, Paraiyas in Tamil Nadu, and Chamars in North India. This invariably gives rise to criticism of the movement as being in fact a "single caste" movement, and it is true that it does lead to tendencies to enclose the movement within the limitations of what we might call the "foundation caste." But given the nature of caste in India, it is inevitable that all movement including rural (and many urban) economic movements, should have such a "foundation caste" (or tribal group) as their base. Criticisms of the fact that such a "foundation caste" exists are meaningless and in fact destructive because they pose an abstract unreality against the Concrete historical reality. The more realistic question is to what degree such a "foundation caste" in fact serves as a vanguard to help a movement move beyond its limitations and draw in oppressed/exploited sections of other castes?

The Chamars are perhaps the largest scheduled caste in India. With leather working as their traditional caste occupation, they can be compared with such groups as the Chambhars in Maharashtra, or the Madigas in the Telugu-speaking region. However, it would be erroneous to see the North Indian Chamars as simply or mainly leather workers. Infact, as the largest untouchable caste in their region, they hold a position within the agrarians structure similar to that of Mahars (in Maharashtra), Malas, Paraiyans, etc., as the main purveyors of agricultural labour, and the main caste responsible for "village service" work (*vethbegar*) of all kinds. As such, in West Uttar Pradesh Punjab and Haryana, they confront primarily Jats as the traditional landholding and cultivating peasant caste while in East Uttar Pradesh and Bihar they have to face the power of Rajputs as a non-cultivating, landlord caste and intermediary cultivating tenant castes like Kurmis, Yadavas, etc.

In return for performance of agricultural and other village services, it seems that the Chamars like Mahars and others traditionally, were given some land for cultivation. Therefore, they were not simply "landless labourers" but also had a small but important whenever they were threatened by the non-Brahmin peasantry. Put in other terms, the Congress capitalists tried to use agricultural labourers against peasants and the Congress Brahmins tried to use dalits against the non-Brahmin middle castes, and they were quite successful in doing so. Gandhi's Harijan Sevak Sangh was not the only (or even main) effort in 1930s to appeal to *dalits*. Perhaps just as significant, though overlooked, was the role of Jagjivan Ram. He founded an agricultural labourers organisation to split the Bihar Kisan Sabha, and Depressed Classes League as a counter to Ambedkar's ILP and Depressed Classes Federation—both in the same year 1936.

Thus, Indira Gandhi's rhetoric of *garibi hatao* and appeals to the rural poor and harijans was no new political creation. Coming in the late 1960s after the massive political alienation of middle caste peasants which had shaken Congress strongholds in North India, it was simply the perfection of many decades-long Congress strategy. Pro-Congress progressives (needless to say, invariably urban, salaried Brahmins) described "Kulaks" and the "Rich and middle peasantry" as the sole beneficiaries of agricultural progress and the main exploiters of agricultural labourers and *dalits*. Indira Gandhi and Congress leaders perfected "KHAM" alliance in many states referring to Kshatriyas, Harijans, Adivasis and Muslims (where as Kshatriyas referred to various backward castes in Gujarat)— but the bidden, unnamed term of the KHAM alliance was the Brahmins. It was really renewed effort to united the upper castes with the lowest castes against the politically assertive middle castes.

In the face of this political strategy, the *dalit* movement by and large wilted. Even in Ambedkar's own time, of course, large sections of the scheduled castes were entrapped enough in their Hindu identity and traditional subordination and they were pulled into organisation like Congress and even Hindu Mahasabha. The appeal to *dalit* poor peasants/agricultural labourers to see the village dominant peasants/middle castes as their main enemies and exploiters did of course have a base in the day-to-day forms of subordination and exploitation—and the power of this appeal and the ideology of the "rural poor" took on even more force when backed up by the very substantive political/ economic benefits which Congress had to offer (at least to *dalit* leaders). Congress did manage to capture the Harijan vote bank in most states, and most of the various factions of the RPI were pulled eventually into some kind of open or indirect alliance with the Congress. *Dalit* interests got expressed only in sectional lobbying. Even the explosion of the "Dalit panthers" in the early 1970s got dissipated into factionalism, with a good proportion of the leadership getting reabsorbed into Congress.

In this background, the rise, from the early 1980s, of an independent, largely anti-Congress political force, firmly based on *dalits* but with a broader appeal to all backwards and exploited, can in fact, be seen as a renewal of the earlier political thrust of the Ambedkarite movement. Kanshi Ram's Bahujan Samaj Party and Prakash Ambedkar's Bharatiya Republican Party have numerous differences in strategy and rhetoric, but they both represent the new political assertion, in which dalits seek to emerge as leaders in a wider coalition of the exploited and marginalised. A comparison here can even be made with the phenomenon of Jesse Jackson and his "rainbow coalition" in the where perhaps for the first time in history a black leader emerged with an impressive degree of success. In this sense, whatever the differences and limitations, the harbingers of a new era seem to be with us.

Chamars as a Leading Force in North India

The Chamars are perhaps the largest scheduled caste in India. With leather working as their traditional caste occupation, they can be compared with such groups as the Chambhars in Maharashtra, or the Madigas in the Telugu-speaking region. However, it would be erroneous to see the North Indian Chamars as simply or mainly leather workers. Infact, as the largest untouchable caste in their region, they hold a position within the agrarian structure similar to that of Mahars (in Maharashtra), Malas, Paraiyans, etc., as the main purveyors of agricultural labour, and the main caste responsible for "village service" work (*vethbegar*) of all kinds. As such, in West Uttar Pradesh, Punjab and Haryana, they confront primarily Jats as the traditional landholding and cultivating peasant caste while in East Uttar Pradesh and Bihar they have to face the power of Rajputs as a non-cultivating, landlord caste and intermediary cultivating tenant castes like Kurmis, Yadavas, etc.

TABLE 8.1: Caste and Agrarian Occupations

Province and Caste	*Actual workers*	*Income from Rent of Land %*	*Cultivators %*	*Field Labourers %*
Mysore State				*(1921)*
Brahmin	51221	17.13	21.79	0.35
Lingayat	1,42,366	3.15	79.43	2.62
Vokkaliga	2,46,329	0.44	89.83	2.08
Holeya	1,57,289	0.97	35,95	37.72
Madiga	63,364	1.58	45.13	26.17
Hyderabad State (1921)				
Brahmin	79,345	7.37	17.52	0.32
Maratha	5,00,638	6.99	60.90	16.33
Kapu	2,91,130	1.60	51.56	26.15
Telaga	1,46,230	1.01	61.22	15.68
Mahar/Mala	1,30,008	3.79	8.40	8.25
(Menial Service)				(65.33)
Madiga	203,492	0.65	10.28	10.16
(Menial Services)				(83.54)
Chambhar	37,591	1.07	4.21	7.69
Madras State (1911)				
Brahmin, Telugu	27,029	34.53	32.37	0.29
Brahmin, Canarese	10,647	13.96	71.89	0.08
Holeya	29,696	—	3.29	75.46
Mala	1,96,256	0.18	14.78	71.79
Madiga	79,924	1.17	10.71	54.71
Bombay Residency (1911)				
Brahmin, Chitpavan	10,407	19.00	2.47	0.13
Brahmin, Deshashtha	14,494	18.68	64.55	2.69
Lingayat	2,05,813	3.24	83.54	22.39
Maratha	4,26,649	1.58	47.63	14.93
Kunbi	3,19,813	1.59	66.88	20.67

Mahar, Holeya, Dhed	69,542	0.75	48.79	22.63
Mang, Madiga	22,672	0.52	16.60	41.71
Central Provinces and Berar (1921)				
Brahmin	1,49,193	3.22	36.67	6.22
Maratha	65,520	4.29	46.00	27.78
Kunbi	3,85,268	55.00	—	34.08
Mahar/Mehra	3,80,101	2.09	22.37	41.02
(Cotton weavers)				(11.33)
Mang	26,007	1.25	3.42	47.73
(native musicians)				(21.97)
United Provinces (1921)				
Brahmin	16,36,446	2.17	77.47	1.78
Rajput	12,63,373	(34.19)	49.57	0.56
Jat	2,75,752	—	78.21	5.31
Gujar	1,23,863	1.76	74.02	3.93
(herding)				
Chamar	19,98,105	0.42	45.64	25.35
				(5.96)

* Figures given under "traditional occupation," in the case of Hyderabad Malas and Madigas these can legitimately be assimilated into "field labour."

** Figures for "traditional occupation;" almost all were most likely landlords.

Source: Census of India, 1921; Census of India, 1911; figures given only for male workers.

In return for performance of agricultural and other village services, it seems that the Chamars like Mahars and others traditionally, were given some land for cultivation. Therefore, they were not simply "landless labourers" but also had a small but important foothold as small peasants. This, along with some economic position as leather workers and an ability to claim other labour, gave them some economic basis to assert themselves against exploitation and casteism by the beginning of the twentieth century.

Table 8.1, which is based on 1921 and 1911 census data on caste and occupation, gives a comparative look at the agrarian economic position of the Brahmins, the main peasant caste, and the major *dalit* castes in different provinces.

Cultivators also, in the case of castes such as Rajputs and perhaps some of the Marathas, include those who used hired labourers and did not work on the land themselves. However, in spite of such inadequacies, the pattern they show is interesting. Chamars and Mahars in particular, in Uttar Pradesh and Bombay presidency, did have a fairly significant foothold as cultivators and not simply as field labourers. One important difference, on the other hand, is in terms of the middle caste they were related to, namely, Jats, who had no agricultural labourers worth speaking of among them, whereas Maratha-Kunbis had a fairly significant number, in the context of a much higher proportion of agricultural labourers to cultivators in Central and Southern India. Thus, where Chamars made up by far the largest majority of field labourers in Uttar Pradesh, in the Marathi-speaking region, the Mahars shared the agricultural labourer role to a significant extent with castes such as the Kunbi-Marathas. This has perhaps made the economic differentiation/contradiction between Chamars and Jats in North-West India sharper than that between Mahars and Kumbi-Maraths in Maharashtra. However, the social similarities are equally important, and it has to be stressed that a full analysis in either case would take account of all the *jatis* and their inter-relationships. Maharashtrian Brahmins, for instance, were traditionally a much more dominating elite as compared to Uttar Pradesh Brahmins.

A crucial historical difference was the role in Maharashtra of Jotiba Phule and the Satyashodhak Samaj in spreading among the broad rural masses a radical, anti-caste ideology and movement. In contrast, the Arya Samaj in North-West India was much more conservative in its approach of rationalising and modernising Hinduism.

Still, the pattern of development of the *dalit* movements was similar, and the Chamar-based movement in North India has as much historical importance as that based on the Mahars in Maharashtra. In both cases, early Christianising attempts gave some outlets to the untouchables and helped to provoke similar Hindu attempts. In North India, it was the Arya Samaj that played the role, in a sense, took up the "challenge" on behalf of Hinduism of reincorporating those they had excluded for so long. A *shuddhi* programme initially undertaken in the later nineteenth century by Arya Samajists to convert or reconvert individuals was turned at the initiative of *dalits* themselves into a collective programme for upward mobility of *dalit* castes accompanied by incorporation into Arya Samaj activists. By 1910, between 60 to 70 thousand *shuddhi* ceremonies had been performed in Punjab and Uttar Pradesh and the Aryas had risen from a small number to 205,000, mostly apparently "purified" untouchables. It is infact this tradition that radical Hindu reformers like Swami Agnivesh represent today.

However, it was not and is not enough radicalism for *dalits,* who found that even after *shuddhi* their position in the caste system and their treatment by caste Hindus had undergone little change. A major revolt against Arya Samajist identification with Hinduism took place, and by the mid-1920s movements like Ad-Dharm and the Adi-Hindu were becoming the vanguard voice of the assertive Chamars. Similar movements elsewhere (Adi-Dravida, Adi-Karnataka, Adi-Andhra), asserted that *dalits* were part of an originally egalitarian and prosperous community of original inhabitants of India, turned into slaves in the caste system as a result of Aryan invasion and conquest. These Adi-Hindu groups began to bold conferences establishing links with emerging dalit leaders elsewhere. Through most of the 1920s they worked in some kind of co-ordination with other non-Brahmin groups and by the 1940s were drawn into Ambedkar's movement. Outside Maharashtra, it was the North Indian Chamars who provided the strongest base for the Scheduled Caste Federation.

Towards the Bahujan Samaj Party

By the middle of 1960s, India was enveloped in an all-round economic and political crisis. Strikes and all forms of political agitation took place from that period on and in the 1967 elections. The Congress lost heavily in several northern states as disaffected peasants and middle castes turned to the opposition. Disaffection hit every political party including the Communists as the apparently revolutionary message of Mao helped to spark the "Naxalite" revolt.

TABLE 8.2
Scheduled Caste and Scheduled Tribal Occupations, 1981

	SC		*ST*		*Other*		*Total*	
	Lakh	*%*	*Lakh*	*%*	*Lakh*	*%*	*Lakh*	*%*
1. Agricultural Sector	289	76.4	192	87.1	999	61.4	1,480	66.5
(a+b)	(19.5)		(13.0)		(67..5)		(100.0)	
(a) cultivators	107	28.2	120	54.4	698	42.9	925	41.6
	(33.8)		(13.0)		(75.4)		(100.0)	
(b) Agricultural	182	482	72	32.7	301	18.5	555	24.9
Labourers	(33.8)		(13.0)		(53.2)		(100.0)	
2. Non-Agricultural	89	23.6	8	12.9	628	38.6	745	33.5
Sector	(12.0)		(3.8)		(84.2)		(100.0)	
Total (1+2)	378	100.0	220	100.0	1,627	100.0	2,225	100.0
(Total in Population)	(17.0)		(10.0)		(730)		(100.0)	

Notes: 1. This table gives percentages both across and down, it shown what % of SCs are agricultural labourers (48.2%) and also what % of agricultural labourers are SCs (33.8%), thus giving an overall picture.

2. The largest section of both SCs and STs are, first, in the more impoverished agricultural sector. SCs are much more highly agricultural labourers than cultivators, though they still make up a significant proportion of cultivators. Here we should remember that the Census underestimates the proportion of cultivators by vastly undercountiug women cultivators and thus probably underestimates also the proportion of SCs and STs who are at least small peasants.

3. Of course no official statistics are available which separate "backward" or middle castes or minorities from the upper castes in the "Other" category which makes it practically impossible to get data on the general economic and social section which the BSP seeks to appeal to.

Source: CMIE.

Dalits were affected by the crisis in a variety of ways. As rural agricultural labourers and poor peasants, they suffered both from overall rural poverty and backwardness, a legacy of the "Nehru model" of heavy industrial, over centralised industrial development and from the increasing economic and social tensions between the landowning middle and upper castes and the lower caste rural poor. The fact was that those who benefitted from agrarian development as "Kulaks" might have been, in fact, a small minority, and they were in reality the holders of rural political power and influence who ruled the villages. The large majority of middle castes and backwards were as much a victim of the system as the *dalits*. In any case the dalits were at the receiving end of most of the attacks, confronting aggressive backlash whenever they tried to move ahead. Atrocities on Harijans committed in practice by a wide range of caste-groups from traditional upper caste elites like Thakurs and Bhumihars, Brahmins to middle castes and lower middle castes (Kunbi-Maraths, Kurmis, Yadavas, Dhangars, Vanniyars), went on an upward swing.

Dalit middle classes were in an equally tension-ridden and in a more ambivalent position. As beneficiaries of the reservation policies that had resulted from the earlier *dalit* movement, they had a *bit more economic security than their lower-class brethren* and hence could aspire for considerable upward mobility. But they faced on a continual score, condescension and opposition from their upper caste co-workers. Their economic position was often fragile particularly with large number of *poorer relatives* around. Within the Indian caste-community context, it was in fact eternally difficult for a "middle class" or "petty bourgeoisie" to escape from the rural an urban working class conditions which enveloped the majority of the scheduled castes.

Out of this situation, it was in fact middle class, educated or semi-educated *dalit* youth who provided impetus to most of the militant organisations that arose from the late 1960s.—the dalit panthers in Maharashtra, Bheem Sena and *Dalit* Sangarsh Samiti in Karnataka, etc.

The Bahujan Samaj Party had its roots in the same period, but with an entirely different history. Kanshi Ram, a young Punjabi *dalit* from a Sikh Chamar background employed in a Pune laboratory resigned his job in 1964 following a long-drawn dispute on caste issues and following a discovery of Ambedkar, determined to dedicate his life to the movement. After seven years of working for the Republican Party, he apparently concluded that it was worthless, and with little temptation towards the type of militancy offered by the *Dalit* Panthers began working towards a different kind of organisation. And when BAMCEF (Backward and Minority Communities Employees Federation) was officially formed on December 6,1978, it was, in several clear ways, a unique exploit.

First, in contrast to almost all other dalit and *dalit-based* organisations of the time, its formation and structure appear as deliberate and not reactive, emerging fourteen years after Kanshi Ram's resignation from government service. It has consistently refused a "reactive" agitational stance which has meant, in practice, staying out of many major *dalit* struggles. Perhaps the biggest example of this was the Namantar agitation for the remaining of Marathwada University after Dr. Ambedkar, which Kanshi Ram characterised as dominated by Poona Brahmins. This refusal to join ongoing agitational struggles has been more of an orientation by BAMCEF to decide its own political direction than simply due to the fact that as a government employees organisation, BAMCEF itself could not engage in struggle activities.

Second, while it has *dalits* (scheduled castes) as its strongest base, there was a concerted effort from the beginning to include all backwards and minorities; the term "scheduled castes" does not even appear in the name of the organisation. While the scheduled castes probably have the majority among the claimed two lakh educated employees including 3,000 holders of MBBS/ MD degrees, 15,000 scientists members of BAMCEF. It remains true that all public functions of BAMCEF have sought to include leaders of various backward castes and minority communities.

Kanshi Ram's major organisational and rhetorical thrust was, in fact, to develop BAMCEF as the major support organisation for a later, if indefinite, political thrust. It is significant to know that it is conducted by the newly formed DS-4 (Dalit Shoshit

Samaj Sangarsh Samiti) from September 24, 1982. It was a denunciation of the Poona Pact. This Pact, signed in 1932 by Ambedkar as a result of Gandhi's fast unto death to achieve the integration of dalits with the majority Hindu community, resulted in changing the separate electorates allotted by the British into reserved seats although with a largely increased number. It fiftieth anniversary had been intended by the Congress Party for a major celebration, and it is noteworthy that DS's denunciation campaign was condemned by almost all the other *dalit* organisations in Maharashtra. But Kanshi Ram's message published in perhaps his only book—The *Chamcha Age*—was simple; the Poona Pact was the beginning of a process in which the educated elites of scheduled caste and backward caste communities were turned into simple puppets (*chamchas*) of the upper caste, they must reject this role and instead direct their services and talents towards organisation of their total community towards breaking caste heirarchy and inequality. In its own description, "BAMCEF is considered a brain-bank, a talent-bank and a financial-bank of the oppressed and exploited society to move its mission ahead. The basic objective of this organisation is to pay back to the oppressed and exploited society to which they belong" ("*The New Messiah*," 1988, p. 5).

From this point, the direction towards political action based in Northern India developed quite rapidly. In what it called "limited political action," DS-4 put up forty-six candidates for assembly election in Haryana in 1982 (*Oppressed Indian*, June, 1982). The BSP, founded on April 15, 1985, contested Lok Sabha elections in December 1984, and then UP Vidhan Sabha elections in March 1985. It lost all seats contested in both elections, but win over a million votes in the Lok Sabha elections, and in Uttar Pradesh it was thought to have played a decisive enough role in drawing votes away from Congress, throwing fifty-one seats to Lok Dal and Janata Party candidates (*Illustrated Weekly*, March 1987). It repeated this performance in the Punjab Vidhan Sabha elections six months later when it was thought to have played a decisive role in turning the tide for the Akali

Dal. Then, in the Bijnore Lok Sabha by-elections in December 1985, the Ruling Party's prestigious candidate Meera Kumari (Daughter of Jagjivan Ram) could barely manage to win the seat with only a five thousand vote margin over the BSP candidate. Throughout this period, the DS-4 and BSP were organising increasingly huge rallies, and in the process increasing their bold over scheduled castes and backward caste government employees.

What really projected Kanshi Ram as a national figure was, of course, the crucial Allahabad Lok Sabha by-election of July 1987, when he decided to contest against Sunil Shastri of the Congress and V.P. Singh of the opposition. Kanshi Ram's objective was to make this into a genuine three-sided contest, and throughout most of the campaign infact it appeared as if the BSP, with relatively low funding, had the most enthusiastic and vigorous campaign centered on the rhetoric of overthrowing upper caste political power: *vote hamara, raj tumara nahin chalega, nahin chalega.* And he emerged with eighteen percent of the total vote (compared to Shastri's twenty-four percent and Singh's fifty-two percent), including sixteen percent of the backward castes. (*India Today*, July 15, 1988, p. 35). A new political force had indeed taken it root on the national scene.

Political Ideology: Advantages of Vagueness

In all of this, what is striking is the nearly total lack of any clear ideology in the programmes and functioning of BAMCEF, BSP, etc. The thrust is solely on breaking the caste system to overthrow the rule of the three upper castes by organising the "oppressed and exploited" for "equality." "Changing" and "destroying the system" are stressed, but the system is described almost solely in social terms. An economic programme is absent, so is any concrete outlines of what dalits and backwards might do once they gain political power, of what kind of society might be built. According to Kanshi Ram: We have not laid down an ideology for our struggle. We are in the process of formulating it. Our struggle for annihilation of caste has begun all over India. At the end of the campaign we will hold a seminar in Delhi where people from different caste groups, interests and political parties will be invited. We shall seek a common approach on the basis of a consensus (Surya India, May 1987; quoted in "The New Messiah.")

In this sense it can also be noted that all the agitational and other campaigns of DS-4, BAMCEF might have been at the symbolic and culturally-political level; they have not dealt with any economic issues; they have been *jagruti* (awakening) campaigns. Massive bicycle tours from the far ends of India into remote villages, *melas* and "people's parliaments" were organised. The only issue taken up has been the 1987–88 anti-drink (alcohol) campaign.

Another aspect of this might be stressed. There is also little negative aspect to the BSP propaganda and campaigning. In contrast to some other *dalit* publications (*e.g., Dalit Voice*) and its regional language variants there is a little tendency to vitriolic attack on upper castes as "Nazis" or whatever, and there is also a little specific attack on individual upper caste politicians and other leaders. The basis thrust is rather the positive one of the *dalits* and backward castes organising themselves. This characteristic gives the literature a vagueness and even a certain amount of vacuity, with almost no commentary on specific events, movements, issues; it also leaves it much more open-ended.

Although the attempt is to unite the minorities with *dalits* and backward caste, Kanshi Ram does not sho the kind of "prominority" line which undones all minority fundamentalism on the pretext that Hinduism is the main enemy there is a wariness about Islam, for example, or rather the positive stress (and this is consistent with Ambedkar) on Buddhism (with some references to the nationalism humanism, atheism of Phule, Periyar and all). Similarly, there is no ideological interpretation of the origins of caste and untouchability, specifically, little of the "non-Aryan" theory which interprets all of Indian history in terms of Aryan (white) conquest of originally non-Aryan equalitarian civilisation; the most recent expositions of such a view have identified India's *dalits* with "blacks" the world over, they have also added a strong racist time to the *dalit* movement.

This orientation was quite understandable in Ambedkar's times. There was no practical, seemingly viable alternative to the Nehru model and the left ideology underlying it. Gandhism, the practical, available alternative in India, stood forth (only as based) on backwardness, Hindu *vedanta* avoidance of life, and acceptance of caste hierarchy/inequality.

Today, however, the "Crisis of Marxism" is quite special and calls into question most of these orientations, including technological development (seen as environmentally destructive), heavy industrialisation (seen as leading to an overcentralised, unbalanced, uneven development which leaves the majority in poverty and backwardness), nationalism and collectivisations, seen as creating statist bureaucracies). Since these uncertainties extend to post-revolutionary societies themselves, it is not so surprising that a current anti-caste movement should remain silent on such issues.

Further, there are some specific reasons why the currently available form of Marxist economic ideology should be unacceptable to an organisation like BAMCEF/BSP. The first is the tendency onwards discussing interpret on *dalits* or caste conflict in the village, to inperpret these in terms of a basic class conflict between rich and middle peasants (Kulaks, capitalist farmers, but the emphasis on "property ownership" as basic to "class" leads to a tendency to lump together all land owning peasants) and agricultural labourers and poor, peasants.

However, this assumed class conflict is in contradiction to the caste alliance which Kanshi Ram is seeking to build between *dalits* and backward castes. With some exceptions, the majority of "rich and middle peasants" (and certainly the majority of those actually involved in attacks on dalits—the "foot-soldiers" of atrocities) are those classified as Sudras and falling in the eighty-five percent majority the BSP wants to represent.

The second issue is that the general "Leftist" solution to the problems of the rural poor and dalits has been in terms of land distribution and collectivisation and nationalisation of industries at the broader societal level. Now in one sense, this "statism" might be seen to be in the interest of the governmental (bureaucratic) employees who are the main "brain-bank, talent bank and financial bank" for the BSP. However, the fact remains that the scheduled caste and the backward caste government employees are subordinates and a minority force in the bureaucracy, a move towards "Statism" in the Indian context clearly brings with it Brahminism, the control of the upper castes. It is not surprising that there would be an ambiguity on this issue. Nor is it surprising that the lower middle-class support base of the BSP with its strong urban foothold could be sceptial about the tendency of urban Brahmin salaried intellectuals to tell them that the main enemy of *dalits* are the rural "dominant caste" peasantry. They confront more immediately the "dominant caste of the cities and the bureaucracy and its much subtler forms of daily domination.

In the face of these complexities and uncertainties, then, the lack of ideology of the BSP may be a kind of advantage— an open-endedness in an era of uncertainty. There is also something to be said for the assertion that bringing the low-caste "oppressed and exploited" into political power, into organisational leadership and intellectual competence, is a prerequisite to any real building of ideology.

In many ways, the Bahujan Samaj Party is a product of the contemporary era of profound ideological uncertainties and political crisis of all established systems. It can be said to be the political expression of dalit and low caste communities, standing shakily on the base of partial gains won as result of past movements. In many ways also, the BSP appears as an "anti-party" rather than a party. Its refusal of ideology, refusal of alliances, refusal to "place" itself in the political spectrum its assessment of all parties by the single criterion of their orientation to break the caste system prove it to be an "anti-party" entity. In this sense also it appears "modern," a not untypical example of many such "new social movements" world-wide. At another level, of course, it can be noted that the vagueness of rhetoric and lack of sharp political definition is helpful, perhaps even necessary for a party striving to unite the divided, even warring eighty-five percent. It is a way of keeping options open for whatever may be necessary to move ahead.

To call the BSP "fascist" is clearly nonsense. Fascism of course has an ideology, and the racial appeals that are integral to fascism are also signally lacking in BSP rhetoric. It is erroneous to call it "casteist" unless appeals to break down the caste system and a recognition of the caste-divided reality are to be stamped as "casteist." Here the point is: does one accept the material reality of caste in India or not?

Vague as its rhetoric may be, and any be lacking as a clear ideology, the whole thrust of the BSP nevertheless appears to be *anti-systemic* (to use Wallersteinian terminology), "left" in the traditional sense. Even the often bitter critiques of the Communists (The Communist parties have become the biggest stumbling block in this regard). They keep talking about change but work for status quo. The BJP is better, they never talk about change. So people never feel duped (Kanshi Ram, *Illustrated Weekly*, March 8, 1987). They are like almost all *dalit* critiques, which are not of Communist ideals but of Communist failures to live up to ideals or do anything really practical about them. Obviously, the claims to unite and represent the eighty-five percent "oppressed and exploited," the massive for reaching awakening campaigns directed against "untouchability, inhumanity, injustice, insecurity, inequality," the continual attacks on the Congress Party and the state, the characterisation of "rural feudal lords and slum *dadas*" as the enemy—all of these do not contain easily fit the usual "class" rhetoric of the Left. But they should at least leave the ground open for a dialogue.

REFERENCES

Centre for Monitoring the Indian Economy. (1985). *Basic Statistics: Volume I All India* (Worli. Bombay).

Kanshi Ram., (1982). *The Chamcha Age: An Era of the Stooges* (New Delhi), Khare, R.S., (1984). *The Untouchable as Himself: Ideology, Identity and Pragmatism among the Lucknow chamars*, London: Cambridge Press.

Nikhil Lakhaman. (1987). Sudden Impact:" Illustrates Weekly, March 18.

Lynch, Owen. (1969). *The Politics of Untouchability*, New York: Columbia University Press.

Jorden, J.T.F., (1970. "Reconversion of Hinduism: The Shuddhi of the Arya Samaj: in G.A. Oddie. (ed.) *Religion in South Asia*. London: Curzon Press.

Joshi, Barbara. (1977). "The Buddhist Movement of Western Uttar Pradesh: (mimeographed paper). March. 27.

——, (1986). Editor. *Untouchable: Voices of the Dalit*: Liberation Movement London: Zed Press.

——, (1987). "Recent Developments of Inter-Regional Mobilisation of dalit protest in India." South Asia Bulletin 7.

Juergensmeier. Mark (1979). *Religion as Social Vision The Movement Against Untouchability in 20th Century Punjab*. University of California Press.

Assorted issues of Oppressed Indian. *Bahujan Nayak (Marathi), Bahujan Sangathak* (Hindi). Dalit Voice. Bheem Patrika and others.

Bibliography

Alter, James P. and Herbert Jai Singh, 1961. *The Church in Delhi,* Lucknow: National Christian Council of India.

Ambedkar, B.R. 1946. *What Congress and Gandhi Have Done to the Untouchables* (Second edition). Bombay: Thacker & Co.

Ambedkar, B.R., 1969. *The Untouchables* (Second edition) Balrampur: Jelavan Mahavir.

Ambedkar, B.R., 1989. 'The Condition of the Convert,' in Vasant Moon (Compiler,), *Dr. Babasaheb Ambedkar, Writings and Speeches*. Bombay: Education Department, Government of Maharashtra.

Ambedkar, B.R.,1945a. *Annihilation of Caste*. Bangalore: Dalit Sahitya Akademy.

Ambedkar, B.R., 1945b. *What Congress and Gandhi have done to the Untouchable*. Bombay: Thacker Publications.

Anderson,W.K. and S.D. Damle. 1987. *The Brotherhood in Saffron. The Rashtriya Swayamsevak Sangh and Hindu Revivalism*. New Delhi: Vistaar Publications.

Ayrookuzhel, Abraham, A.M. 1990. 'The Ideological Nature of the Emerging Dalit Consciousness,' *Religion and Society* XXXVII (3) September 14–23.

Babb Lawrence, A. 1975. *The Divine Hierarchy: Popular Hinduism in Central India*. New York: Columbia University Press.

Baxi, Upendra, 1994. 'Emancipation as Justice: Babasaheb Ambedkar's Legacy ad Vision,' in *Ambedkar and Social Justice*, Vol. 1. Edited by Ministry of Information and Broadcasting, Government of India, Delhi.

Caplan, Lionel, 1987. *Class and Culture in Urban India: Fundamentalism in a Christian Community*, Oxford: oxford University Press.

Census of India, 1931, 1933. Volume xxviii, *Travancore Part I*: Report, Delhi: Manager of Publications, Government Press, p. 439.

Chitinis, Suma, 1981. *A Long Way to Go*: *Report on a Survey of Scheduled Caste High School and College Students in Fifteen States of India*. New Delhi: Allied Publishers.

Damle, Y.B. and Jacob Aikara, 1982. *Caste, Religion and Politics in India*. New Delhi: Oxford & IBH Publishing Co.

Das, Bhagwan and James Massey, 1995. *Dait Solidarity* Delhi: The India Society for Promoting Christina Knowledge (ISPCK).

Devanandan, P.D. 1960. *The Dravida Kazagham: A Revolt against Brahmanism*. Bangalore: Christian Institute for the Study of Religion and Society.

Forrester, Duncan B., 1979. *Caste and Christianity*. London: Curzon Press.

Frykenberg, Bober Eric., 1989. 'The Emergence of Modern "Hinduism" as a Conceptas an Institution: A Reappraisal with Special Reference to South India,' in Gunther, D. Sontheimer and Hermann Kulke (eds.), *Hinduism Reconsidered*. Delhi: Manohar.

Fuller, C.J., 1976. 'Kerala Christians and the Caste System,' *Man* 11: 63–65.

Gandhi, M.K. 1949. *Communal Unity*. Ahmedabad: Navjivan.

Galanter, Marc., 1968. 'Changing Legal Conceptions of Caste,' in, Milton Singer and Bernard S. (eds), *Structure and Change in Indian Society*, Chicago: Aldine Publishing Co.

Gladstone, J.W., 1984. *Protestant Christianity and People's Movements in Kerala 1850-1936*. Trivandrum: Seminary Publications.

Gupta, S.K. 1985. *The Scheduled Castes in Modern Indian Politics*: Their Emergence as a Political Power Delhi: Munshiram Manoharlal.

Godbole, Madhav, 1997. 'Crime and Punishment: Trying Times for Tribal Peoples,' *The Times of India*, 14 February, p. 14 (Mumbai).

Golwalkar, M.S. 1947. *We or Our Nationhood Defined* (Fourth edition). Nagpur: Bharat Prakashan.

——, 1968. *Bunch of Thoughts*. Bangalore: Bharat Prakashan.

Gore, M.S. 1993. *The Social Context of an Ideology. Ambedkar's Political and Social Thought*, New Delhi: Sage Publications.

Hardgrave, Jr. Robert L. 1965. *The Dravidian Movement*, Bombay: Popular Prakashan.

Harrison, Seling, 1960. *India: The Most Dangerous Decades*. Princeton: Princeton University Press.

Hutton, J.H., 1933. *Census of India, 1931*. Vol. 1-India: Part 1-Report. Delhi: Manager of Publications, Government Press, Indian Statutory Commission Oral Evidence. 1929, Fourteenth Meeting, Madras. 1 March.

Irudayaraj, Xavier (ed.), 1990. *Emerging Dalit Theology*, Madras; Jesuit Theological Secretariat.

Japhet, S., 1987. 'Christian Dalits: A sociological Study on the Problem of Gaining a New Identity,' *Religion and Society* XXXIV, deptember: 59-87.

Joshi, Barbara R., 1982. *Democracy in Search of Equality:*

Untouchable Politics and Indian Social Change, Delhi: Hindustan Publishing Corp.

Juergensmeyer, Mark, 1982. *Religion as Social Vision: The Movement Against Untouchability in 20th-century Punjab*. Berkeley: University of California Press.

Kamble, J.R. 1979. *Rise and Awakening of Depressed Classes in India*. New Delhi: National Publishing House.

Kananaikil, Jose, 1986. *Scheduled Castes insearch of Justice*, Part II: *The Verdict of the Supreme Court*,New Delhi: Indian Social Institute.

Koilparampil, George, 1982. *Caste in the Catholic Community in Kerala*, Kochin: C.I.S.R.

Kooiman, Dick n.d. *Conversion and Social Equality in India*. Columbia: South Asian Publications.

Koshi, Ninan, 1968. *Caste in Kerala Churches*, Bangalore: C.I.S.R.S.

Keer, Dhananjay, 1964. *Mahatma Jotirao Phooley, Father of Indian Social Revolution*, Bombay: Popular Prakashan.

——, 1974. *Dr. Ambedkar: Life and Mission*, Bombay: Popular Prakashan.

Kejariwal, O.P., 1988. *The Asiatic Society of Bengal and the Discovery of India's Past*. Delhi: Oxford University Press.

Kothari, Rajni, 1988. 'Integration and Exclusion in Indian Polities,' *Economic and Political Weekly*. XXIII (43), 22 October: 223–229.

Kothari, Rajni, 1997. 'Rise of the dalits and the Renewed debate on Caste,' in Partha Chatterjee (ed.), *State and Politics in India*. New Delhi: Oxford.

Kshirsagar, R.K. 1994. *Dalit-Movement in India and Its Leaders*. New Delhi: M.D. Publications.

Mathew, Joseph, 1986. *Ideology, Protest and Social Mobility:*

Case Study of Mahars and Pulayas, New Delhi: Inter-India Publications.

Marshall, P.J. 1970. *The British Discovery of Hindusim in the Eighteenth Century*. Cambridge: Cambridge University Press.

Massey, James, 1990. 'Christian Dalits in India: An Analysis,' *Religion and Society* XXXIII (3), September 40–53.

Michael, S.M. 1986. 'Politicisation of Ganapathi Festival,' *Social Compass* XXXVII(2—3): 185–97.

Mosse, C.D.F., 1986. 'Caste, Christianity and Hinduism: A Study of Social Organisation and Religion in Rural Ramnad' Unpublished D.Phil. Thesis, University of Oxford.

Nath, Trilok, 1987. *Politics of the Depresed Classes*, Delhi: D e p u t y Publications.

Naicker, Ramaswaray, E.V. 1959. *The Ramayana: A True Reading*. Madras: Rationalist Publications.

O'Hanlon, Rosalind. 1985. *Caste, Conflict and Ideology., Mahatma Jotirao Phule and Low Caste Protest in Nineteenth-Century Western India*. Cambridge: Cambridge University Press.

Omvedt, Gail. 1976. *Cultural Revolt in a Colonial Society: The Non-Brahmin movment in Western India*. 1873 to 1930. Poona: Scientific Socialist Education Trust.

——, 1994. *Dalit and Democratic Revolution: Dr. Ambedkar and the Dalit Movement in Colonial India*, New Delhi: Sage Publications.

——, 1996. *Dalit Visions, The Anti-caste, Movement and the construction of an Indian Identity*, New Delhi: Orient Longman, Tracts for the Times/8.

Oddie, G.A., 1969. 'Protestant Missions, Caste and Social Change in India,' *Indian Economic and Social History Review* VI, September, 259–91.

——, 1975. 'Christian Conversions in the Telugu Country 1860–1900: A Caste Study of One Protestant Indian Movement in the Godavery Krishna Delta,' *Indian Economic and Social History Review* XII, January-March: 61–69.

Omvedt, Gail, 1994. *Dalits and the Democratic Revolution Dr. Ambedkar and Dalit Movement in Colonial India*, New Delhi: Sage Publications.

——, 1995. *Dalit Visions: The Anti-Caste Movement and the Construction of an Indian Identity.* Hyderabad: Orient Longman.

Parvate, T.V. 1959. *Gopal Krishna Gokhale* Ambedabad: Navjivan Publishing House.

Prabhakar, M.E. 1990. 'Developing a common Ideology for Dalits of Christian and Other Faiths', *Religion and Society* XXXVII (3) September 24–39.

Pradhan, Atul Chandra, 1986. *The Emergence of the Depressed Classes.* Bhubaneswar:Bookland International.

Rajasekharian, A.M. 1971. *B.R. Ambedkar: The Politics of Emancipation.* Bombay: Sindhu Publications.

Ram, Nandu, 1988. *The Mobile Scheduled Castes: Rise of a New Middle Class*, Delhi: Hindustan Publishing Corporation.

Shah, Ghanshyam, 1995. 'Dalit Movements and Search for Identity,' in Manorama Savur and Indra Munshi (eds), *Contraditions in Indian Society.* Jaipur Rawat Publications, pp. 23–45.

Shashi, S.S. (ed.), 1992. *Ambedkar and Social Justice*, New Delhi: Government of India.

Shourie, Arun, 1997. *Worshipping False Gods: Ambedkar and the Facts which have been Erased*, New Delhi: ASA Publications.

Smith, William Roy, 1938. *Nationalism and Reform in India.* London: Yale University Press.

Smith, Donald Eugene. 1963. *India as a Seculr State.* London:

Prince-ton Unviersity Press.

Thapar, Romila, 1985. 'Syndicated Moksha', *Seminar* 313, September: 13–22.

Thorat, S.K., 1996. Dalits and the New Economic Policy,' *Dalit International Newsletter* 1(2): 1 and 4.

Throat, Vimal. 1997. 'Dalit Women,' *Dalit Internatioinal Newsletter* 2(I): 1 and 10.

Vanaik, Achin, 1997. *Communalism Contested: Religion, Modernity and Secularisation*, New Delhi: Vistaar Publications.

Weber, Max, 1958. *The Religion of India*. Hans H. Gertha and Don Martindale, eds. and trans., New York: Free Press.

Webster, John, C.B. 1976. *The Christian Community and Change in Nineteenth Century North Indian*, New Delhi, Macmillan.

——, 1994. *The Dalit Christians: A History* (Second edition). Delhi: I.S. P.C.K.

Zelliot, Eleanor, 1992. *From Untouchable to Dalit: Essays on the Ambedkar Movement*. Delhi: Manohar.

——, 1996. 'The Dalit Movement,' *Dalit International Newsletter* 1 (1): and 4.